3 1168 00073 0620

CENTRAL

Library Association of Portland, OR

Books are due on the latest date stamped below.
Fines are 10¢ per day for adult materials; 5¢ per
day for juvenile materials.

MAY 11 1989 MB

MULTNOMAH COUNTY
LIBRARY

F76 12/88

F76R

Purchased
Multnomah C
Title Wave
216 NE Knott S
503-988-

D1011298

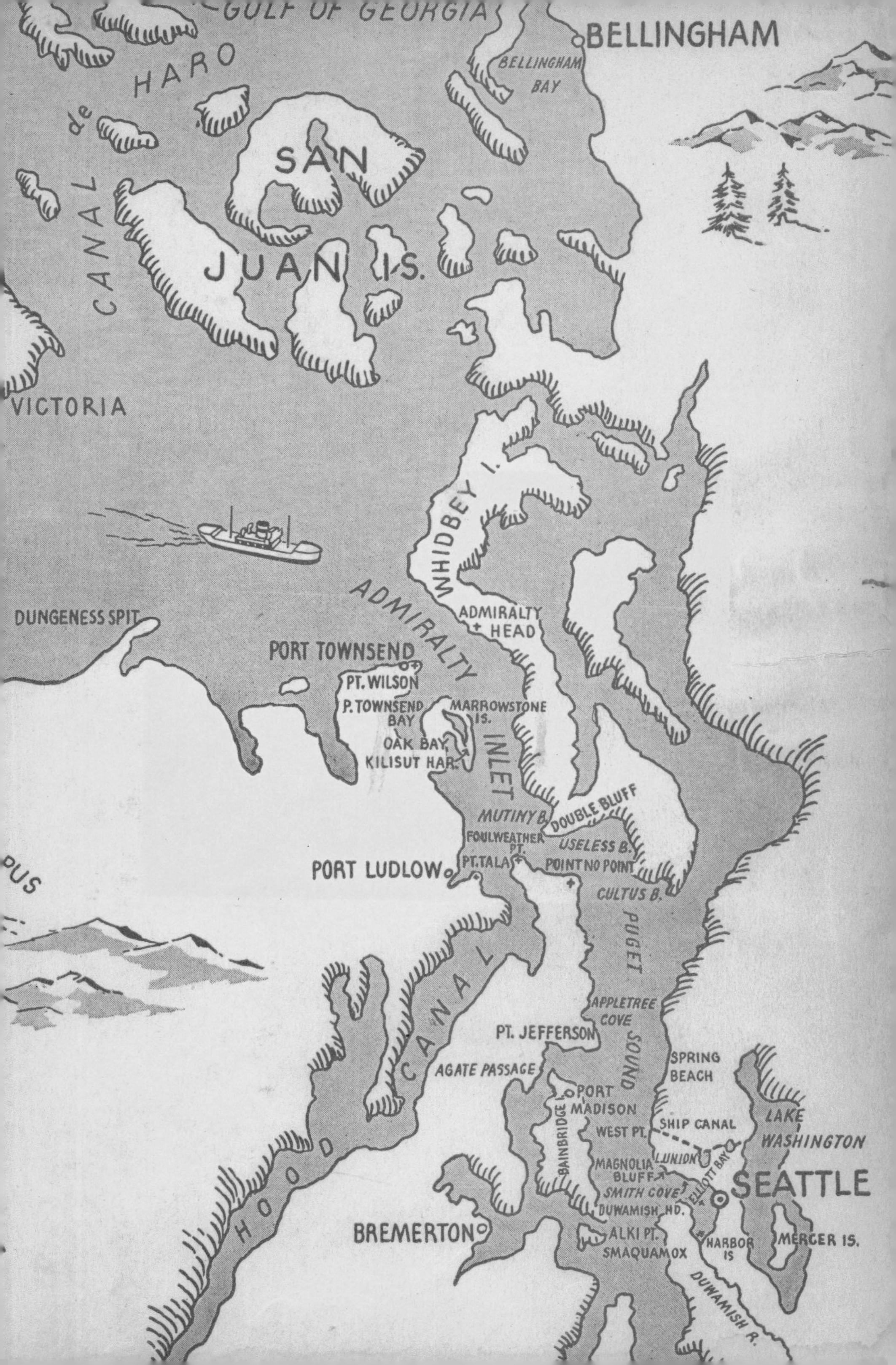
GULF OF GEORGIA
BELLINGHAM
BELLINGHAM BAY
HARO
CANAL de
SAN JUAN IS.
VICTORIA
WHIDBEY I.
ADMIRALTY
INLET
DUNGENESS SPIT
ADMIRALTY HEAD
PORT TOWNSEND
PT. WILSON
P. TOWNSEND BAY
MARROWSTONE IS.
OAK BAY
KILISUT HAR.
MUTINY B.
DOUBLE BLUFF
FOULWEATHER PT.
USELESS B.
PORT LUDLOW
PT. TALA
POINT NO POINT
CULTUS B.
PUGET
SOUND
HOOD
CANAL
APPLETREE COVE
PT. JEFFERSON
AGATE PASSAGE
SPRING BEACH
PORT MADISON
BAINBRIDGE
SHIP CANAL
WEST PT.
LAKE WASHINGTON
L. UNION
ELLIOTT BAY
MAGNOLIA BLUFF
SMITH COVE
SEATTLE
DUWAMISH HD.
BREMERTON
ALKI PT.
SMAQUAMOX
HARBOR IS
MERCER IS.
DUWAMISH R.

LIBRARY ASSOCIATION
PORTLAND OREGON
ILLUMINO
1864

Northwest Gateway

BOOKS BY
ARCHIE BINNS

Northwest Gateway

Mighty Mountain

The Land Is Bright

The Laurels Are Cut Down

Lightship

Northwest Gateway

THE STORY OF THE PORT OF SEATTLE

By
ARCHIE BINNS

ILLUSTRATED

Doubleday, Doran & Company, Inc.

GARDEN CITY, N. Y.   1941

LIBRARY ASSOCIATION OF PORTLAND ORE

PRINTED AT THE *Country Life Press*, GARDEN CITY, N. Y., U. S. A.

CL
COPYRIGHT, 1941
BY ARCHIE BINNS
ALL RIGHTS RESERVED

MAR 1 0 1953

To

FRANK BINNS
who carried a Home Guard rifle
during Seattle's anti-Chinese riots
so that the processes of democracy
might be preserved.

AUG 2 7 1941

Contents

Contents

Illustrations

[ix]

Northwest Gateway

CHAPTER I

The Mythical Strait

GOING INTO SEATTLE from the Pacific a ship must pass between authentic Cape Flattery and the Graveyard. The Graveyard is the hard and harborless lee shore toward which a strong northerly current sets, and where great Pacific swells break and thunder at the foot of the mountains on Vancouver Island.

Like Cape Flattery and the forested hills of the Olympic Peninsula, Vancouver Island is authenticated. But historically the fifteen-mile width of water between is a myth. The Strait of Juan de Fuca is a companion piece with dragons and boiling seas and the jumping-off place at the end of the flat earth.

The explanation for this state of affairs goes back to Italy and ancient history. Italy was the place to dream of unexplored seas. There, in Genoa, Columbus dreamed of voyages that took him to the New World. There, in Venice, history says, Juan de Fuca dreamed the strait that bears his name.

Northwest Gateway

Historians tell us it happened this way: In 1596, on the Rialto, an Elizabethan gentleman named Michael Lok met a seafaring man who was down on his luck. The old sea dog was a Greek pilot by the name of Apostolus Valerianos. But he was better known as Juan de Fuca, having spent forty years in the Spanish service.

Juan de Fuca's best story was about a voyage to the Puget Sound country.

In 1592 the Viceroy of Mexico sent him on a voyage of discovery to the North West coast of America. Hee followed the coast of California and Oregon, etc., until hee came to the latitude of forty-eight degrees, and there finding that the land trended North and North East, with a broad Inlet of sea between 48 and 49 degrees of latitude, hee entered thereinto, sayling therein more than twenty days, and found that the land trended sometimes North West and North East and also East and South Eastward, and was very much broader sea than was at said entrance, and hee passed divers islands in that sayling. . . . And also hee said that hee being entered thus farre into said strait, and being come into the North Sea already, and finding the sea wide enough everywhere, and to be about thirtie or fortie leagues wide in the mouth of the strait where hee entered [where he entered the supposed North Sea or Atlantic Ocean] hee thought that hee had now well discharged his office and done the thing hee was sent to doe, and that hee not being armed to resist the force of the savage people that might happen, hee therefore set sayle and returned homeward againe towards Nova Spain, where hee arrived at Acapulco Anno 1592.

Juan de Fuca's voyage, as reported by Lok, describes the circumnavigation of Vancouver Island by way of the

The Mythical Strait

Strait of Juan de Fuca, Canal de Haro, the Gulf of Georgia, Johnson's Strait, Goleto Channel and the Pacific. It includes a creditable description of Mount Lemon, at the northwest end of Vancouver Island:

And at the entrance of the said strait [where he re-entered the Pacific] there is on the North West coast thereof a great Headland or Island, with an exceeding high Pinnacle of spired rock like a pillar thereupon.

The Viceroy of Mexico promised Juan de Fuca a princely reward for his discovery, and gave him nothing. Juan de Fuca left the Spanish service and was now open to offers of employment from the English, who did not love Spain.

Lok tried and failed to get the old pilot into the English service, and de Fuca died on the beach. Nothing was done about his discovery for a hundred and seventy-odd years. In 1775 the Spanish sent an expedition north from San Blas, under Heceta and Quadra. The expedition followed the coast to Alaska, but failed to find the strait described by Juan de Fuca. The man was a Greek and, *quién sabe?*

Three years later the great Captain Cook followed the Northwest Coast in search of the same strait and the Northwest Passage. Between the latitudes of forty-eight and forty-nine degrees he sighted a bold cape. The cape and the latitude checked with de Fuca's story. Inside that cape there should be the Greek pilot's strait, sketched on Cook's Spanish chart. Cook was fresh from his discovery of the Hawaiian Islands, and he had with him such able men as William Bligh, who was later in command of H.M.S. *Bounty*, and George Vancouver, who became a discoverer in his own right. Cook passed the cape, where Juan de Fuca's strait should have been—and was—but he failed to see it. He sailed on, into the Arctic, naming the headland "Cape Flattery" for the story of the discredited Greek pilot.

Ten years later, in 1788, Captain John Mears was exploring in a handy little vessel, the *North West America*, which he had built at Nootka, on Vancouver Island. Between forty-eight and forty-nine degrees of latitude he sailed into the broad inlet of sea which the Viceroy's Greek pilot had described, and where he had located it nearly two hundred years before. Mears named the great inlet the "Strait of Juan de Fuca." And he named the beautiful mountain on the mainland, to the south, "Mount Olympus."

The beachcombing Greek pilot was vindicated at last, or seemed to be. But historians went on a voyage of discovery of their own. With Juan de Fuca's mythical strait a proven fact, they proved that Juan de Fuca was a myth. He had never been near the northwest coast, and he had fabricated everything he described: his strait and the Haro Canal; the San Juan Islands and the Gulf of Georgia; Johnson's Strait and Goleto Channel. All that historians concede de Fuca is a gifted imagination. They observe it is remarkable that the great inland sea was found precisely where he located it, and much as he described it. Remarkable, indeed!

So it happens that on a voyage from the Pacific to

The Mythical Strait

Seattle a ship must pass through seas that are mythical, or
at most a coincidence.

Since we are sailing mythical seas, we might as well
make it a mythical and unnautical voyage. Assume a summer day and yourself in command of a steamship. You
nose in toward the Strait, followed by big Pacific swells
that rise out of the west like shadows, assume gray reality
as they overtake your vessel, and go dim again as they
pass and heave into muffled oblivion a few seas ahead.
Between the blasts of your whistle you hear the great
air diaphone on Tatoosh. Once through rifted veils of fog
a great shape looms up to starboard: the broken white
of a receding sea lacing over rocks; sheer, fog-wet walls
of rock; and, two hundred feet above the sea, green grass
and the neat white buildings of the lighthouse and radio
station. You see them through gauze veils of fog that
thicken. They dim and are gone like things in a dream.
There remain the long, overtaking seas that come up
astern and go away ahead like shadows, real only for the
moment when they heave through the little circle of
reality about your fog-wet ship. There is only that, and
the roar of your whistle answering the horn on Tatoosh.

There is not much to see, but what can you expect, entering waters that have no right to be; a strait invented by
one of the ancients who dreamed and sleeps on the other
side of the earth? At least you know where you are. And
having sailed these mythical waters on other summer days
you have reason to expect clearer weather.

The shadow of another long Pacific swell rises out of
oblivion astern. It takes shape, like a sea in the pearl dawn,

[5]

and becomes real as it passes under your ship. Smoothly it heaves away, ahead, not shadowy this time, but brightening. Almost abruptly you steam into blue waters and bright sunshine.

Astern, that yellowish bank of fog over the Pacific is stopped by the gentle summer easterly blowing out of the Strait. Ahead of you are waters that an old Greek pilot dreamed by the Adriatic Sea.

This is to be an unnautical voyage. You do not want to be encumbered by details and the responsibilities of a command, and you have a diverting thought. You send the surprised watch officer on an errand, and he returns with a passenger who is on his first voyage. You say to the landlubber, "Relieve the quartermaster at the wheel and take over the navigation; pilot us through the Strait of Juan de Fuca."

The passenger takes the wheel, eagerly. "Thank you," he says, "I've always wanted to steer a boat." His calling the ship a boat is proof that he is a landlubber, and you are disconcerted by the confidence with which he takes over without even asking where or how. Then you learn that he is an historian, and the joke is on you. You volunteer the necessary information: "It's straight ahead for ninety miles, and don't run into the mountains on either side." With that, you give the mate and the quartermaster a holiday, and you go up on the flying bridge to enjoy the scenery.

No pilot is required on a ship going from the Pacific to Seattle, and there is no reason why the lubber cannot get you there. He does not even need any more directions for navigating the Strait. It is ninety miles, without a bend or inlet where he can go astray, and fifteen miles wide, with no outlying dangers. Barring fog and collision, your amateur helmsman has only to distinguish between level waters and mountainous shores. Juan de Fuca dreamed generously and was kind to seamen.

In the wheelhouse below the flying bridge the historian is making out well enough. Roughly, he is taking a mid-channel course along the international boundary, and the generous sea erases the meandering wake he steers. The Pacific swells have dropped to a gentle undulation, and in fine summer weather you steam southeast through waters as blue as the Adriatic. To port you see the blue-green and blue mountainous shores of Vancouver Island. To starboard, the still-untamed Olympic Peninsula, with its crescendo of forested hills rolling up like organ music to the Olympic Mountains and the white peak of Mount Olympus.

In the Strait you meet and overtake other ships: an oil tanker from Los Angeles; the American *Flying Fish* from Buenos Aires; the *Satarita* with general cargo for Manila; the Russian *Uralmash* from Vladivostok; the light motor ship *Hie Maru* for Kobe; and one of the Luckenbach family from Boston.

In narrower waters this might be considered traffic, but the Strait is wide and deep, and the closest passing ship gives you a berth of a mile. Even the largest does not have the whale-in-a-bathtub look of a third-rate liner in a steamship advertisement. Here vessels are seen in their proper setting and proportions, like things in nature. Only an advertising artist would pretend that a ship is more impressive than the sea and mightier than the mountainous shore.

The shores have not changed much since Juan de Fuca's day. In three hours of steaming at eighteen knots you do not pass a settlement bigger than a modest village. And now, to draw on Lok's interview with the Greek impostor, the land to port trends northeast toward the Strait of Georgia, and to starboard it trends east and southeastward toward Admiralty Inlet. There is very much broader sea than was at said entrance, and off to the northeast, beyond the smoke of Victoria, are the divers San Juan Islands, which Juan de Fuca passed in that "sayling". . . .

Is history mistaken, and did the Greek pilot really discover these waters for an ungrateful Viceroy? Or did he dream them, an exile on the beach at Venice? There is one fragile clue, overlooked for centuries. Compare maps and charts. Thus far, Juan de Fuca's Strait follows the shape and general trend of the Adriatic Sea, looking from Venice. Here it opens into broader waters, much as the Adriatic opens into the Ionian Sea. And those rocky San Juan Islands, so lovely and so bold, shimmering in the enchanted distance, might be the Islands of Greece.

Truly, historians may be right that Juan de Fuca invented this lovely inland sea. Here may be a clue to the material from which he shaped his dream. Threadbare and old, in the twilight of a glittering century, he stood on the shore of the Adriatic and looked toward home. . . .

The Mythical Strait

The thought makes you feel more kind toward history. You descend to the wheelhouse, where the historian is having a good time.

"These are remarkable waters," he says, "really remarkable! I've been going straight ahead for three-and-a-half hours without running into anything. I'm trying to see how long I can keep it up."

"For another hour," you say. "It's ninety miles from the Cape to Admiralty Head. There you turn a bit more to the south. If necessary you could raise Seattle with one more compass course."

"Remarkable waters!" Then he observes, "Old Juan de Fuca had the imagination, describing all this two hundred years before it was discovered!"

"Yah," you say, "he was a good one."

At a pinch, two compass courses from Cape Flattery would bring your vessel within sight of Seattle, a hundred and thirty-odd miles inland. But there is no use pinching. Between low Wilson Point and the old tower on Admiralty Head you tell the historian to keep a mid-channel course. Your vessel is now in more restricted waters. Even then there is room enough with reasonable caution. Between here and Seattle, Admiralty Inlet is nowhere less than three miles wide, and for two miles of that width a vessel would never be in less than twenty fathoms at low tide. The shores of the Olympic Peninsula to starboard and Whidbey Island to port rise abruptly two hundred and three hundred feet. With visibility good, navigating the Inlet with a ship of any size is a simple matter of not ramming the unmistakable shore.

[9]

Northwest Gateway

Admiralty Inlet is narrower than the Strait, but it makes up the difference with the harbors that honeycomb its western shore. Passing Wilson Point at the moment of entering the Inlet, you open up the fine harbor of Port Townsend, two miles wide and six miles long. The east shore of the bay is hollow; land wrapped on four sides of Kilisut Harbor, which is so thoroughly protected that it is not of much use. From the narrowed southern end of Port Townsend Bay a dredged channel cuts through the peninsula to Oak Bay on the other side. To the south, Oak Bay curves into the harbor of Port Ludlow, and around Tala Point from Ludlow is the entrance to the inlet that Vancouver named Hood Canal. The Canal is a landlocked, deep water harbor, seventy-five miles long.

All that is hung on the first harbor you open entering Admiralty Inlet, and there are many more.

On the bluff at the entrance to its fine harbor sits the ghost city of Port Townsend—older than Seattle.

"Small for its age," the historian remarks.

You agree. The city is smaller than it looks. Many of those buildings have never been occupied—never will be. They are the fine brick warehouses built for the golden harvest that never came. For sixty years they have been empty, except for accumulating dust. Seattle was not the only village that dreamed of being the city of destiny. That ghost city on top of its three-hundred-foot bluff had the grandest dream of them all; incredibly grand. Those brick warehouses, with their dust and virginal seals of spider web, were built for the grain harvest of the Columbia River Valley. Port Townsend was to be the seaport of Oregon as well as Washington. How? Why?

The fathers of Port Townsend figured it out. They had a formula that seemed foolproof. Grain would be shipped by water. The undredged bar of the Columbia River left Oregon without a seaport. The grain would have to be shipped by rail to water, which meant Puget Sound. It would be carried by sailing ships, which meant the closest harbor assured of good winds. That meant Port Townsend. The town proprietors believed in their formula passionately. They believed in it enough to pour fortunes into the echoing walls of warehouses. And when others were drawn by the glamor of the scheme and flocked there, they were rebuffed. Their money was not enough to buy lots in the city of destiny. Gold, and a harvest of dust. . . .

"That's right, Historian, give that freighter a good berth." Things have happened in these waters, and simultaneously launched investigations have not always converged at the heart of the mystery.

In the last minutes of March 1921 two vessels sighted each other out here: the *Governor* and the *West Hartland*. The *Governor* was a big, two-funnel liner, on her way from San Francisco and Victoria to Seattle. The *West Hartland* was a Shipping Board freighter, outward bound from Port Townsend and loaded deep with lumber and railroad ties for India. There were shreds of mist in the night air, and visibility was not the best, but it was fair. When they were two miles apart the lookout on the *West Hartland* struck the fo'c'sle bell twice to signify a vessel to port, and the *Governor's* lookout struck his bell once for a vessel to starboard. After they were reported, the vessels never lost sight of each other.

The *Hartland* had the right of way, and she held her course and speed. And the *Governor*, with plenty of room and time to cross the freighter's bow, kept her course and speed.

The *Governor* always had a farewell dance on her last night at sea, but the dance had broken up a little while before midnight. The ship's orchestra had put its instruments away, and most of the passengers had turned in. In one stateroom a mother and her two daughters went to bed, amused by the fact that they were already more than home. Early in the evening they had passed Neah Bay, but the liner did not stop there and they would have to come back from Seattle in a smaller vessel. But at least they had seen it clearly, and for the benefit of other passengers the three pointed out their home, which they never saw again.

A few late passengers were still on deck, although the fun was over and there was nothing to see but the flashing white light on Point Wilson to starboard, and the high and lonely shore of Whidbey Island to port. Ahead there was only the flashing green light on shadowy Marrowstone Island, with Mystery Bay in its heart. Between its dark shores Admiralty Inlet was deserted except for the mast lights of a steamer coming out of Port Townsend.

Eight bells struck and it was midnight and April first. Above and below decks the watches changed, and in the pilothouse of the *Governor*, Second Mate Kellenberg relieved Third Mate Hage, but the navigation was in charge

The Mythical Strait

of Pilot Marden. It was a calm night and the weather was clear, except for wisps of fog that did not dim the mast lights and red port running light of the outward-bound freighter. There was plenty of room to cross her bow.

Suddenly there was not plenty of room, and the freighter bellowed its warning. Give her a whistle blast in answer. Port your helm a little. Port a little more. Port a little—— HARD APORT! Slash the telegraph handle to *Stop*, to *Full Speed Astern.* . . .

On both vessels it was the same. They saw the misty smile of the sea change to a leer as something distorted. Not distorted; straightened out, as the mirage of safety disappeared, the illusion of ample searoom. The hazy atmosphere, with its light banners of mist, was like a tide sweeping the vessels toward each other with infinite speed. But it was only the straightening of a distortion; an illusion vanishing in air that had the quality of a mirage. Neither ship had been where she appeared to be.

The desperation of short whistle blasts exploded in the air, with its waiting shrouds of mist. Below, steering engines roared and gongs clanged. Engineers leaped to throttles and reversing levers. Engines stopped with a hissing sigh, then pounded into action with a flash of great piston and connecting rods and outward-tilted eccentric rods. The great, racing thunder of propellers going astern—— But all the speed of desperation was not quick enough for the vanishing of an illusion.

Afterward some of the dead were washed ashore on the lonely Whidbey beach. Children came down from the heights of the island and found treasures: cases of grapefruit and steamer chairs, and some of the fortunate found fur coats.

Things have happened here. You steam past Marrowstone Point, and the fine harbor of Port Townsend closes behind you. To starboard you have the yellow bluffs and two-hundred-foot wooded shore of Marrowstone Island, wrapped so tightly around its harbor as to make it unusable. Like the fathers of Port Townsend who guarded their treasure too jealously.

"Keep her in mid-channel, Historian." The navigable channel here is three miles wide; six hundred feet deep in the middle. There is deep water close to the high, lonely shore of Whidbey Island.

Once, boys playing on that golden shore saw a thing they never forgot. When they were men they recalled it, undimmed by time and still mysterious. They felt the urge to tell about it because, in a way, it was always new. Each time was a new attempt to communicate feelings that could not be communicated. But they never reached the heart of the mystery.

The boys were wading close to the deep clear water of the outgoing tide when they saw something coming toward them, just beyond the edge of the shore. Really, they felt it before they saw anything; the way, playing in bright sunshine, you feel the shadow of a moving cloud before you see it or know what it is. You have only the feeling of change—of some darkness coming toward you.

It was not the shadow of a cloud, but it was like a shadow passing in the deep clear water, making it not clear, and coming between them and underwater sand and stones, and seaweed waving in the depths of the tide. Those things were blotted out, as by a moving shadow. Then the boys saw that it was a ship passing under water, almost at their feet. It was a sailing ship, with its masts gone, and it was hove down with its deck toward them. They could see the fo'c'sle head, the rail and hatches, and the planking of the deck. The ship was close to the surface of the water, but it never broke the surface, never came through. Ghosting by in that deep tide, the derelict went as if it knew its course and was confident of its destination. And the boys who stared at it knew they were watching something in another world. If any part of it had showed above the water—but it glided by under the surface, belonging wholly to the sea. Two worlds were separated by a few feet of water, transparent as glass. But then, and in the rest of their lives, speculating about it, they never got through those few feet of clear water.

It was so close, they said afterward, almost close enough to touch. If they had had a rope they could have got it on the ship, somehow, and ended her sleepwalking voyage. They would have beached her on the outgoing tide and found out what ship she was, and from what port, and what dead men or cargo were below. But they had no rope with which they could pull her from one world to another in order that they might come to the heart of her mystery. Then, and thinking about her afterward, they always saw her sailing under that stately tide, separated from them by a few feet of water as clear as air and, alas, impenetrable forever. . . .

This west coast of Whidbey Island is a lonely shore,

harborless except for open bays: Admiralty Bay, as grand and open as a palace without a roof; the poor shelter of Mutiny Bay; Useless Bay, which condemns itself; and Cultus Bay, which means "worthless."

"Keep a mid-channel course, Historian." Long ago the clipper ship *Windward* piled up on that lonely shore. But there is no use looking for her bones here or in the deep flowing tide. She had a land burial, under roaring city streets. Seattle has a clipper ship buried in her heart.

There, to port, are the twin points of Double Bluff, like a woman's breasts. To starboard is Foulweather Bluff, two hundred and fifty feet, protecting the entrance to Hood Canal. Beyond Foulweather and Double Bluff is Vancouver's Puget Sound, but the name hasn't stayed put. Except to mariners, Puget Sound is from Olympia to the Pacific.

"No, keep the wheel, Historian. Puget Sound isn't anything ticklish." Inside the entrance it's five miles wide. That next headland, with the light, is Point No Point. From there the Sound fans out to ten miles wide, and there will be better than six hundred feet of water under our keel. The unmistakable, wooded shores go up steeply three hundred and four hundred feet above waters as blue as the Adriatic. Juan de Fuca dreamed in an age of magnificence.

Off the riddle of Point No Point, we open up the great reach of Puget Sound, running due south. Twenty miles ahead, on the eastern shore, there is the unmistakable loom of a city: sky line and smoke, and the smoke of steamers entering and leaving a harbor beyond a tremendous headland.

The Mythical Strait

Steering carefully, the historian says, "Until now we haven't seen anything bigger than a village, but I can recognize a great city from far off. There had to be one for this area, but how did it happen to be Seattle?"

"Because of its harbor," you say.

"This country seems to be all harbors," the historian says. "Is Seattle's so much bigger and better than the others?"

"We've passed others as good," you tell him, "and some of them much bigger."

"Then it isn't the harbor."

You say, "A harbor isn't only what it is, it's also where it is. The most important thing about a harbor is the land. Water's good in the right place, but you can have too much of it."

"Like Ophelia," the historian suggests.

"Exactly," you say, though the name is unfamiliar. "We've passed half a dozen good harbors; one of them with a hundred and fifty square miles of sheltered anchorage, but all of them with miles of water between them and the rest of the United States. Even the open bays we saw on the other side are on an island. Seattle is the first real harbor on the mainland, except Bellingham Bay up toward Canada. Bellingham upsets the theory, because it has a harbor four times as big as Seattle's Elliott Bay, and it had a brief gold-rush population of ten thousand when Seattle was just a village of twenty families."

The historian suggests, "Seattle is nearer the western center of gravity of the state."

"It's near the center of everything," you agree.

Northwest Gateway

Steaming south, you open up the fine harbor of Port Madison with its snug inner harbor, and Agate Passage on the west opening into fifty miles of still more-inland waterways. All of them are on the wrong side of the Sound for a great city, though one of them has Bremerton and the Navy Yard.

Still you have not seen one real harbor on the continental side, though the signs keep multiplying. You meet a ferry loaded to its shovelnose with motor cars; a big freighter slides out from behind the headland of West Point and swings toward you. Flying high, an air liner for Victoria passes over your ship. A silver ferry, as streamlined as any car it carries, shuttles across the Sound past Bainbridge Island; a passenger steamer for Alaska plows out from behind the great headland; and a four-motored bomber rumbles overhead on a trial flight from Boeing Field. Between you and West Point, surprisingly, a sightseeing steamer pokes out of the high, yellow bluff and passes confidently between buoys that mark the entrance of the Lake Washington ship canal.

If we were to follow the sight-seer's course in reverse, our big steamship would go comfortably through the Government locks at Ballard and through the ship canal. The canal would open out and we would find ourselves in a mile-long lake in the heart of the city; a lake with wharves, drydocks and yards where new ships are built and older ones are repaired, and mooring grounds where still older ships, steamers and windjammers, lie enchanted in the still dark water, overtaken by the synthetic death of obsolescence.

The Mythical Strait

From Lake Union we would sail on through the city, through the campus of the University of Washington. When it seemed we had already sailed too far and could go no farther, our ship would steam out of the narrow, dredged channel of reedy Union Bay into a deep, fresh-water lake on the other side of the city; a lake twenty miles long, surrounded by the city and shipyards and fir forests, sawmills and cabins and homes of elegance with yachts anchored out in front and seaplanes parked in front yards. That would be Lake Washington. In the lake there would be Mercer Island, five miles long and a mile wide, rising to three hundred feet high, with city streets and homes and fir forests. A floating bridge links it with the city and a fixed bridge spans the distance to the opposite shore.

This is part of the harbor of Seattle, with its infinite variety of waterways through land and land in water, and salt water harbors and fresh: canals and lakes and rivers leading from security to security. That is what we would find if we turned in at the door in the yellow bluff and sailed our steamship into the heart of the city and out on the other side.

But we are still in Puget Sound, between Point Jefferson and Spring Beach, and we are on a more conventional voyage. The wheelhouse clock is striking eight bells, four in the afternoon. Pinch-hitting for your amateur helmsman, you take the lanyard above the wheel and give it eight smart jerks, in pairs. The clangs are answered in deeper tones by the big bell on the fo'c'sle head, and the first officer and a quartermaster step into the wheelhouse.

They are coming on their appointed watch, ignorant of the trick you have been playing on history.

The historian relinquishes the wheel to the quartermaster with a sigh of relief. Following you out onto the bridge, he says, "Thank goodness, that's over. I was scared stiff that I might run into some of this shipping, or aground."

"Not aground," you say. "Right here we're in the greatest depth of all, with nearly a thousand feet of water under us."

"Remarkable waters," the historian says, "truly remarkable!"

You stand on the port wing of the bridge as your ship steams around West Point, opening up Elliott Bay, with a great city rising before you. And still the Sound is three miles wide, and better than eight hundred feet deep. Off to the west a freighter is passing close to the beautiful shore of Bainbridge Island, with the smoke from her stack drifting before her in the light southerly blowing out of the Sound. The freighter is a big one of ten thousand tons, but she does not look big or small. Against the high, forested shore she looks a part of nature, comfortably at home, as a ship should look. Above the ship and the wooded hills of the island there is the long range of the Olympic Mountains, blue and crested with snow like long seas breaking in the sky.

To port, that three-hundred-foot cliff, golden in the sunshine, is Magnolia Bluff, crowned with madroña trees. By now there may be magnolias around some of the fine residences, but there were only madroñas when it was named by some amateur botanist who was confused by somewhat similar foliages. Like Appletree Cove back there beyond Point Jefferson. One of Vancouver's men saw dogwood in bloom and predicted apples in the fall. Among discoverers the first to arrive is awarded the palm, even though he has left his glasses at home and accepts it for a pine.

Those madroña trees have never borne magnolia blossoms, but they have done something even more remarkable. Notice how some of them lean out over the edge of the bluff toward the sun and this water of Adriatic blue. Remember their wood is weak and brittle and tremendously heavy. By all laws they should break in the first good breeze. But they do not break, even in a rare gale. They accomplish that by adopting the principles of engineering and growing their trunks in the shape of "I-beam" girders. You are not expected to believe that, but drive out there sometime and look for yourself. As the trees grow older and heavier, their cylindrical trunks flatten on two sides. And as they grow still older and heavier, the flattened sides become concave until the cross section of the trunk has an unmistakable I-beam shape.

The flora is remarkable in other ways. With a good telescope used at the right moment you could make out date palms up there in someone's garden, out of doors the year round and making a go of it. On Queen Anne Hill ahead, you could see fig trees ripening their fruit, and hedges of bamboo. Sometimes roses bloom on Christmas Day. Admittedly, such things are strange in the latitude of Maine.

Northwest Gateway

The warm Japan Current has something to do with it, but the real explanation lies in your own field, Historian. We have it from history that Juan de Fuca invented these mythical waters in Venice. Never having been near the Puget Sound country, he could not be expected to get everything right. It was only natural that some of the trees and flowers of the Adriatic should slip in; and some of the climate; and the color on those golden cliffs and on the deep waters of this gentle northern sea—waters as blue as the Adriatic, forever with the quality of a dream.

There, to port, is Smith Cove Terminal and the Great Northern Docks that were a part of Jim Hill's empire. Not part of the real harbor, but a port big enough for a fair-sized city: piers half a mile long and channels dredged through mud flats. Japanese steamers load there mostly, sometimes a dozen of them at a time, and Smith Cove longshoremen are a breed of their own.

It has a tough sound, Smith Cove, but Henry Smith was another sort. He was a medical doctor and a literary man who wrote good prose and better verse. One was about "Time that blows a wreath of wrinkles to us all. . . ." But that was when he was an old man. When he was young he had his share of adventure. On the night the Indian War broke he rowed out of the cove with his mother in a boat with muffled oarlocks, and escaped to the Seattle blockhouse. Then he came back with two runaway sailors and harvested the crop in his clearing— the crop that the Indians burned along with his house before his harvest sweat was dry. Like the doctor whom they could have killed a dozen times, they had a sense of humor, and they let him garner everything into the house and barn before they fired the flaming arrows. No, Smith wouldn't be surprised to see the freight terminal and those piers. He settled in that wilderness cove in the belief that it would be a railroad terminal—and he lived to see it happen.

Beyond Seattle, protecting the harbor from the south, that long, low headland with the fir trees is Alki Point, where the pilgrims landed. Protecting the harbor from the west, the inner point we see, nose on, is Duwamish Head. Between it and the main city, the Duwamish River is split by Harbor Island, which divides the East Waterway from the West Waterway. Between there and here is the main harbor, with deep water up to five miles of curved harbor shore, finned with piers that lie from east to west. The depth of water is authenticated. The Denny brothers and Boren and Bell took soundings from an Indian dugout before they decided to build a city here. Mary Denny supplied the clothesline, with a warning to bring it back. They had a horseshoe for a sounding lead, and their city was fortunate.

There it is, on its seven hills; a city of upwards of half a million people, with all the trappings of a modern metropolis, and a sky line something like New York's. But its personality is its own. And its history is not like that of any other city, Historian. It is a piece of American mythology. The guardian spirits of the city are two horses that came out of the sea at the beginning: a docile black mare and a milk-white stallion with an unbroken spirit and a disposition toward violence.

That is not folklore. It was such a little while ago that there are men living on those hills, keeping office hours in those skyscrapers, who remember the man who drove Seattle's first horses from the sea. His name was Thomas Mercer. Mercer Street and Mercer Island are named after him. He named Lake Union and Lake Washington, and first proposed the ship canal. Discreet and factual histories mention and praise the docile mare and give her name, which is "Tib." They record that Mercer brought two horses, but they do not say much about the other one, because they want their city to have a good name. But the spirits of those two still gallop over the mighty hills of the city: the impatient, pale stallion and the docile black mare.

Madame Damnable, turned to stone, sleeps under one of those hills where invisible horses gallop. On her indestructible face there is a Mona Lisa smile of satisfaction, because she is going to outlast all the generations of Seattle, if it takes a million years. And it is also because no one ever dared to ask the riddle of Fells Point, Baltimore, which was the Achilles' heel of her mortal life. She and Seattle have a long way to go in their race, because the city is only at the beginning, ninety years away from the landing of its pilgrims on an unknown shore.

CHAPTER II

The Pilgrim Ship

SEATTLE, too, had its Puritans and pilgrims and gentlemen adventurers, and adventurers who were no gentlemen. The city acted out the building of America accurately, but with the growing momentum of more than two centuries. At the far end of telescoped time, Seattle's beginning was the same as the beginning of the nation. The pilgrims of Seattle landed from their little sailing ship on a shore as unknown and forbidding as the shore of Plymouth, and as isolated from the home states as Plymouth was from England, at the edge of a denser forest, as well supplied with Indians and wild beasts. And though the Indians, ignorant of history, were friendly at the time, that flaw in the parallel was soon corrected.

On November twelfth, 1851, the stage was set for the arrival of the pilgrims who founded Seattle. From unnamed Smith Cove to Duwamish Head the bluff shore and mud flats of Elliott Bay were walled by a heavy fir forest that had never been penetrated by a white man. A

[25]

few miles up the Duwamish River, on meadow lands and little prairies, there were the Collins, two Maples and Van Asselt claims. All of the men were bachelors except Collins. His wife and fourteen-year-old daughter, Lucinda, were the first white women in the region. West of the divided mouth of the Duwamish River, near Duwamish Head, was the only settlement on Elliott Bay. That was a temporary fishing camp where Chief Seattle and some of his tribe were catching salmon for their winter food supply. The place was called "Skwudux," a name that never would have done for a great city.

From bold Duwamish Head the heavily timbered shore inclined southwest and diminished to low-shored Alki Point, which was then called "Smaquamox." There, on Alki Point, was the beginning of a city, and one white resident. The beginning of a city was a log cabin, complete as to walls but without a roof. That evening the heavy November rain roared down into the building and ran out of the doorway. It was no place to live, and the one white resident huddled under a leaking shelter of cedar boughs, with his blanket around him like an Indian, while he kept his fire alive under the kettle in which he was cooking his supper.

The white resident was a young man who had crossed the plains that year from Illinois. He was nineteen and his name was David Denny. For three weeks he had been alone, except for visits from the Indians. There was a certain amount of discomfort in his situation that November evening. An older man in the same fix would have considered the situation desperate. A few days before, working on the unfinished cabin, he had cut his foot with the ax. He had managed to stop the bleeding, but the wound left him too crippled to work or hunt. Along with the wound he had a return of malarial chills and fever, brought in his blood from Illinois. On top of malaria he had a bad case of neuralgia. And that afternoon, hobbling back from a look at the roofless cabin, he had found a family of wild animals in possession of his shelter. He was not afraid, but neither was he a fool, and he stood patiently in the rain while the skunk tribe ate up the last of his food. When they were gone, the comforts of life were vigorously reduced. About all David Denny had were a leaking shelter of thatched boughs, a handful of tea that the skunks had left and his hopeful youth.

A sad song might be written about a boy of nineteen, sick and wounded, without food and almost without shelter, deserted on an unexplored shore among the Indians and battered by the icy rain of northern autumn. But David Denny did not feel deserted or sorry for himself. He was at the beginning of manhood, at the beginning of great things. Not many young men have the opportunity to keep vigil in such a primeval place, with the knowledge that it is the beginning of a great city. John Low and Lee Terry had decided that six weeks before, when the exploring party of three landed at Smaquamox. They decided to build a city there, and their plans went ahead so fast that within a few days Terry had decided on a name for their city. They would call it "New York," after his birthplace, which their city would shortly rival. So John Low left young Terry and David to build the first house while he walked back to Portland, two hundred miles away, to bring his family. David Denny's father and four brothers were also there, and he sent a letter to his married brother, Arthur, to come at once to Puget Sound. Arthur had already decided on that region, but chills and fever had kept him helpless in Portland while his young brother and John Low had gone to drive Low's cattle north for winter range and to spy out the country.

At the village of Olympia, in northern Oregon, the two explorers met Lee Terry, the boy from New York, and the three of them joined forces with Captain Fay, who had a boat and who was setting out to buy salmon from the Indians to ship to San Francisco. The four sailed down the Sound as far as Elliott Bay and up the Duwamish as far as the four newly staked claims. Then Captain Fay left the others at Smaquamox, which later became Alki, and the party was reduced to three. Low went back to Portland to bring some population for his city, and the party was reduced to two. David Denny and Lee Terry built the city as far as one cabin without a roof. Then they discovered they had no frow for splitting shakes. Luther Collins came down the Duwamish in his scow, on the way to the Hudson's Bay station at Nisqually, and Terry caught a ride with him. The settlement was thus reduced to one man of nineteen and a roofless cabin. And after three weeks of solitude and an invasion of skunks, the food supply of the budding city was reduced to a handful of tea.

When his pot boiled, young David made some tea and drank it, hot and strong and straight. Then he muffled himself in his damp blanket and crawled out of his shelter for the evening look around, which had become part of his Robinson Crusoe life.

There was not much to see but night coming down fast with the autumn rain. On the wide reach of the Sound there was no sail or running lights of any ship. To the northeast there was the luminous smoke of an Indian fire on Duwamish Head. All the other shores were black with the impenetrable darkness of the forest, where night came early and materialized into a solid thing of multiplied blackness. There was nothing to hear but a breath of wind passing through the great fir trees on the point and the cold wash of waves on the gravel beach. Inherently there was not much comfort in standing there alone at the edge of the primeval world in the roaring cold rain. But the young man did not feel cold. He was full of hot tea and burning with malarial fever that made him light-headed, and he did not feel like a lonely castaway. From Alki to Duwamish Head and across Elliott Bay, north to West Point, he saw the lighted buildings of a great city. It was the city that he and young Terry had dreamed, and it was real because Lee Terry was from New York and he had described the city and the gas-lit windows, seen from the opposite shore across dark water at night. Terry, gone for three weeks now, was sure they could build as big a city out here. Low, the cautious, middle-aged man of thirty-one, had said it would take years. But David and Lee were both in their teens. Working on the cabin or lying under their shelter of boughs at night, they had talked as if the city were already a fact. This night David

[29]

could see it at last: the dark bulk of buildings walling the shore like a forest, shot with the twinkling lights of countless windows. It was so vast and grand that it made him feel delirious, and he could even hear the roar of traffic, like wind going through great trees. . . . The city faded and the countless lighted windows dwindled to dancing fever sparks inside his eyes. He was alone at the edge of the forest, beside a roofless cabin in the rain. Sick and wounded and supperless, with no food left for breakfast, he crawled into the shelter of boughs and went to bed under his damp blankets. He was not sorry for himself, because he was young and holding the fort where a great city was about to spring up at the edge of the unexplored forest.

When John Low reached Portland with David Denny's letter and his own endorsement of northern Oregon, he found everything favorable. Arthur Denny and his wife had somewhat recovered from their malaria. Between chills and fevers, Arthur had learned more about Puget Sound, and he was eager to start north at once. His brother-in-law, Carson Boren, also wanted to go, and Boren's attractive young sister, Louisa, was of the same mind. She and Arthur Denny's wife were sisters, and she and David had crossed the plains together and were good friends. An emigrant by the name of William Bell had also caught the "Northern Oregon Fever," and in the small world of Portland, which had a population of two thousand, another man had joined the party. He was a California gold miner of 'forty-nine, and he already had some experience in the west although he was only twenty-two. He was Charles Terry of New York, and he joined the main party without knowing that his young brother, Lee, had already joined the advance guard. It was a party of young people for a young country. The oldest member was John Low, who was thirty-one, and the youngest was Arthur Denny's son, Roland, born in Portland two months before.

Everything had gone well for John Low's plan to round up a population for his city at Smaquamox. He had found more willing recruits than he had expected, and there was no difficulty about transportation. The *Exact* was at Portland, fitting out for an expedition to the Queen Charlotte Islands, and on the way she was entering Puget Sound with emigrants for Olympia. Captain Folger agreed to take the city builders to Smaquamox, if they could find it. He had never seen Puget Sound, which was only sketchily charted, and he could not be expected to recognize a spot the Indians called Smaquamox unless it was pointed out to him.

Carrying emigrants to Puget Sound was only a sideline for Captain Folger. The real destination of the *Exact*, Queen Charlotte Islands, was the home of the fierce Haidahs, who terrorized the Indians of Puget Sound on their raids for slaves and plunder. A discovery of gold in the Queen Charlottes had been reported, and now it was the Haidahs' turn to be plundered. Most of the passengers in the little schooner were miners on their way to the islands of a strange and splendid race that wore armor and helmets in battle, and carved great totem poles and tombs for their dead, which were raised on cedar columns five feet through and ornamented with great, brooding figures of the Thunderbird. The Haidahs also carved beautiful canoes that were sometimes seventy feet long and carried upwards of a hundred trouble-loving warriors. Only the lure of gold would have tempted men in their right senses to their forbidding islands.

The founders of Seattle were hitching onto the star of a gold rush, and it was a good omen.

The pilgrim ship was the schooner *Exact,* and she hailed from Nantucket, not very far away from where the *Mayflower* landed. She was not so big as the *Mayflower*, and probably no easier on the stomach, but she was a better, more seaworthy ship for those who could stay with her. The *Exact* was a two-masted, bald-headed schooner, seventy-three feet long, twenty feet in beam and six feet deep in the hold, of about seventy tons burden. She was the product of generations of pilgrim descendants: English colonists becoming Yankees and developing fast and handy smuggling craft to outsmart the revenue cutters of the mother country, and outright Yankees developing still faster craft for outright competition.

The *Exact* had the profile of a Gloucester fisherman and, except for the lack of topsails, she had the same rig; and she could sail. In her day she was one of the smallest craft to round Cape Horn, and she made a better passage of it than some of the big ships. And she was easier on her crew. With her bald-headed rig there was no occasion for men to go aloft, and when the wind piped up and the helm threatened to take charge, they clapped tackles on the tiller and drove her like a clipper ship.

The Pilgrim Ship

The *Exact* was commanded by Captain Isaiah Folger of Nantucket. Isaiah was the son of Walter Folger, the scholar and inventor, and one of his crew was his young son, George, who was there by way of a health experiment. All the other Folger children had died, and when the youngest began to pine away, the captain said to his wife, "Sarah, we won't have a doctor to George. I'll take him with me in the schooner." Sea life and salt horse and Cape Horn weather and hard chances did the trick, and George lived to be a man.

Captain Fay had brought the advance guard for the founding of the city, and Grandma Fay was in the pilgrim ship, but she was not called that until long afterward. Captain Fay and she had not even met. At the time she was Mrs Alexander, and she and her husband and their two little boys were on their way to Olympia. But Grandma Fay was the right woman to be on board. She was the only one of that party of inland people who would ever talk about the voyage of the pilgrim ship. She had gone on observing, no matter what, and she should have been a novelist because she remembered the right things; for instance, how the women prepared for the voyage, and what they had for breakfast on the fifth of November 1851, and how Charlie Terry got seasick, and what the gold miners sang on their way to the island of the Haidahs.

The *Exact* was to sail on November fifth, and on the fourth the pilgrims brought their belongings on board and the women primped up for the voyage. Grandma Fay, who remembered the right things, observed that they starched their sunbonnets very stiffly and ironed them against the firm, short grass on the river bank.

Charles Terry had decided to go into business at the new city, and in the morning his stock of goods came on board, and he wrote in his memorandum book:

> schooner
> Shipped on the brig *Exact*
> 1 Box Tin ware
> 1 " Axes
> 1 " tobacco
> 1 Keg Brandy
> 1 " Whiskey
> 1 Box Raisins
> Portland Nov 5 1851

His first calling the *Exact* a brig has the flavor of his earlier days in San Francisco, where nearly every small vessel was a brig. It also suggests that he was no seaman, and while it required only a few seconds to correct the error on paper, it took him years to correct an error in city planning that came from the same ignorance of maritime matters.

While Terry checked the goods for his store, Indians came on board offering fresh salmon. All the emigrants bought some, and as many women as could get frying pans on the stove began frying salmon cutlets for breakfast. The one small stove was in the center of the *Exact's* cabin, and the double tier of berths around the cabin were filled with emigrant families and household goods, and fish waiting to be cooked. The packed cabin was hazy with grease smoke and the smell of raw and cooking salmon, and through it all there was the undefined but ever-present smell of the ship, which none of the landsmen commented on, and none of them failed to note.

From above there came the sound of creaking halyard blocks as the sails were hoisted, and the clatter of capstan pawls as the cable was hove in short and the anchor broken out. The *Exact* dropped down the Willamette River toward the Columbia, with the emigrant women cooking salmon on the little stove or quieting their hungry children and trying to make order out of cramped chaos while they waited their turn to cook. All of them had learned patience in the hard school of wagon trains across the continent, and everyone was good natured in the family confusion and cooking smoke and smells of the crowded little cabin. Now and then a bearded face looked down from the hatch, and the miner made relishing comments on the good smell of frying salmon, but the miners did not add themselves to the uproar below.

Considerately the miners stayed on deck where they sang and played poker. The miners for the Queen Charlotte Islands were fine fellows. Some of them were from the California diggings and some were not; but all of them followed the cut and pattern of the 'Forty-niners: disreputable slouch hats, all the beards their faces would raise and all the dirt they could collect, heavy flannel shirts and trousers tucked into high cowhide boots. And at least everyone who could justify the repair had the seat of his trousers patched with the choice cut of flour sacking that bore the legend XXXX, like kisses appended to a letter.

The miners stayed on deck, playing poker and singing "Three Blind Mice," and in the cabin below the relays of pilgrims waited their turn and fried their salmon and ate, precariously, in their crowded bunks. The hardy little *Exact* reached down the Willamette to the Columbia, with a freshening wind, and came into the great, rolling river.

Mrs Alexander, later Fay, had a long wait for the stove, but she was a young woman of cheerful patience. She fixed up her little boys so they would be clean and neat for breakfast, and had a go at the impossible task of arranging her housekeeping affairs in quarters so cramped that everything had to be on top of something else, with something else on top of it. And nothing could be moved without moving everything, and there was no room to move anything. After that, she sliced her fine fat salmon and fixed her coffeepot. All the time there was the disturbing, foreign smell of the ship and the rich smell of salmon sizzling in fat. All around her in the jammed cabin people were eating salmon, and on deck the miners were singing "Three Blind Mice." It sounded innocent at first, but it became exhausting and made her head ache as it went on endlessly, with the parts of the round overlapping. It was such a short song and it went on forever, like identical waves running after the farmer's—running after each other, and it made her a little dizzy. *"Three blind mice, three blind mice——"* The round went on in successive waves, and it seemed to make waves as the little schooner surged along in the rolling Columbia. *"Three blind mice——"* One of the women took her breakfast from the stove, and it was Mrs Alexander's chance to cook her mice—to cook her salmon.

She started for the stove with her frying pan and coffeepot. The cabin floor heaved under her feet, and the air of the cabin swam with the smells of fat salmon, raw and fried, and the awful smell of disturbed bilge water. Mrs Alexander knew that she was about to be very sick.

With a second to decide where, and wondering sickly what the others would think, she gave one glance and saw and heard them pushing their breakfasts away and hanging over the edge of their bunks. She stumbled vaguely to her own, and they were all sick in unison. Abandoned coffee-pots and pans of salmon drifted about the reeling cabin floor as the little schooner surged along in the rolling river. And on deck the heartless miners roared their round, un-ceasingly, and the three blind mice ran round and round in the aching heads of the pilgrims and in their retching stomachs.

The Dennys had a bunk on one side of the stove, and Mrs Alexander and her boys were on the opposite side. Arthur Denny was very sick, but he was also under the spell of something ludicrous he had seen. Whenever he found time to speak, he looked at the prostrate woman on the other side of the cabin and gasped, with a wan twinkle in his eyes: "What are you lying there for, Mrs Alexander? Why don't you get up and cook your fish?" And Mrs Alexander could not answer because each mention of the word "fish" brought on a new wave of nausea.

All of the pilgrims were seasick except Charles Terry. He was on deck, visiting with the miners and feeling very good indeed. He was a man of the world, and he could be with the happy-go-lucky gold miners in spirit though he was not with them in a business way because he knew something better. He had had his try at the diggings on the Sacramento, and he had observed that the man who runs the store has the best chance of getting rich. He was an experienced man of twenty-two, and that was why he was sailing with store goods in the hold instead of a pick and shovel and gold pan on deck. But Terry could talk the miners' language and he felt generous toward them. So he said, "Boys, how about a smoke to celebrate our sailing? I have some good cigars downstairs."

The miners cheered the suggestion, and Terry descended, whistling, into the cabin of affliction. While he bent over his traveling chest and had a struggle with the lock, the schooner rose and fell and rolled, mixing strange odors, and derelict coffeepots and pans of fish skated about the slippery cabin floor.

Leaning over the chest, Terry began to vomit. And while he vomited, the heartless miners crowded round the companion hatch and called, "Hurry up with them cigars you went after, Terry! What are you doing down there, Terry?" They kept it up long after Terry had crawled into a bunk. Then they gave him up, loudly, as a stingy four-flusher who promised good cigars and did not give them even a civil word. They went back to playing poker and singing "Three Blind Mice" in rhythm with the plunge and roll of the schooner, and the pilgrims, with mice running around in their aching heads and convulsed stomachs, loathed the healthy sound of their singing. In a seasick world the unnatural monsters are the healthy ones. "Did ever you see such a sight in your life as three blind mice?"

It was a voyage of blind mice and blind destiny. The

by-product was the founding of a great city, and the main expedition came to nothing. The Queen Charlotte Islands gold strike was a false alarm, and the *Exact's* miners sailed back without one nugget. At that, they were fortunate. The other schooner in search of gold was wrecked on one of the islands. When a rescue party went in search of them, long afterward, they found that the fierce Haidahs had a sense of humor. They had made slaves of the shipwrecked men, and the schooner crew and miners served a long apprenticeship at menial work usually reserved for old women and Indians captured on Puget Sound.

With her passenger list of gold-seekers and home-seekers, the *Exact* was cleared by the custom's authorities at Astoria on November seventh. The same day she bucked and rolled her way across the bar between the furious breakers on the sands south of Point Adams and the furious breakers on the sands east of Cape Disappointment. After that terrifying introduction to the sea, the Pacific looked quite reasonable to the pilgrims. They were only normally seasick as the little schooner sailed up the coast of northern Oregon, which is now the coast of Washington.

On November eleventh the *Exact* rounded Cape Flattery and sailed in the generous Strait of Juan de Fuca to where it opens into a much wider sea. There the wind deserted her altogether and she lay becalmed for twenty-four hours off Dungeness Spit.

At three o'clock on the rainy morning of the thirteenth a northwesterly breeze stirred and freshened, and Captain Folger tumbled his crew out to make sail. By the time they had the anchor catted, half a gale was blowing and the little Nantucket schooner was running off before it with a bone of gleaming spray in her teeth. At daybreak she was storming along between the towering, forested shores of Admiralty Inlet, making better than ten knots.

Captain Folger called passenger John Low and told him to keep a good lookout for Smaquamox. Low was the only man on board who had ever been on Puget Sound, and he was one of the half-dozen white men in the world who could vouch for the existence of Smaquamox. If he could not identify the place, the *Exact* would pass it up as one of the lost cities of the earth.

With half a gale behind her, the *Exact* roared past Point No Point against the push of the outgoing tide. The great reach of the inland sea opened still wider, and the little schooner ran due south in Puget Sound. While she stormed along, John Low stood in the wind and rain forward, steadying himself against the port foreshrouds and keeping an anxious lookout. The honor of his city was at stake. He knew it was somewhere on the left side of the Sound, but he did not know exactly where. And the left shore was ten miles away, blotted out by drifting rain clouds and gray rain.

As the *Exact* raced on, the Sound narrowed to a five-mile width and the left shore came within eye's reach: three-hundred-foot yellow bluffs topped by two-hundred-and three-hundred-foot fir forests that seemed to be sailing through the rain clouds. The shore at Smaquamox was low and gently sloping. They were not yet there, unless they had already passed it.

The *Exact* passed an Indian camp at the mouth of a river

that looked something like one of the mouths of the Duwamish, but the rest of the landscape did not fit, and the
point of land beyond was tremendously high. They roared
past the high point and opened up a great bay. Half the
bay was surrounded by steep bluffs that left off suddenly,
and the rest of it was bordered by wet, gray mud flats un-
covered by the outgoing tide. Above the bluffs and beyond the misty ooze of the mud flats was the tremendous,
unbroken forest, with rain clouds sailing past the great
trees; about everything there was the primeval look of a
world at the beginning of time. At the head of the bay mud
flats and marshy land and water and mist were mixed up at
the edge of the wet northern jungle. It looked as if there
might be a river mouth in there; maybe the twin mouths
of the Duwamish. Then, looking ahead, up the Sound,
Low saw a long, wooded point of land with a gently
sloping shore that thinned to nothing where it met the exposed beach. It looked like the point the Indians called
"Smaquamox," but there should be the beginnings of a city
there if young Denny and Lee Terry had done their part.
Then, between the forest and the beach, he caught the wet
shine of peeled logs. Low ran aft, calling to Captain Folger
that Smaquamox was dead ahead.

He had found the obscure port of call, but on closer
look he was disappointed. The new cabin was roofless in
the driving rain, and there was no sign of life about the
point. It looked as if the boys had abandoned the place,
unfinished, or been killed by the Indians.

While Low pondered the mystery, Captain Folger
shouted commands. The long tiller was swung over and the

Exact rounded up into the wind, well off the point. The big single jib crumpled and came down, and the anchor was let go with a harsh roar of cable chain that echoed from the lonely woods. It was then eight o'clock on the morning of November thirteenth, 1851.

CHAPTER III

A City Is Born

IN HIS LEAKING BOWER of cedar boughs David Denny was awakened by the sudden harsh roar of cable chain. He crawled out and saw the schooner lying off the point, with her crew smothering the wet, threshing sails as they came down. The deck of the little pilgrim ship was dark with bearded men and shawl-wrapped women with their sunbonnets flapping in the wind and rain. The population for the city had arrived, and the hungry boy hobbled to the outer edge of the wide beach, with his neuralgic head tied up in a cloth and his damp blanket drawn around him Indian style. He was so excited and happy that it did not occur to him that the women might not be thrilled by the prospect ashore.

Actually, the women had considered the new city from the *Exact*, and they were crushed by what they saw: one roofless cabin at the edge of the tremendous forest, in the rain; something like a sick Indian waving to them from the edge of the wet beach; and a rabble of naked and half-naked Indians hurrying along the beach toward the landing place.

The men in the party did not notice the temporary lack of conveniences ashore, and they were busy and excited getting their possessions out of the hold to start their new life in a new world. Louisa Boren was the only woman who was not in tears by the time they crowded into the longboat. The cold autumn rain had wilted the sunbonnets they had starched so stiffly and ironed with such care on the grassy bank of the Willamette. Mrs Alexander, who was going on to Olympia, saw them crying as they were rowed ashore, with their stricken sunbonnets going flip-flap, flip-flap in the wind and rain. Mrs Denny and Mrs Bell and Mrs Boren each carried a baby in her arms, and Mrs Low held a two-year-old girl. Among them, the four had twelve children, nine of them girls, and the oldest was nine. Mrs Alexander was sorry for them all, but she was sorriest for Mrs Denny. Her baby was only two months old, she was weak from chills and fever and seasickness, and she was going ashore in a storm of rain to a city of one house with no roof.

For Captain Folger the stop at Alki was a side issue. The Queen Charlotte Islands were his real destination; he still had emigrants for Olympia, and he wanted to make use of the strong fair wind. Smartly, the remainder of the party and their belongings were landed on the beach. Sails were hoisted and the anchor hove, and the *Exact* stood away to the south. From the deck Mrs Alexander saw the pilgrim women diminishing into the distance. They were standing under a tree in the pouring rain, their wilted sunbonnets lopped down over their faces and their aprons to their eyes.

The men of the party had no time to cry, even if they had felt like it. Their goods had been dumped on the beach at low tide, and now the tide was coming in. They were fully occupied saving their belongings from the sea. After that was accomplished Arthur Denny went to see how the women were making out. They were not doing very well. They had crawled into the brush at the edge of the woods, under the shelter of a piece of canvas they had spread, and made a fire. They were huddled together with their children, crying, while naked and partly draped Indians squatted about them and their fire, waiting to see what would happen next. Even then, Denny said afterward, he did not realize that he had gone a step too far and embarked on a desperate adventure from which there was no turning back.

That day the men split cedar blocks into shakes for a roof. They were still working with hammer and frow when darkness closed down on them, and that night the twenty-four pilgrims huddled in the roofless cabin under a piece of canvas and some Indian mats that gave the illusion of shelter.

That was one of the temporary inconveniences of building a city. By the next night the settlement had a roof over its head, and the men had begun felling trees for Arthur Denny's cabin. While the pilgrims built their city, the floating population swelled. The Indians came by the hundred to camp on the beach and on the land the white men had cleared of trees, and they brought their portable houses

with them. The houses they assembled in the new city
were of split cedar boards and mats woven from the inner
bark of the cedar, with roof boards grooved to fit together.
The Indians were squat Salishes of the Duwamish and Suquamish tribes. Many of them had flattened skulls that
slanted back from the eyebrows to a point at the top of the
head, and some of their babies, strapped to boards, had
other boards pressed against their foreheads for the flatten-
ing process. The Indians, in search of beauty, bound their
children's heads somewhat as the Chinese bound the feet
of their girls.

The Indians were helpful and annoying. They helped
the settlers with their work, traded salmon and venison for
ship's bread, taught the inlanders to dig clams from the
teeming beach and gave them transportation in their
canoes. They also distressed the pilgrims with their naked-
ness and the strong smell of smoked salmon on which and
among which they lived, and with their curiosity. Sometimes when the twenty-four white inhabitants were gathered in Low's one-room log cabin where they ate and
slept, Indians would wander in for a *nanitch* (a look
around), and presently there would be fifty or more of
them in the room, strong with salmon and sprightly with
fleas. As more crowded in there would not be even room
to scratch. The Indians were immensely interested in the
fair-haired children, and in what the citizens ate and how
they cooked it, and where they slept and how they managed. The more they crowded in to see, the less the citizens
were able to manage. But it never occurred to the simple
Indians that they were intruding. Neither did it ever occur

to the pilgrims that they were intruding on an Indian camp ground, on Indian land.

The Indians had strange-sounding names for things. The door, which they entered without knocking, was *le pote*. The pitch they recommended for starting fires was *le gome*. Head was *le tate;* the tongue, *le lang;* and the teeth, *le dents*. At first the settlers thought those were Indian words, but it turned out to be the language worked out by traders and trappers and their Indian customers, and the settlers began to learn the useful Chinook jargon.

Another thing they learned from the Indians was the splitting of long, wide boards from cedar logs. The cedar trees of Oregon were often two hundred feet tall and ten or more feet through, and the soft, straight-grained wood split so easily and so true that it seemed improbable. When Arthur Denny's log house was finished and there were no more suitable logs within reach of men without teams, they resorted to the methods of the aborigines. Houses of split cedar boards were built for William Bell and Carson Boren. When they were finished, "New York" had four buildings, and the great housing shortage was over.

From their point of land that jutted out into the Sound the settlers saw an occasional vessel pass: an open sloop, known as a "plunger," a small trading bark or brig; and occasionally they saw and heard a little steamer. She had high free board and a frigate bow and wide transom stern, and a tall, thin smokestack. Her hull was painted black, with white upperworks. Her paddle wheels were up at the bow and sponsoned out so that at some angles she looked like a grasshopper poised for a leap; at other angles she looked like a squirrel with its cheeks full of nuts. She was the Hudson's Bay steamer, *Beaver*, plying on company business between the Nisqually station and the station at Victoria. The *Beaver* had been launched in England in 1836, in the presence of King William and a hundred thousand of his subjects. She had come under sail to the northwest coast and donned her paddle wheels at Fort Vancouver. When she crossed the Columbia bar on her way to Puget Sound she was the first steamer to enter the Pacific Ocean.

They saw vessels pass, but none came within speaking distance until December tenth. On that day a brig sailed so close to the point that those on board could see the four cabins at the edge of the woods and white men on the beach. The mainsail of the brig was backed with a gesture of surprise; the gig was lowered, and the master rowed ashore.

The master introduced himself as Captain Howard, of the brig *Leonesa,* and he asked what place it was.

They told him it was New York.

Captain Howard told the citizens that the shack town of San Francisco was booming with the stream of gold from the diggings, and was threatening to become a permanent city. New piers were being built, and he had been sent to Puget Sound for a cargo of piles. But Puget Sound was a big place and he did not know where to begin.

The young men looked at one another and nodded, and John Low became their spokesman. He assured Captain Howard that he had come to the right place, and that the men of New York were ready to get out a cargo of piles for the *Leonesa*. They signed a contract on the spot, and the men got out their axes. It was then less than a month since the *Exact* had landed the pilgrims on the beach, and the city already had its sea-borne commerce.

In some ways the young men were well prepared for supplying the brig with a cargo. They all had axes, and there were plenty of trees about suitable for the fifty-foot piles required. For hauling they had only one yoke of oxen, which Low had brought up from their winter pasture on the Chehalis, but since the landing of the pilgrim ship Lee Terry had returned with the frow he had gone to buy in October. He now left posthaste for the Puyallup Valley to buy another yoke of oxen, and the remaining men set to work with what they had. Lee Terry returned a few days before Christmas, driving his new oxen along the beach, and the loading of the *Leonesa* was completed on New Year's Day, 1852.

Captain Howard was pleased with the dispatch with which his brig had been loaded. He agreed to return for another cargo, and he took with him the money the citizens had earned and their orders for goods from San Francisco: pork and flour and hard bread, boots and brogan shoes and domestics, hickory shirts, window sash and glass, grindstones and cross-cut saws and files.

New York, Oregon, was booming, but there was handwriting on the wall. The Denny brothers and Boren and Bell had already decided it was not the place for a seaport. They were inland people who had never seen salt water until three months before, but the exposed point and shoal water did not seem right to them. The Terry brothers from New York, with its magnificent harbor, became the champions of the place, but the inlanders looked elsewhere for a permanent location.

A few days after the *Leonesa* sailed north toward the Pacific, the dissenters paddled south in an Indian dugout, exploring. They went as far as the mouth of the Puyallup River without finding anything to their liking, and paddled back again. Arthur Denny, from the prairies of Illinois, sounds like a poor bet for the leader of a party setting out to locate a seaport, but he had an eye for the practical and he put the needs of the party into concise words. Their only immediate means of making a living was the supplying of ships with cargoes of timber, and that meant two things: a good supply of timber and a good harbor for the vessels that carried it.

The day after the dissenters returned from their expedition south they paddled two miles northeast from New York, around Duwamish Head, and found themselves in what appeared to be a magnificent harbor. They had rejected New York for sound reasons. One of them was the exposed point that jutted out into Puget Sound. But now they saw that what was bad for New York was good for Elliott Bay. While the point took the pounding of southern storms it protected the entrance to the bay. The funnel-shaped entrance was six miles across, and on the north it was formed by bluffs three hundred and four hundred feet high. Inside the shelter of Duwamish Head the bay trended southeast to the mouths of the Duwamish River; thus the southern half was sheltered in every direction. The rest was open only to the west and northwest, from which no storms had come during the winter, and it was open only as far as the high, wooded hills of Bainbridge Island a few miles away.

The four explorers in the dugout canoe had found a wonderful and wonderfully sheltered expanse of water, and they had found it two miles from where they were wintering. It was walled on three sides by an apparently inexhaustible supply of timber, and the only unanswered question was whether the water was deep enough for ships to enter.

Arthur Denny had brought his wife's clothesline, and a horseshoe for a sounding lead. While the others managed the nervous Indian canoe he took repeated soundings, but the horseshoe always took the hundred-foot line down to the bitter end. And that is not surprising, because the water is nearly six hundred feet deep at the entrance to the bay proper, and in the bay it averages around two hundred and fifty feet. The horseshoe never touched bottom anywhere until the canoe was close to shore. The prairie people had found their harbor and their timber supply. And thinking over what the Indians had told him in jargon and in signs, Arthur Denny thought he saw something else in favor of the place. From somewhere on the bay a trail led east over the mountains by way of an easy pass. It was only a thought and a thread of trail through the tremendous forest to the east, but that way lay the rest of America, and it was something that might come in handy some day.

On February fifteenth, 1852, Arthur Denny and William Bell and Carson Boren located their claims on Elliott Bay. The northern half of the shore they had explored was bordered by bluffs, some of them honeycombed with the graves of Indians and others notched by falling streams of good water. The bluffs diminished toward the south and ended at a wooded point of land, which was an island at high tide. South of the point there were mud flats. The three men staked out claims that fronted on the solid shore from the peninsula northward.

When spring came the Dennys and Bells and Borens were going pioneering on their new claims on Elliott Bay. But conditions were primitive enough at New York, where a thousand Indians had gathered around the little white settlement, and some of the necessities of life were missing. There was no milk for the children. Mrs Denny was down with malaria and her baby, Roland, was only a few months old. Having nothing else, they fed him clam juice and he did very well nursed by the sea, which was the first mother of all living things.

Late in March the schooner *Exact* sailed back up the Sound and let her anchor go off Alki Point. While her gold miners had been finding nothing on the Queen Charlotte Islands the settlement of New York had grown up and split, and a new one was about to be founded. Carson Boren and David Denny were ready to start for the Willamette Valley after their stock and they went in the schooner as far as Olympia.

A few days afterward a big canoe came up from the south, standing in toward the point, with her crew singing a canoe song to which they kept time by striking the sides of the craft with their paddles. In the canoe there was a striking, dapper white man accompanied by Chief Seattle and a retinue of paddlers.

The stranger introduced himself as Doctor David Maynard. He was from, but not of, Olympia, and the great dugout canoe was loaded with his goods and gear. He was looking for a place to make barrels and salt salmon, which Chief Seattle's Indians would catch for him. He would then ship the salmon by lumber vessels to San Francisco, and it would surely become a great industry. Maynard was also a physician and he had had a store in Olympia, but he had given that up. According to one story he was in the habit of lowering his prices with each drink, and when he had had enough he envisioned Utopia and gave his goods away. His competitors, who were sober, did not see anything except that he was hurting their business, and they asked him to get out of town.

Doctor Maynard was a legitimate hero and a romantic figure, and he afterward paid for it through the nose. He was a true pioneer according to the definition of being strong on the attack and weak on the defense. He had crossed the plains in 1850 under circumstances that might have made all the people in the wagon train hate one another cordially. But the emigrants who crossed with Maynard acknowledged him as a hero who was never in bad temper or downcast or exhausted by the ordeal. He came through undefeated, and that was because the great trek had caught his imagination. In it he saw the journey of life made visible: the journey from dawn to sunset; the procession of men and beasts all moving in the same direction, weeded out by death and replenished by birth, and menaced by dangers as they journeyed west, under the wide sky, with visible time. It was the kind of world for which Maynard was built, and if life had always stayed visible and kept its forward motion he might have been a great man.

But afterward things became less clear. There were delays and counterattacks, and in the confusion he was done to death. There had even been a confusing note in the wagon train. Her name was Catherine Broshears, and the doctor had befriended her after her husband had died of cholera. She was on her way to Tumwater, where her brother, Michael Simmons, had been the first American settler north of the Columbia River. It was part of the journey that Doctor Maynard should fall in love with the young woman from Kentucky, who grew stronger and more sure of herself while others crumbled. Back in the East the doctor had a wife from whom he was separated, but not divorced. When he arrived at New York with his Indian retinue the matter was still unresolved. He did not get it settled until that fall, when he went to Oregon City and had the Legislature decree that he was no longer married to his eastern wife. And the matter stayed settled only until the forward motion of life halted and time and the East caught up with him.

David S. Maynard was an interesting gentleman and he was a physician and the head of a salmon-packing enterprise. The Terrys wanted him for their city, but he did not like the location. Arthur Denny and Bell also wanted the doctor for their city, and they took him across the bay

to show him what a fine place they had. At that time the
only building in their city was the ruin of an Indian hut
from past times and the only inhabitants were the dead en-
tombed in the bluff with their possessions; but Doctor
Maynard approved of the place. And Seattle said the bay
was a good place for salmon. It was not at all new to him,
or newly discovered; he and his people had often camped
on the little wooded peninsula that separated the mud flats
from the deep water and the bold shore.

The three claims already staked began at the point and
extended north, taking in the best three miles of water
front. As an inducement to their first prospect, Denny
and Bell offered to move their stakes north in order that
Maynard's claim would include the peninsula, which he
had chosen for his salmon packing. At first the doctor was
interested in the place only as a temporary site. Then he
changed his mind and decided to take up the six-hundred-
and-forty-acre donation claim that the law allowed him (as
an emigrant of 1850) and his not yet divorced wife. The
other stakes were moved and Doctor Maynard staked out a
claim that took in "The Point" and extended for a mile
south along the mud flats.

The winter of 1851–52 had been mild, with plenty of
rain but little freezing weather, and spring came early. On
April third William Bell and the Boren family and Doctor
Maynard were off to found the new settlement. They
went in Indian dugouts loaded with their possessions and
landed on the uninhabited shore of Elliott Bay, which has
never been uninhabited for a moment since. Arthur Denny
had been the leader in exploring the land about the bay,

and he had surveyed the claims, but he was not in the party. He and his wife were down with the ague again, shaking with chills on alternate days, and while, as they said, that made it convenient for them to take care of each other, it was inconvenient for everything else.

The landing party included Mrs Boren and her baby, Gertrude, and Boren's unmarried sister, Louisa. As yet the new city did not even boast a cabin without a roof, but the party found it good to be pioneering again. New York and their cabins were only a few miles away, but they were not inclined to turn back from the new adventure even for overnight shelter. They camped out until their new homes were built.

Boren's cabin of split cedar was the first to be completed. Bell's cabin was a close second, and Doctor Maynard's, on the Point, was the last of the three. But, in the act of being last the doctor took two firsts: his big cabin, eighteen by twenty-six feet, was divided between living quarters and the first drugstore and the first general store. Maynard also had a name for the city. He proposed that it be named after his friend and fishing companion, Chief Seattle. Thanks to the pioneering doctor, Seattle was born with a fish-packing industry, a drugstore and a general store, and a name that was not imported from England or Spain or brought around the Horn from the East. It was a name as native as the fir forest. But not much attention was paid to the name by outsiders; that summer the Legislature classified the region about the bay as "Duwamps," and its mail address was "Olympia, Oregon."

When the first three houses were finished the citizens

worked together on a fourth for Arthur Denny. They built it near the northern end of his water front, on the imposing bluff. But unfortunately the site was better suited for a lighthouse than for a dwelling. When Arthur Denny was well enough to move over to his new home he found the location too difficult, and later in the summer he built another cabin on the lower shore to the south.

Soon after the settlement was established, Captain Plummer of the passing brig *John Davis* observed that the shore was inhabited by white people. So he put in to see if the settlement could supply him with a cargo of timber. The settlement could, and the men proceeded to fell trees and cut logs, which they rolled off the bluff into the water and towed out to the brig.

The *John Davis* was followed by the brig *Franklin Adams*, Captain Felker, and the two alternated during the summer, carrying building materials to insatiable San Francisco. The men of Seattle were kept busy felling the smaller firs for piles and squaring larger logs into timbers with broadaxes. They also worked with hammer and frow and drawknife, splitting bolts of cedar into shakes and shaving them into shingles. There was work for everyone, and when a brig was in the harbor the crew came ashore and helped with the logging, just as earlier crews of the same brigs had gone ashore to help with the curing of hides on the California coast.

While prairie-bred citizens worked at lumbering, Doctor Maynard looked after the fishery, brine-pickling the salmon brought in to the Point by fleets of Indian dugouts. During the summer he packed a thousand barrels of salmon, which he shipped to San Francisco in the two brigs. But the pioneering doctor did not understand the business very well. He killed but did not cure the salmon, and all of them were spoiled by the time they reached San Francisco. The venture was a total loss.

That was a summer of great industry, and the citizens of Seattle were too busy to drum up additional population for their city; but a few people joined the settlement of their own accord. Doctor Henry A. Smith came from Olympia in a dugout, and a lumber brig brought George McConaha and his family. Smith, at twenty-two, was a physician and a scholar and a man of letters. Within the next two years he mastered the complicated Duwamish language and thereby preserved one of the greatest of American orations. He also wrote excellent prose and better poems than some that have been perpetuated in schoolbooks.

McConaha was a lawyer who achieved the too-expensive glamour of dying young. At the time he was drowned he was president of the first council of the Territorial Legislature. He was rated as a man of great promise and a brilliant speaker, and his older fellow legislators were very proud of him. McConaha built a house in Seattle, and that summer his wife gave birth to a daughter, Eugenia, who was the first white child to be born in the city.

Doctor Smith took up a claim far north on the bay, where mud flats filled a bight in the land. There, at what became Smith's Cove, he built a cabin on the bluff and brought his mother to keep house for him, and he began clearing a farm. He had already decided that in such a healthful country there was not much future for a doctor; and there was even less future for a poet.

It was in the woods between the Cove and Seattle that Smith had his adventure through the looking glass, which became one of the classic stories of the town. He had always gone to Seattle in a "Chinook buggy," otherwise an Indian dugout, but on this occasion he decided to do some pioneering and find his way to Seattle on foot. He took a compass and his rifle and started southeast through the unexplored woods.

He made out well enough at first, and then he was amazed to see that the needle of his compass had reversed itself. When he stopped to ponder over that his scientific mind told him that the only explanation could be the presence of a large body of ferrous metal. Undoubtedly he was standing over a deposit of iron ore. He broke branches to mark the spot, and when he pushed on the needle of the compass remained reversed. The iron deposit was evidently of great extent, and as he hurried toward Seattle he broke more branches to mark the location of his iron mine. He envisioned a smelter and blast furnaces and the rolling mills of a great industry at Smith's Cove, where he had originally planned nothing more than the terminus of a transcontinental railroad.

Pushing on farther, Doctor Smith came upon a second mystery, as great as the first. In the depths of the forest, where no human habitation should have been, he found a fenced clearing and buildings that were certainly the work of a white man. Forgetting all about his iron mine he sat on the rail fence looking at the place and wondering whose it was and how it could have got there. And the more he looked the more amazed he became. The clearing was about the size of his own, surrounded by the same kind of fence. In the clearing there were a cabin and a barn and a chicken house, just as he had in his own clearing. The buildings were a little smaller and shabbier than his own, but otherwise they were identical except for their arrangement. And even in that there was a similarity. To the last detail, everything was opposite, like a reflection of his own claim seen in a mirror. The cabin faced east instead of west; the barn was southwest of the cabin instead of northeast; and the chicken house was on the north side instead of on the south.

While the doctor sat on the fence, wondering, he saw his own mother come out of the cabin and begin feeding the chickens. Evidently she was familiar with the mysterious neighboring claim and had been keeping it from him, but he could not understand how she had managed to get there before him when he had left her busy at home.

Then, as the doctor told it, the landscape suddenly wheeled in a half circle and stopped with everything in its proper place; and he knew that he had walked in a circle and come back to his own claim as an objective-eyed stranger.

In 1852 colorful and great figures came up from the inland city to join the new city. Maynard was the first, and then there were McConaha and Doctor Smith. In October another stranger landed from his Indian canoe and walked up the beach to where the men of Seattle were cutting spar timber in what is now Pioneer Place. The stranger was a massive, heavy-featured man of forty-five, with a well-fed and prosperous look about him. As he came up from the inland sea he loomed big against the sky; and he loomed big in Seattle until the end of his long life.

The stranger introduced himself as Henry Yesler, of Baltimore, Maryland, and more recently of Portland, Oregon. He was a millwright and he was looking for a location for a steam sawmill. Yesler inquired about claims, and when he learned that all the water front on the east side of the bay had been taken, he ambled cheerfully to his canoe. Leaning on the handles of their axes the citizens of Seattle saw him paddle across to the west shore, near Duwamish Head. He still loomed up big, out of the slender dugout, and the idea of a steam sawmill loomed up big. There were a few water-power mills on Puget Sound, but not one steam plant, which would be a triumph for any city.

The city builders had already moved the boundaries of their claims to accommodate Doctor Maynard's fish packing, and they could move them again to accommodate another industry. They sent a committee over to Du-wamish Head, where the big millwright was staking out a claim, and invited him to build on any site he chose in Seattle. Yesler returned and chose the spot where he had first landed. The claim he staked out was mostly inland, but it had a long panhandle or corridor to the sea, which was contributed out of Boren's and Maynard's claims. The citizens helped build a large log cookhouse, which was the last log house built in the city. Then Yesler took passage for San Francisco in a lumber brig to buy his mill machinery.

Yesler's mill was in operation early the following year, and from the standpoint of Seattle it was the mill of the gods. It brought more vessels to the bay, and produced ready money, which kept the town going. Directly or indirectly the mill gave employment to all the male citizens and to a fair number of Indians. Some of the mill hands lived to own mills of their own, ten times as big, and expensive mansions. Seattle is full of streets and parks and skyscrapers named after men who used to tumble out of their log cabins in the dark of early morning when they heard the shrill whistle of Yesler's mill.

CHAPTER IV

Horses from the Sea

IN THE WINTER OF 1852 Thomas Mercer came to town looking for land he had seen in a dream. Ideas and dreams are the most refined products of man, and they have a way of leading to rough places and rougher adventures.

Tom Mercer was born in Ohio and learned the weaver's trade. At twenty-one he was still working in the woolen mill where he started as a boy. But one day, in the dusty loom, he saw the map of the United States pushing west while he stayed at home, weaving, like a woman. The next spring he was pioneering on the wild frontier of Illinois.

His parents followed him west, and his youngest brother was born near Princeton, Illinois; Asa Mercer was twenty-five years younger than his brother Tom. The weaver's hands grew thick with callouses, but what they lost in skill they made up in strength. The wild frontier became more settled and less wild, and there were neighborhood gatherings at the Mercers' house. The Dexter Hortons and the Reverend Daniel Bagley and his wife were favorites, and sometimes the young lawyer, Abe Lincoln, would ride up and tie his horse at the hitching rail and join the party—an indolent and unsuccessful young giant. He would sit with little Asa on his lap and tell stories in his whimsical sad nasal voice—stories that always ended in a roar of laughter and left an afterglow of warmth and an echo of sadness.

Tom Mercer married and begot four daughters, and there were good seasons and bad in Illinois. Autumn was a good season, with its clear air and rich color and rich harvest. Winter was a bad season, with its blizzards and savage cold; and spring was a bad season, with its flooded lands and new-hatched mosquitoes rising in clouds. And summer was a bad season, with its savage heat and more savage mosquitoes; everyone burned with fever or shook with the chills of malaria.

In the late 'forties another kind of fever swept the state: the "Oregon Fever," and everyone talked of going west. Tom Mercer had a mind for ideas. He read histories and guidebooks and newspaper accounts and letters from people who had already followed the overland trail. He remembered everything and wove the fragments together until he had a living map in his mind. He became an authority on Oregon, which he had never seen; men shaking with the chills of malaria and burning with the fever of Oregon came from miles to learn from him what the territory was like and what possessions they should take with them and what equipment and what seed.

Horses from the Sea

It was true only in a way that Mercer had never seen the Oregon country. One spring morning he saw it in a dream. He heard the crying of myriad frogs and found himself in a sidehill swamp at the edge of a lake. The lake was surrounded by a forest, and the dark reflection of trees went down into the mirror of the lake as into the depths of a dream. Tom Mercer climbed the hill, through the forest, and from the top he saw a great bay on the other side. He knew it was salt water, which he had never seen, and he thought how fortunate he was to have a claim to which he could come home in a boat from either side. The crying of frogs was still in his ears when he woke up on the farm in Illinois. He looked out the window at the dawn over flooded fields, where the galley-nippers would soon be rising in clouds. He knew it was time to get out of there. He had already given his mind to Oregon, and Oregon had come to him in a dream.

Most of the emigrants headed for the Willamette Valley with ox teams, the almost universal goal and the traditional method of travel. But Tom Mercer had made himself an authority on the subject and he varied the pattern, after the manner of experts. He drove a team of horses: "Tib," a docile black mare used mostly for bucking straw from the thresher, and a powerful white stallion of a different disposition. Mercer's goal was Puget Sound.

The Dexter Hortons and the Daniel Bagleys went with him and they started in the spring of 1852, the year of the greatest migration of all time and the year of the great cholera epidemic. For all his studies on the subject Mercer was not able to foresee a kind of crossing that had never happened before and never happened afterward. Before they reached the Platte River emigrants were dying, and the living seemed numberless. As far as a man could look ahead or behind there was a swaying stream of white-covered wagons and cattle and horses on the move. The stream reached the Platte and flowed along its northern shore like another river between the thickening lines of drift that marked its course: broken-down wagons and abandoned furniture and new graves. On the opposite side of the river there was another unending stream, like a reflection, with its way marked by broken-down wagons and wagons that stopped while men dug graves, and its columns of dusty clouds by day and its pillars of campfires by night.

Polluting the springs as they went, the emigrants died by the score. The southern migration crossed the Platte and the two unending streams merged into one great river of wagons and livestock and grim humanity. The grass was eaten away and the trees were cut down for fuel and the germs of cholera spread. Starving cattle lay down and did not get up again, and emigrants died by the hundred.

In that slow-moving river that flowed uphill toward the Rockies the Mercers went west: the grim-faced weaver following his dream, the anxious young wife and the four little girls with wide eyes and trusting faces under their sunbonnets. With charmed lives they went west in that pilgrimage of death, with the black mare and the pale stallion stalking on through the wreckage of a migration, between the graves of the dead.

No family was more fortunate on the overland trail.

Horses from the Sea

They reached The Dalles in Oregon, untouched by sickness or death. After days of waiting they got passage on a batteau to the Cascades. The open scow was packed with emigrants, and as they floated down the Columbia the icy November rain poured down on them. At the mouth of the Hood River they saw the mountains going up steeply out of the river, and on the mountainside above them the rain was powdering down in snow.

The mother of the little girls shook with a chill and then burned with fever, as if there were still malaria in her blood. But she also had a cough, and it was pneumonia, and they buried her at the Cascades, where the Bridge of the Gods had once spanned the River of the West.

That winter Tom Mercer boarded his motherless girls in Salem and went up the Cowlitz River in a dugout with Indian boatmen. Puget Sound was his destination, and his calculations led him to believe that the village of Seattle had a future. It had a thriving air, with half a dozen houses built and more going up. A tier of four donation claims had already been taken up along the bay. The village was sprinkled over three of these. The fourth was considered altogether in the woods, and Mercer would have to go still farther out.

The last claim touched the southern end of a small lake, *tenas chuck*. In the wilderness beyond that last claim Tom Mercer found himself in a sidehill swamp at the edge of a lake. The lake was surrounded by forest, and the reflection of great fir trees went down into the mirror of water as into the depths of a dream. Mercer blazed his way through the wet woods to the top of the hill, and through

[67]

a break in the forest he had a glimpse of Elliott Bay. It was his claim and the next day he began the journey to the Land Office in Oregon City.

Mercer filed on a donation claim of three hundred and twenty acres and went back to Salem, where sympathetic families offered to adopt the four motherless girls. The father didn't want to part with them, but he knew it wouldn't be much of a life for little girls in the uttermost wilderness, with Indians and black bears and cougars for neighbors. He told the children how it was, and Susan, who was fourteen and the eldest, made the decision. She said, "We're a family and we must stay together. Seattle can't be as bad as crossing the plains, or people wouldn't live there. I'll keep house and be mother to the rest."

In April Tom Mercer took the Cowlitz road to Puget Sound and the Dexter Hortons went with him. Mercer brought his horses and wagon. The last stage of the journey was made in a scow, and the village turned out to see them arrive. New settlers were a cause for celebration, but the horses got most of the attention. Against the water and the April sky they looked like more than horses as they came snorting up the bank—horses that came out of the sea. The citizens crowded around and patted the comfortable black mare and they admired the pale stallion, beyond the reach of his teeth and rough-shod heels. Tom Mercer joked about the pair and said they were a perfect match. And the citizens admired the fine, well-tried wagon. They had seen horses and wagons in their time, but these were the first that had ever appeared in their village. That fact gave them a significance that could not be denied, and a touch of the miraculous. Seen there at the moment of their arrival, against the sea and the rolling white clouds of the April sky, the outfit looked like a wagon and horses of destiny.

There were advantages and disadvantages in bringing the first horses to Seattle. They got a great deal of attention, but there was not one road on which they could be driven. Still, they were Seattle's first and they deserved tribute. Besides, there were the four quiet children, with trusting faces under their sunbonnets, waiting to see their father's claim. The men got out their saws and sharpened their axes and cut a wagon road through the forest to Mercer's claim on *tenas chuck*. The road went through dense brush and wound between the trunks of trees six and eight feet through. It was wide enough for only one wagon, but that was safe because there was no other wagon to meet.

In Illinois the weaver had dreamed of a claim that reached from a lake to salt water. Since then he had crossed the plains and found the claim. On the winter trip he had filed on it—three hundred and twenty acres. That was the double claim allowed a married couple, and in practice when one of a couple died after reaching the territory, the survivor was allowed to file on the full amount, half of it in the name of the minor children. It was usage, not a law, and when Mercer arrived in April he found that another settler had filed on the west half of his claim. The filing was made on the contention that Mercer was a single man.

Tom Mercer had dreamed his claim on a dark spring morning in Illinois, with his young wife asleep beside him.

Now she was asleep beside the Bridge of the Gods, and half his dream was gone.

He might or might not have regained the land by going to court, but he was a peaceable man. He made the best of the half that was left and felled trees at the edge of *tenas chuck*. There he built his log cabin and began clearing land. While he made his claim inhabitable his oldest daughter kept house in the Bell's original cabin in the village and was mother to the younger children.

The father was away from his claim a great deal because of his horses and wagon, which were his fortune. They were the only ones about the village, and whenever there was something to be hauled there was a call for Tom Mercer and his team. And there was a great deal of hauling to be done. Yesler's steam sawmill was operating, and houses of sawn lumber were going up. Twenty-five were built between spring and autumn, and Mercer hauled the lumber for all of them. There were goods to be hauled from Yesler's wharf, too, where lumber barks and brigs came and went. The only things Tom Mercer did not haul were the logs that fed the mill. They were cut on Doctor Maynard's claim and rolled down the hill to the bay with handspikes and floated to the mill boom. Some of the lumber was sent to China. Seattle had begun her foreign trade with the other side of the earth, but the farthest one could go by road was to the claim on *tenas chuck*.

At first, with Mercer away so much, his clearing grew slowly. Then he hired Indians for the work, and things went better. The Indians did not look promising and they moved slowly and were seldom seen in the act of exerting themselves, but the trees came down and stumps were grubbed out and ashes fell like rain over the waters of *tenas chuck:* gray-white ashes and black ashes in the shape of fern leaves.

Mercer was exceptionally kind to his Indians. He paid them well and doctored their ailments and listened to their troubles. He treated them as human beings and exchanged information with them. He was a stranger in their land, and there were many things they could teach him; and in a different sense they were strangers in their own land, among alien invaders, whom Mercer understood better than they.

It was a contemporary opinion that Siwashes did not possess a spark of gratitude, but Mercer kept faith with the Indians, who called him "Old Tom Mercer" affectionately. His conscience was good, and after a while he moved his four little girls out to the claim at the end of the world. He was often gone all day, but when he drove out of the darkness of the woods into the clearing, where there was still some daylight left, there was always chimney smoke, and the light of a fish oil lamp in the window of the cabin where the little mother and her sisters were getting supper. They led a charmed life out there, where the forest was fading back from the cabin beside the waters of *tenas chuck.*

By the following summer Mercer and his Indians had made a fine clearing, and there were cows grazing in the stumpy hillside pasture. Tom Mercer was adding dairying to his transfer business. He had been an important citizen since the day he brought his horses out of the sea and he was becoming more important.

On the Fourth of July the people of Seattle had a celebration. They wanted to get out into the real country, so they went through the woods to Mercer's claim and had a picnic on the shore of *tenas chuck*. There were Fourth of July speeches, and Arthur Denny suggested that the lakes should be named. Seattle was growing into a town, and still the big lake to the east was *hyas chuck* and the little lake between the big one and the Sound was *tenas chuck*. Those were not even proper Indian names. They were Chinook jargon for "big water" and "little water"; identifications, but not names.

Everyone at the picnic thought up lake names. Some of them were ridiculous and some commonplace, and some were good names but they did not seem to fit. Then Tom Mercer got up and said, "We might not be celebrating here except for George Washington. This is a good day to remember the father of our country with more than speeches. I suggest that *hyas chuck* be named 'Lake Washington' in his honor."

No patriotic gathering could have been cold to the suggestion, and there were cheers for Lake Washington. Mercer had paid his respects to history and now he turned to prophecy for the future. "This little lake," he said, "this *tenas chuck*, is important because of its location between Lake Washington and the bay. In time to come there will be a canal between Lake Washington and Puget Sound. The canal will go through *tenas chuck*, which should be called 'Lake Union,' because it will unite the two larger bodies of water." He sat down while they were still cheering for Lake Union.

That is when and how the lakes were named, one for the past and the other for times to come. That was July fourth, 1854, at a village picnic beside a lake in the depths of the northern jungle. Some of the younger picnickers lived to see ocean steamers sail into Lake Union, in the heart of a great city, and out into Lake Washington on the other side.

In Illinois the weaver had dreamed of a claim that he could reach in a boat by fresh water or salt. Death had cheated him of half the dream, but if he had lived long enough he would have been able to reach his diminished claim by ocean steamer. But that was not really necessary. He was a man of imagination and his mind always had its outlet to the sea.

The Hortons had crossed the plains in the same wagon train with the Mercer family and they accompanied Mercer to Seattle that spring. Dexter Horton intended to establish himself as a merchant, but he did not have anything to start on. He and his wife were sick and broke, and it was not a good time to start on borrowed capital. The usual interest rate was thirty-six per cent, but sometimes it was higher. Wages were also high, and help was wanted at Port Gamble, in the great wilderness of the Olympic Peninsula, where a sawmill was being built.

Dexter Horton worked at putting up the mill and his wife cooked for the hands. They found their health improved by hard and unaccustomed work, and they made out very well. Later in the same year they came back to Seattle, and Dexter Horton and David Phillips went into partnership in a general store. Horton went to San Francisco in a lumber brig to select a stock of goods while his partner supervised the building of the store. When the new store was opened for business, Dexter Horton thought he was launched on his life work. But he had brought a safe with him, and a safe suggests banking just as horses and a wagon suggest hauling things. It was the only safe in Seattle, and the citizens welcomed it with cheers. They went to their cabins and dug up their money bags, heavy with silver dollars and eight-cornered slugs of California gold. Dexter Horton wrote out a tag with each man's name and put it on the proper sack, which he tossed into the safe. Then he closed the solemn iron door and turned the knob. Seattle breathed easier with its money safely banked.

Dexter Horton did not even worry about forgetting the combination. If that had happened he would have gone behind the safe and taken out its contents. He had bought the safe cheap because it had no back. But it had a bold front, and in time Dexter Horton became a famous banker.

CHAPTER V

Boom Days

THE YEAR 1853 was the one in which things took their present shape. Northern Oregon became Washington Territory; northern Thurston County became King County; the plat of the town of Seattle was filed; and the town got a log-cabin post office. At the beginning of the year Seattle was a part of Duwamps in Thurston County; its mail address was "Olympia, Oregon," and citizens paid twenty-five cents a letter for mail brought from the capital by Moxlie's Weekly Canoe Express. Before the end of the year the address became Seattle, King County, Washington Territory, which is what it is today, except that "Territory" has become "State." In the plats that were filed the streets of downtown Seattle were laid out as they are today, and they had their present names.

A few weeks after the citizens learned that Northern Oregon had become Washington Territory, they had news that their newly appointed Governor, Isaac Stevens, was on his way. While Stevens traveled overland he was surveying a railroad from the headwaters of the Missouri to Puget Sound. Only two years earlier, while Arthur Denny was considering the shore of Elliott Bay for his city, he had heard from the Indians of a trail that led east over the Cascade Mountains by an easy pass. He had thought of it as something that might come in handy for his city some day, because beyond that vast wild hinterland lay the rest of America. Now the tenuous dream of 'fifty-one had broadened into the transcontinental railroad survey of 'fifty-three; and, suitably, Denny received a letter with additional news from the Governor: Captain George McClellan, in charge of the western end of the railroad survey, would build a military wagon road over the Cascade Mountains from Fort Walla Walla to Puget Sound. The road was to be completed for the fall immigration, and wagon trains that were now rumbling west from the Missouri River would be able to come direct to Puget Sound.

In 1853 all things seemed possible and within reach. A flood of emigrants and a railroad were coming, and Seattle would be the terminus of the railroad and a great city. There was feverish speculation in town lots, and within two years patches of land sixty by one hundred and twenty feet, studded with tremendous stumps, were selling for as high as $250.

Arthur Denny and Carson Boren filed their plat of the city on May twenty-third, 1853. Doctor Maynard filed his plat next day. That was because he got drunk in celebration of the official birth of Seattle.

There were differences of more than temperament between Denny and Maynard. Writing about the incident afterward, Denny observed that the doctor had taken enough to make him feel that he was not only monarch of all that he surveyed but of what Denny and Boren had surveyed as well. Because of their temperamental differences the two plats did not harmonize. In Denny's and Boren's plat the north and south streets paralleled the shore line; in Maynard's they conformed with the points of the compass, and there was a jog in the streets where the two halves of the town met but did not fit. To this day, in the snarl of traffic where cross-purpose streets run into Yesler Way, the differences between Boren and Denny and Doctor Maynard continue unresolved. Perhaps it is only right that the two sections of the city should bring their differences to Yesler Way. Henry Yesler was probate clerk in 1853, and the conflicting plats were filed in his cookhouse-office at the foot of what is now Yesler Way.

In January 1853 Seattle had its first wedding. David Denny was nineteen when he kept his vigil at Alki Point, waiting for civilization and Louisa Boren to arrive. When he came of age he and Louisa were married in Arthur Denny's cabin and they went to live on their new claim between the bay and *tenas chuck*. The marriage ceremony was performed by Doctor Maynard, who was, among other things, the first justice of the peace. It was a kind of hail and farewell to marriage, because Maynard had recently secured the first divorce. But presently he married Catherine Broshears, with whom he had fallen in love on the Overland Trail. She brought the first dandelions, which are now so common in the lawns of western Washington.

In that booming year of 1853 Seattle got its first hotel. The year before, Captain Felker, of the brig *Samuel Adams*, had been the second shipmaster to discover that the shore of Elliott Bay was inhabited by white people; and he had been busy ever since, carrying Seattle timber and lumber to San Francisco, and San Francisco goods to Seattle. Observing how the town grew while he made voyages, the captain decided to have a stake in it. He built the Felker House on the Point, where he had a good view of it as he came in from the sea. The Felker House was a two-story frame building with a wing and a stately porch across the front. It was painted white outside and hard-finished inside, and structurally it was centuries removed from the older buildings of the two-year-old city. The first log cabins were identical with those built by the Pilgrims in Plymouth, Massachusetts, and the split cedar cabins followed the still older construction of the houses of the Puget Sound Indians. But the captain's hotel was porched and painted and hard-finished, and the citizens were proud of the luxurious place.

The water-front hotel brought a water-front person to town, as cook and manager. Her name was Mary Ann Conklin, but sometimes she called herself Mary Ann Boyer, to show her independence of her absent husband, who was a whaling captain. She was also called other names, including "Mother Damnable" and "Madame Damnable." That was because of her vicious disposition and her vocabulary collected on older water fronts. For those who offended her she kept three savage Indian mongrels, which she would let slip like the dogs of war; and she had considerable striking power of her own. It was her custom to appear suddenly with an armful of stovewood or an apronful of rocks and pelt and curse her enemy from the premises.

Captain Felker's brig, *Samuel Adams*, was only one of the many sailing vessels that visited Seattle that year. Yesler's mill was working two twelve-hour shifts a day to turn out its capacity of fourteen thousand feet of rough lumber, and gangs were busy in the woods with saws and axes and broadaxes and ox teams, getting out piling and ships' spars and squaring timbers. There were fewer brigs in Elliott Bay, and more barks and more and larger schooners; and ships were beginning to appear. The ships *Tuskina* and *Potomac* became regular callers at Seattle. The bark *Louisiana*, Alfred Drew, sailed for China with a cargo of spars, and the *Mary Adams*, Captain Harding, for Singapore. The following year four lines of sailing vessels were touching regularly at Seattle.

In the rush of traffic with San Francisco and the far side of the world local traffic was neglected, and there was no regular means of reaching other parts of Puget Sound unless one owned a sloop or Indian canoe. Seattle did not have her first steamer service until the fall of 1853. The steamer was the *Fairy*, Captain Gove. She was built in San Francisco and brought north on the deck of the bark *Sarah Warren*. She was put in operation between Olympia and Seattle in November, and the fare for the sixty-mile trip was ten dollars. Arthur Denny was Seattle agent and Charles Terry the agent for Alki.

Alki, served by the same steamer as Seattle, had started life as New York; but a captain had added the Chinook jargon "Alki," meaning "bye and bye." That year Terry had dropped the "New York," and the town was doing very well with the more modest name; Seattle and Alki were neck-and-neck rivals. Seattle attracted as many lumber vessels as she could supply with cargoes, but the *Leonesa*, which the pilgrims had first loaded, was faithful to the original settlement, which also attracted other vessels. Seattle had Yesler's sawmill, but Captain William Renton had built another steam sawmill at Alki. The Terry-Renton mill was on the north side of the point, protected from southern storms, but exposed to storms from the north, which played havoc with the mill boom and threatened to drown out the mill. Also, there was not enough fresh water for the boiler. Between too much water and not enough, the mill had an uneasy and brief existence on the Point, and the following year it was moved across the Sound. The name of "bye and bye" became more derisive, and Alki failed because it had accepted the outer breakwater of a great harbor for the harbor itself.

The year 1853 was a period of great progress, with minor discouragements. One of them was the military road that Captain McClellan, later of Civil War fame, was to have built over the Cascades. McClellan arrived too late to build the road; he also made a discouraging report on the railroad survey through the mountains.

Boom Days

McClellan did nothing toward building the road across the Cascades, but when he arrived the settlers of the upper Sound were already at work on one. With money from their own pockets and with their own saws and axes they were hacking a road from the Steilacoom plains to high Naches Pass. Money and enthusiasm gave out while the road was still a rough sketch, and only one wagon train crossed the Cascades that fall. That was the Biles Party, and at one stage of their journey they killed some of their oxen and braided strips of the hide into ropes with which they let their wagons down the face of Summit Mountain. They averaged less than three miles a day on that part of their journey, and of the seventy wagons with which the party had started over the mountains they reached the Sound with one.

Not all the bright promises of 1853 were fulfilled, but still brighter ones were made. Governor Stevens arrived in September, enthusiastic about his new territory and about his railroad survey. He predicted that the railroad would be built and operating within five years. It would come through Snoqualmie Pass, at Seattle's back door, and it would bring undreamed-of wealth. The railroad would be the shortest distance across the continent, and from Puget Sound to Asia is the shortest distance across the Pacific. Together that meant the shortest distance between Asia and the markets of the United States and Europe. The trade routes of the world would be redrawn, and the wealth of India and China, now crawling in caravans across the deserts of Asia, would flow through Puget Sound and Snoqualmie Pass.

Northwest Gateway

Actually things did not happen so swiftly or turn out so perfectly. The railroad got lost in political jockeying and rehearsing for the Civil War. Stevens' railroad survey was submitted to Secretary of War Jefferson Davis. Slavery was the great issue, and Southern interests were set on having the transcontinental railroad pass through slave states. In his report to Congress Jefferson Davis misrepresented the nature and geography of the continent west of the Missouri River, and he did it so well that to this day the eastern half of the United States has erroneous ideas about what the western half is like. Secretary Davis represented Stevens' survey as a failure; and while he made much of McClellan's opinion that the Cascade Mountains were impassable even in summer, he neglected to mention another surveyor's demonstration that they were passable even in winter.

The defeat of Governor Stevens' northern route for the railway was only a symptom of gathering trouble that exploded in the Civil War. In the kind of orderly world necessary for building, McClellan's report would have been of small consequence. As it was, the transcontinental railroad did not come for another generation, and the settlers' road over the mountains was so heartbreaking and wagon-breaking that only one small wagon train followed the Biles Party, and the road fell into disuse. But all things seemed possible and within reach in 1853, and the pioneers had official encouragement in their dreams of wealth.

Plenty has been written to suggest that the westward pioneers suffered incredible hardships in order to carry out some vague but sacred mission personally entrusted to them. If they could hear the suggestion the old pioneers would be puzzled. Then, as now, people moved across the continent or across the street for the purpose of avoiding discomfort or bettering their condition. And while there were hardships, it seemed better to put up with temporary discomforts on the journey than with inescapable ones at home.

The founders of Seattle crossed the continent to escape malaria at home and to better their condition in the new world. In the forthright little book Arthur Denny wrote in his later years, he made it clear that it was his ambition to become a capitalist, and he took satisfaction in being one. He also opined that the old pioneers deserved all they got.

In the 'fifties the opportunity never seemed more promising for bettering one's condition. Americans of the period have been called "the speed-mad, money-drunk mob." Seattle had its full measure of the strong drink of booming expansion. Even Doctor Smith, the gentle poet of Smith's Cove, had chosen his isolated claim on the long-range guess that the Cove would be the terminus of the railroad.

Perhaps the only early citizens who came without much thought of temporal things were the missionary Blaines, who reached Seattle in the winter of 1853.

The Reverend David Blaine was a Methodist who built the first church in Seattle. It was painted white and was known as the "White Church." Catherine Blaine kept house under difficulties while she taught the first school in her one-room house. She often sat up until past midnight, by the light of a dogfish-oil lamp, writing excellent letters to her relatives in New York. Her letters record some of the strained and hectic spirit of young Seattle, where people were striving to better their condition. Soon after her arrival, she wrote:

There are, as I wrote before, two or three town proprietors here, and there exists between them a jealous spirit, which affects us rather unfavorably in the effort to build a church. Each is afraid that the other will have some preference shown him or will derive more than his share of the benefits from the locality of the church. This will necessarily retard our movements, but we trust will not prevent the accomplishment of our purpose to get a church in the course of the coming season. . . .

The following May Catherine wrote:

Things work strangely here. Nobody has any confidence in anybody else and there is but little ground for any. So large a population of our citizens are here only for a time and they do not feel any desire to secure a good reputation and are almost reckless.

A letter written on August eighteenth, 1854, touches on Seattle's growing trans-Pacific commerce:

We have a vessel in now from the Sandwich Islands. They now, I suppose, form a part of our wide spreading country. Among other things she brought a quantity of sweet potatoes which surpass any ever brought from the Carolinas to your place. . . . She also brought some fowls. I have not seen them and so do not know whether they are superior or not. There has a vessel gone from the Sound taking a load of lumber to China and when she returns will bring a quantity of products of that country, fowls among the rest, so we can get some "pure breeds" direct from home.

In September Catherine wrote:

Business is very dull here at present, but it is thought the present dullness will be for the good of the country, as those who are here only to make their "piles" and return to the states will be driven away, and the permanent settlers that remain will feel interested in doing all they can for the improvement of the country. These transient persons only impoverish the country as they carry away all they can get by fair means or foul. . . .

In the letter there is a growing distinction between the class of settlers who expected to benefit by stocking the trout stream and those who dynamited it in passing. The Blaines were primarily interested in more eternal streams, but they were human, and with conditions what they were, it was natural that they should run a few degrees of speculative fever. In the same letter Catherine wrote:

Mr. Blaine spoke to our principal business man about that money that Father spoke about. He said that if we had it now he would gladly give 15% for it all, but said it would bring more to let it out in smaller sums. We lent him $200.00. . . . Our house is now painted on the outside and is the admiration of the whole town. The people say that it is by far the handsomest house in town, that it looks like a house in the states.

The following month business picked up:

We have had eight or ten different vessels in here within two or three weeks. Last Saturday was a lively day, there being five vessels in and two came and went. . . . We have one now loading for Australia. The mill runs night and day and cannot supply the demand for lumber. . . .

Another month later David Blaine's speculative fever was up several degrees. He wrote to his brother Saron:

If I had the value of that mill here, or even half of it, I could buy the whole town plat of Seattle that remains unsold, as the times are depressed and money scarce just now, and this in ten years would increase in value ten-fold. The reason for this assertion is simply that now there is only beginning enough made to indicate the certainty of a future city here not unlike New York or London in commercial importance. This may sound and look like castle building, and it may be many years ere such a state of things will be realized, but it is conceived in the womb of the future beyond all reasonable doubt.

Seattle was then a stumpy clearing with one sawmill and about thirty log cabins and Indian-style split cedar cabins and frame houses, lorded over by the Blaines' one-room house with its coat of paint. In such a setting, the prophecy had the sound of castle-building phantasy. And more fantastic still, it was essentially correct. In the same letter David wrote:

If we had the money I should consider it a profitable investment to purchase town lots with it while they can be had so cheaply. I purchased two lots a few days since for Brother Devore, for $15.00 each, very cheap and beautifully located. One of our town proprietors, Dr. Maynard, a good friend to us, has given us some two acres, more or less, a short distance from the town plat, laying on the shore of the bay, for a garden and orchard. The land is very rich and in a few years will be included in the town and needed for building lots. . . .

Boom Days

The two acres, more or less, were given on the condition that the land be cleared by the end of the following summer. The gift was typical of Doctor Maynard, who went on the theory that anything which helped the town helped everyone, including himself. He was right, except in the expectation of sharing in his benefactions. Doctor Maynard was a true pioneer and there was no help for him.

In the spring of 1855 the Blaines had not yet received the money they hoped to invest in Seattle. On March fifteenth Catherine wrote:

We are looking with more than usual anxiety for the mails now, for it is about time we should hear something about the money matters we wrote about some time ago. The last news from San Francisco is not very encouraging. Page, Bacon & Co., Adam and Co., Wells, Fargo & Co., have all suspended payments and if you have sent a draft on either of those firms, it may all be lost. Those who know best about their affairs think their paper not worth 25%. I wish we had the money now for property is rising and probably never will be lower than now. Lots in the business part of town bring from $200.00 to $250.00.

The draft arrived in May, and even then there was a catch. On May twentieth Catherine wrote:

Father writes about the draft. We sent it to San Francisco about two weeks ago with the instruction that if 90% at least could not be paid on it, that it should be protested and we will send it back. It is a great pity that we are to be kept out of the use of it, as we could get from three to six percent a month for it now if we had it. I would rather take 90% for it than send it back and get the whole face value, as we shall be obliged to use it to build after we move. Besides, I have my fears that it might not be paid if sent back. They are a very rascally company. There is a man here who had had $900.00 in gold deposited in their office in St. Louis to be sent on by express. Instead of sending the money, they sent a receipt for the money and a draft for the amount. Now he can not get it without a great deal of trouble, delay and expense. He went over to Portland to see what could be done about it. They offered him 50% for it but he would not take it, and is going to have it protested and sent back. They do not know anything about the first principles of honesty.

It was a glittering time for would-be investors, with interest rates up to seventy-two per cent a year. But private forwarding companies knocked some of the glitter off by giving their customers the choice of doing without their funds from the East or paying tribute as high as fifty cents on the dollar.

CHAPTER VI

Chief Seattle

THE WHITE SETTLERS who came to the West were conditioned by a propaganda of racial superiority, centuries old, which decreed that a country or region was undiscovered and unclaimed until the arrival of white men. It also decreed, in effect, that people of any other color were without property or legal rights.

In Washington Territory there was a pretense at allowing the Indians both. But in the alleged purchase of their land and their removal to reservations the Indians were told, not asked, the price, and they were not consulted as to their taste in reservations. In early Seattle several white men accused of lynching Indians were tried for murder, but all were found innocent, including one simple-minded lyncher with a bad conscience who admitted his guilt. In another, more flagrant case the jury freed the defendant on the grounds that the court had not made it clear that it was talking about the Indian whom the jurors had seen the defendant hang.

People of any color who are without rights are at a disadvantage, and if the Indians did not start as an inferior race they were soon made into one. All the Puget Sound Indians were termed "Siwashes," and it was the prevalent opinion that Siwashes were hardly human or worthy of consideration. Siwash is a corruption of the word "savage." The first white explorers and traders on Puget Sound called the Indians savages, and the Indians, who had received them hospitably, did not understand that they were being stigmatized. They assumed that "savage" was descriptive of their friendly race and they adopted the term for themselves, but "Siwash" was the nearest pronunciation they could manage.

Since the majority of white settlers did not look for any culture among the Indians, it was natural that they did not see much. But even they had to concede the Indians certain abilities in woodlore and canoe making and house building. In the founding of Seattle there was the unusual situation of inland, prairie people set down in isolation between a great forest and salt water. They did not know about clams until the Indians showed them how to dig and cook them. They learned their seamanship firsthand from the Indians, and for local travel on water they had to depend entirely on native dugouts. The Indians were masters in handling canoes and judging weather, and the only recorded instance of any of them being drowned was when members of the superior race forced them to put out against their own better judgment. In one of her letters Catherine Blaine observes:

Chief Seattle

Last Thursday Capt. Barstow, the owner of the vessel in which we came up from San Francisco, together with Colonel McConaha, the speaker of the council of our legislature, were coming down from Olympia in a canoe, manned by six Indians. The sound was rough when they started and the Indians, who are always to be trusted as to the propriety of going out in a storm, were unwilling to start, but were overruled by the white men. They managed to get within a few miles of this place when a violent squall of wind struck as they were in the middle of the sound, upset the canoe and drowned the men. They clung to the canoe as long as they could but at last were obliged to let go. Two Indians were drowned and the other four managed to right the canoe and get into it and so came ashore, but were almost perished. The trunk and hat of Colonel McConaha, the cap of Capt. Barstow came ashore, but nothing can be found of their bodies.

One of the high spots of Puget Sound Indian culture was canoe making. The canoes were burned and hewn out of red cedar logs, and the finished product has never been surpassed for speed or beauty. Their lines and proportions were almost identical with those of the ultimate clipper ships. The concave bow that revolutionized clipper ship design was in use in the Pacific Northwest for generations, and probably centuries, before it appeared in the *Sea Witch*. Seventy-foot canoes of the same model, built by northern Indians, were capable of being paddled at a speed of ten knots.

When the pilgrims completed their first one-room log cabin at Alki they thought of it as the first house on that part of Puget Sound. They were right only in the sense that a house is not a house unless it is built by whites. Northwest across the Sound, on Bainbridge Island, was a building that compared favorably with the crude new cabin. It was an apartment house nine hundred feet long, covering an acre and a quarter of ground. It was divided into forty apartments, each apartment with its fireplace and built-in berths and separate rooms. Each of the forty apartments had its private entrance between great cedar pillars carved with figures of the Thunderbird.

The Oleman House at Port Madison was the headquarters of the Duwamish and Suquamish Indians. There six chiefs lived in adjoining apartments, and there Chief Seattle ruled tolerantly over the tribes he had united. He had got that far in building a civilization when he was stopped by the invasion of the white settlers.

The Oleman House at Port Madison was a remarkable structure in its way, but the early inhabitants of Seattle were honest in not considering it worth a log cabin. It was only a dozen miles away, but few had time to visit it, and very few of those really saw the house or the pictograph legend that recorded its building. Their instructed minds were left cold by the sight of a rustic palace nine hundred feet long and inscrutable characters engraved on a cliff.

With the status of the Indians what it was, it seems remarkable that a "Siwash" should have had a city named after him by his white contemporaries. There were several reasons for this. One was that the degree of contempt in which the Indians were held varied inversely with the intelligence and culture of the individual. Lynchers were recruited from the most dubious class of citizens and the sailors from ships in the harbor. The Indians fared best at the hands of the intelligent and responsible men who founded the city.

But the main reason for the city's indigenous name was the man. Seattle was a great chief and a man of great and complex character, who gave the impression of simplicity because of his capacity for being consistent and because of his integrity, which came from within and was never compromised by outside events.

Physically as well as otherwise Seattle had the advantage over other members of his allied tribes. They were inclined to be short and stocky and bowlegged from almost constant sitting in canoes; and after the Flathead custom, many of them had their skulls deformed. As a chief who traveled in large canoes that others paddled, Seattle's legs had escaped deformity, and his head showed little sign of having been bound. When the advance guard of the pilgrims camped at Alki, Chief Seattle was about sixty-five years old. He was a good physical specimen, straight and vigorous, although he carried a staff in keeping with his age and dignity and peaceful intentions. He was about six feet tall, broad shouldered and deep chested, with a massive head, graying, unbraided hair worn to his shoulders, and a benevolent face. He looked like an aging philosopher who no longer put much trust in physical strength.

Chief Seattle had traveled a long and complex road before the American settlers of the early 'fifties found him waiting to co-operate with them. He was born, as nearly as can be estimated, in the year 1786, on what is now

Bainbridge Island. In his childhood he shared in the generally pleasant and unambitious life that the Puget Sound Indians had led for centuries they had not bothered to count. They hunted with fierce dogs that drove deer into the water, where they were easily killed; dug clams from the squirting beaches; devoted themselves to berries in berry time; camped out about the bays and islands wherever and whenever it seemed agreeable; caught salmon in the salt water in summer and trapped them in the streams in the fall. Their supply of food and shelter was apparently inexhaustible. Sometimes there were battles with neighboring tribes, as fond of life as themselves, and with as little reason for fighting. The battles provided desirable noise and excitement and few casualties, often none at all. Sometimes a battle was limited to name calling, and even the slow-witted ones who got the worst of it soon recovered.

Occasionally, in summer, parties of fierce, sea-roving Haidahs or Tsimpsians would come raiding in their great canoes. They were the ancient enemy from the "Land of Blue Ice and the Home of the Thunderbird," and the Puget Sound Indians did not stop to argue with them. If they were in the home camp, they all piled into the Oleman House. If it was a summer camp, they took what they could manage and retreated into the forest and waited for the enemy to go away. Nothing the raiders took was irreplaceable. They could not take the forest or the beach or the Sound, and those were the only things that mattered. . . .

The Puget Sound Indians were not all noble savages:

not many of them noble and still fewer savages. There was no particular need in their amiable life for universal nobility, and there was still less occasion for meanness. They were human beings who enjoyed life and had fewer urgent problems than peoples who have all the complicated machinery of the world for solving them. One reason for their fortunate state was their considerable measure of laziness in a world of delicate balances, where too much energy in one person can let loose a train of consequences that a thousand cannot overtake. Chief Seattle's ancestors and tribesmen never upset the balance of nature and therefore never had the job of trying to put it on its feet again.

Chief Seattle passed his childhood in the agreeable world of his ancestors, which may not have been so haphazard as it appeared. Neither was it so secure. Ten years before Seattle was born, Spanish Heceta and Quadra had sailed up the coast in search of Juan de Fuca's legendary inland sea. A few years later Captain Cook, with Vancouver and Bligh, sighted and named Cape Flattery. But the strait for which they were searching slept beyond the enchantment of a fog bank that made it invisible. Cook sailed on, to be eaten by natives elsewhere, and Bligh went on to other adventures; but presently Vancouver returned to make a first and thorough exploration of Puget Sound and to name everything in sight.

The summer Seattle was six his people were camped on an island southwest across the Sound from Alki. One morning there was a great explosion of excitement in camp, and the world changed and a way of life ended. From the crowded beach the Indian boy saw a canoe of unearthly size. Growing out of it were three tall trees with branches that spread white wings. From the bow of the canoe something plunged into the water with a great splash and a sudden harsh roar that echoed from the primeval fir forest; and the white wings on the canoe-borne trees were folded as the ship *Discovery* came to anchor off the little, anvil-shaped island, which Captain George Vancouver had already decided to name "Blake Island."

The Indians thought the ship was a winged messenger of the gods, as it was, but it took time for them to decipher the message of doom.

While Seattle was growing up there were trappers and traders in the familiar world, and new gadgets and new diseases, and a drink that produced temporary insanity in the Indians. There were also misunderstandings. When Seattle was established as chief of his tribe and doing his best under difficulties, he was branded a "bad Indian" by the Hudson's Bay people. That was because he went to their station at Nisqually and bought a musket with which he shot another Indian. The Hudson's Bay people said that was wrong—without asking the circumstances. The Indian who died was a doctor who had lost a patient; someone had to kill him—tribal laws demanded it; and Seattle had gone to some trouble and expense to do a thankless job.

Seattle never had much faith in warfare, but he was a practical and able general when necessary. On one occasion his spies brought word that the Green River and White River Indians planned a daybreak raid on his camp. The traditional defense would have been to move or fortify the camp against attack, but Seattle was not steeped in military tradition and he managed an unconventional approach. He paddled up the Duwamish River with his braves to the southern border of his own territory. There the Black River, from Lake Washington, and the White River joined to make the Duwamish, and the resulting river bent sharply around a high, forested point of land. Seattle had his braves hack down a tall fir. The tree was supposed to mark the boundary of his territory, beyond which it was not safe for raiders to come, and when it was felled the party waited to see what would happen.

The raiders came that night, in about twenty canoes, racing down the swift river to fall on the Duwamishes at dawn. They swept around the blind turn of the river at the point of Mox la Push, and their canoes crashed and piled up and overturned on the fallen tree that lay across the river just above the level of the water. While they were floundering, Seattle and his braves waded in with their axes and clubs and beat out as many brains as seemed necessary to victory.

The survivors walked home to the hinterland, and Chief Seattle descended the Duwamish in triumph to the Sound. There he started a political campaign on the strength of his record. When it ended he had united the salt-water Indians into a little nation that recognized him as their leader. And the chiefs of the six warring tribes began living peacefully, in adjoining apartments, in the Oleman House on Bainbridge Island.

That was as far as Chief Seattle was able to go in the direction he had planned. After that it was a case of saving what he could and shaping some kind of course for his people in the tide race of strange times in a familiar world.

From the beginning he saw that there was only destruction in trying to oppose the white invasion. He would go with the tide so willingly that he might be able to manage some saving leeway. He learned about the religion the "Bostons" professed and was baptized by one of the missionary priests. But his own words show that he had no illusions about the white man's god disregarding the color line. Before he was through he had few illusions of any kind left, but he never wavered in his policy of non-resistance and co-operation with the whites.

Even in the early days of the village that bore his name Seattle knew that he had made a hard choice of one-sided co-operation. He saw his high-spirited granddaughter bought from her parents by a drunken and brutal white man. He saw her beaten and pursued and brought back and beaten again when she ran away. He could not interfere because he was an Indian, and the whites did not interfere because the girl was an Indian. Presently the girl killed herself by hanging, leaving a son who turned out no better than his father. A white man could do as he pleased with his squaw. But when one of the Indians killed his squaw the white men hung him to a tree.

Neither the Americans nor the Indians were sufficiently advanced in civilization to be able to live together. Chief Seattle saw that early, and he was relieved rather than otherwise when he heard that the Government was preparing to buy the Indians' land and segregate them on reservations.

On a hurried visit to the Territory in 1854 Stevens de-

Photograph by L. D. Lindsley

Chief Seattle.

The city from Queen Anne Hill, with Mount Rainier in the distance.

voted a month to traveling about the large region west of the Cascade Mountains, "familiarizing" himself with thirty-odd tribes of Indians, "learning their needs" and deciding on the value of their land. The haste was ominous and at best the results could only be tragically superficial. The Governor had been handed a bad situation and he made it worse with haste and bad judgment. He was an ambitious man and he had insisted on having charge of the railroad survey along with his other superhuman tasks. The realization of the railroad was twenty years away and the Indian War only a year, but Governor Stevens made a bad guess. After the hasty survey of his new territory he raced back to Washington, D.C., to fight Jefferson Davis on the routing of the railroad.

In his hurried glance over Indian affairs Governor Stevens visited the village of Seattle, where all the Indians of the Elliott Bay region were called together. The shore was blackened with hundreds of canoes drawn up on the beach, and the narrow forest trails poured out Indians until three thousand of them crowded the village.

The Governor's party arrived in the new Sound steamer *Major Tompkins*, which the canoe-traveling settlers looked on as a miracle of luxury. The small and swarthy Governor addressed the Indians from in front of Doctor Maynard's drugstore-real-estate log cabin. Doctor Maynard was master of ceremonies, and an interpreter hacked and jammed the Governor's English into Procrustean Chinook jargon. The Governor told them how the Great Chief in Washington loved Indians, and he told them that he loved them as much as if they were the children of his own loins. Because of his love for them he was going to have the Great Father buy their lands and he was going to give them fine reservations and the blessings of civilization, such as schools and blacksmith and carpenter shops.

The Governor made a fine speech, but he was outranged and outclassed that day. Chief Seattle, who answered in behalf of the Indians, towered a foot above the Governor. He wore his blanket like the toga of a Roman senator, and he did not have to strain his famous voice, which everyone agreed was audible and distinct at a distance of half a mile.

Seattle's oration was in Duwamish. Doctor Smith, who had learned the language, wrote it down; under the flowery garlands of his translation the speech rolls like an articulate iron engine, grim with meanings that outlasted his generation and may outlast all the generations of men. As the amiable follies of the white race become less amiable, the iron rumble of old Seattle's speech sounds louder and more ominous.

Standing in front of Doctor Maynard's office in the stumpy clearing, with his hand on the little Governor's head, the white invaders about him and his people before him, Chief Seattle said:

Yonder sky that has wept tears of compassion upon my people for centuries untold, and which to us appears changeless and eternal, may change. Today is fair. Tomorrow it may be overcast with clouds. My words are like the stars that never change. Whatever Seattle says the great chief at Washington can rely upon with as much certainty as he can upon the return of the sun or the seasons. The White Chief says

that Big Chief at Washington sends us greetings of friendship and goodwill. That is kind of him for we know he has
little need of our friendship in return. His people are many.
They are like the grass that covers vast prairies. My people
are few. They resemble the scattering trees of a storm-swept
plain. The great, and I presume—good, White Chief sends us
word that he wishes to buy our lands but is willing to allow
us enough to live comfortably. This indeed appears just, even
generous, for the Red Man no longer has rights that he need
respect, and the offer may be wise also, as we are no longer in
need of an extensive country. . . . I will not dwell on, nor
mourn over, our untimely decay, nor reproach our paleface
brothers with hastening it, as we too may have been somewhat to blame.

Youth is impulsive. When our young men grow angry at
some real or imaginary wrong, and disfigure their faces with
black paint, it denotes that their hearts are black, and then
they are often cruel and relentless, and our old men and old
women are unable to restrain them. Thus it has ever been.
Thus it was when the white men first began to push our fore-
fathers further westward. But let us hope that the hostilities
between us may never return. We would have everything
to lose and nothing to gain. Revenge by young men is considered gain, even at the cost of their own lives, but old men
who stay at home in times of war, and mothers who have sons
to lose, know better.

Our good father at Washington—for I presume he is now
our father as well as yours, since King George has moved his
boundaries further north—our great good father, I say, sends
us word that if we do as he desires he will protect us. His
brave warriors will be to us a bristling wall of strength, and
his wonderful ships of war will fill our harbors so that our
ancient enemies far to the northward—the Hydas and Tsimpsians—will cease to frighten our women, children and old men.

Then in reality will he be our father and we his children. But can that ever be? Your God is not our God! Your God loves your people and hates mine. He folds his strong and protecting arms lovingly about the paleface and leads him by the hand as a father leads his infant son—but He has forsaken His red children—if they really are his. Our God, the Great Spirit, seems also to have forsaken us. Your God makes your people wax strong every day. Soon they will fill the land. Our people are ebbing away like a rapidly receding tide that will never return. The white man's God cannot love our people or He would protect them. They seem to be orphans who can look nowhere for help. How then can we be brothers? How can your God become our God and renew our prosperity and awaken in us dreams of returning greatness? If we have a common heavenly father He must be partial—for He came to his paleface children. We never saw Him. He gave you laws but He had no word for His red children whose teeming multitudes once filled this vast continent as stars fill the firmament. No; we are two distinct races with separate origins and separate destinies. There is little in common between us.

To us the ashes of our ancestors are sacred and their resting place is hallowed ground. You wander far from the graves of your ancestors and seemingly without regret. Your religion was written upon tables of stone by the iron finger of your God so that you could not forget. The Red Man could never comprehend nor remember it. Our religion is the traditions of our ancestors—the dreams of our old men, given them in solemn hours of night by the Great Spirit; and the visions of our sachems; and it is written in the hearts of our people.

Your dead cease to love you and the land of their nativity as soon as they pass the portals of the tomb and wander way beyond the stars. They are soon forgotten and never return. Our dead never forget the beautiful world that gave them being.

Chief Seattle

Day and night cannot dwell together. The Red Man has ever fled the approach of the White Man, as the morning mist flees before the morning sun. However, your proposition seems fair and I think that my people will accept it and will retire to the reservation you offer them. Then we will dwell apart in peace, for the words of the Great White Chief seem to be the words of nature speaking to my people out of dense darkness.

It matters little where we pass the remnant of our days. They will not be many. A few more moons; a few more winters—and not one of the descendants of the mighty hosts that once moved over this broad land or lived in happy homes, protected by the Great Spirit, will remain to mourn over the graves of a people once more powerful and hopeful than yours. But why should I mourn at the untimely fate of my people? Tribe follows tribe, and nation follows nation, like the waves of the sea. It is the order of nature, and regret is useless. Your time of decay may be distant, but it will surely come, for even the White Man whose God walked and talked with him as friend with friend, cannot be exempt from the common destiny. We may be brothers after all. We will see.

We will ponder your proposition, and when we decide we will let you know. But should we accept it, I here and now make this condition that we will not be denied the privilege without molestation of visiting at any time the tombs of our ancestors, friends and children. Every part of this soil is sacred in the estimation of my people. Every hillside, every valley, every plain and grove, has been hallowed by some sad or happy event in days long vanished. . . . The very dust upon which you now stand responds more lovingly to their footsteps than to yours, because it is rich with the blood of our ancestors and our bare feet are conscious of the sympathetic touch. . . . Even the little children who lived here and rejoiced here for a brief season will love these somber solitudes and at eventide they greet shadowy returning spirits. And when the last Red Man shall have perished, and the memory of my tribe shall have become a myth among the White Men, these shores will swarm with the invisible dead of my tribe, and when your children's children think themselves alone in the field, the store, the shop, upon the highway, or in the silence of the pathless woods, they will not be alone. . . . At night when the streets of your cities and villages are silent and you think them deserted, they will throng with the returning hosts that once filled and still love this beautiful land. The White Man will never be alone.

Let him be just and deal kindly with my people, for the dead are not powerless. Dead, did I say? There is no death, only a change of worlds.

Soon after this meeting Governor Stevens was on his way east, to be gone for months. He returned to the Territory in November and plunged into the business of extinguishing the Indians' title to the land.

The treaty that included the Indians of the Seattle region was made at Point Elliott on January twenty-second, 1855. About twenty-three hundred Indians met the Governor's party at the Point and were persuaded to sell two million acres of land of incalculable wealth for $150,000. It sounded like a handsome sum to the Indians, who were not good mathematicians, and it was enhanced rather than otherwise by the fact that it was to be paid in yearly installments over a period of twenty years. As in some of the other treaties, the Indians misunderstood the terms and believed that they were to receive that much a year for twenty years. But $150,000 was the full amount, and it came to not much more than $1.80 a year each for

the estimated four thousand members of the tribes represented. This was further diminished by the fact that it was
to be paid in "useful articles."

At the Point Elliott Treaty the Indians did not become
as wealthy as they supposed, but it was one of the best
treaties made. The reservations were comparatively generous and well located, and they included Port Madison,
with Seattle's ancestral Oleman House. At the time only
one tribe of Indians was actively dissatisfied with the
treaty. They were Chief Nelson's Muckleshoot Indians
from the White River region. The treaty required them
to leave their ancestral river within a year and live with
the salt-water tribes, who were their traditional enemies.
The Muckleshoots thought of themselves as being thrown
to the wolves of their enemies and they blamed the white
settlers.

The Indian War began east of the Cascade Mountains
during the treaty-making summer. Whatever the main
cause, the war was undoubtedly hastened by a gold rush
and it began with the Indians picking off isolated prospectors and concealing their bodies.

West of the mountains the summer passed quietly. But
in September the Muckleshoot Indians attacked the claim
of a man named Porter. Porter escaped and warned his
neighbors, and the White River Valley settlers fled down
the river to Seattle, where the citizens decided it was time
to build a blockhouse.

David Denny had a cargo of square-hewn timbers ready
for the next lumber vessel, and he donated them to the
cause. The blockhouse was built on a knoll of the penin-

sula; it was two stories high, with gun ports in the side; the upper floor was for women and children.

While the blockhouse was under construction the citizens of Seattle were pleasantly reminded that they were under the protection of the Government. On the afternoon of October fourth, 1855, a three-masted ship, with gun ports in her sides, sailed around West Point and stood into Elliott Bay. She let her anchor go off the peninsula and fired a gun; and the men, rushing the completion of the blockhouse, were glad to see her.

The ship was the sloop-of-war *Decatur*, Captain Sterrett. She had been at Honolulu, in the Sandwich Islands, when Sterrett received orders to "cruise the coast of Oregon and California for the protection of settlers." It was a broad order, and the commander broadened it still more by deciding to operate in the waters of Puget Sound.

The proprietors of Seattle were pleased by Captain Sterrett's interpretation of his orders. They told him of their fears of an Indian attack and persuaded him to take up his station on Elliott Bay.

Governor Stevens was then somewhere about the Rocky Mountains, negotiating with the Blackfeet Indians. He had worked very fast, but the first of his treaties had blown up before the last was signed. Young Charles Mason, Secretary of State, was acting in the Governor's absence, and he did not want anything unpleasant to happen. He visited the Muckleshoot Indians and was persuaded that Porter had imagined the attack on his house. After that he visited Seattle and persuaded the White River settlers to return to their claims with their women and children. But Acting Governor Mason was not able to persuade Porter to return. And Arthur Denny struck a discordant note by urging the settlers to stay in Seattle. Denny was getting information from Chief Pat Kanim of the Snoqualmies, and he had been warned that trouble was coming. He made himself unpopular with the acting Governor by predicting that the settlers would all be massacred if they returned to the White River country. But Arthur Denny was a town proprietor, and there was the suspicion that he was trying to boom Seattle business by scaring settlers into staying there.

There was the same thought about the presence of the *Decatur*. In all sincerity the acting Governor informed Captain Sterrett that the Indian scare was a hoax, and the only purpose being served by the *Decatur* was that of providing trade for Denny, Horton and Phillips and other firms ashore. Sterrett was only prevented from leaving in anger by the earnest pleas of the accused town proprietors. They were able to convince him of their sincerity and he determined to find out whom to believe. He made his own investigation and decided to stay; but most of the White River settlers returned to their claims.

CHAPTER VII

The Massacre

THE CLEARING IN THE FOREST of the rich White River valley was about twenty miles from Seattle. The original building was a one-room log cabin. Harvey Jones had built it the first year, when he was getting started. The log cabin was now used as a storeroom and the family lived in the new frame house a few rods to the north. There were Mr and Mrs Jones, Johnny King, who was by Mrs Jones's first marriage and going on seven, and the Joneses' children: a girl of not quite four and a boy of not quite two. There was also Enos Cooper, who had the adjoining claim and helped Mr Jones with his work. For neighbors there were the Brannans and Mr Lake and the Thomases. The Thomas claim was farther away than the others, but it was familiar because that was where Johnny King went to school.

For neighbors there were also the Indians. They were generally dirty and rough mannered. Instead of knocking they would make questioning grunts until someone opened the door and let them in. Then they would sit around for a while, visiting and eating anything Mrs Jones offered them. Their chief was a stocky man known as Nelson. He did not look much like a chief, with his dirty blanket and unbraided hair, but he was friendly in a restrained fashion. He spoke some English and was decidedly intelligent. If he resented Harvey Jones and Cooper as intruders on the land of his people, he had less resentment for Mrs Jones, and still less for the children, with their diminishing and vanishing degrees of responsibility. And Nelson was dependable; when Mrs Jones heard his distinctive grunt outside the door she knew almost to the minute how long he would visit; and she knew what he liked to eat and how he would act and what he would talk about.

But when he called on Friday, the twenty-sixth of October, 1855, Nelson did not run true to form. That was a few weeks after the settlers' flight to Seattle and their return. Mrs Jones was baking bread in the Dutch oven, a loaf at a time. One loaf was already done, and bread was the favorite delicacy of the Indians, but when she offered him some he grunted, "Wake" (No); and he continued to sit on the bench, looking into the fire, with his Hudson's Bay flintlock musket leaning against the stone-and-clay fireplace. When Mrs Jones asked if he had been hunting, he said, "Wake." It was like that with all her attempts at conversation, until she saw there was no communicating with him. Instead of staying his usual half-hour he appeared in the morning, just after Mr Jones and Cooper went out to cut wood, and he stayed until almost noon, when the men might be expected home to eat. Whatever

the purpose of his visit, it was for the benefit of the woman
and her children. When Nelson was at the door, going
away, he said, "Soon Siwash will be gone and Bostons will
have all the land here."

Harvey Jones did not come home until late, and he and
his wife could not decide what had been in the chief's
mind. Jones had caught cold during the day, and at the end
of that uneasy evening he went to bed complaining of a
knifelike pain in one side of his chest.

On Sunday morning Jones was suffering from an attack
of pleurisy and unable to leave his bed. Enos Cooper did
the chores and came in to have breakfast with Mrs Jones
and the children. The table was in the center of the large
room, which served as kitchen, dining and living room.
Two bedrooms opened off the large room, and Harvey
Jones was in bed in the southwest room at the front of
the house.

They had just sat down to eat when there was a questioning guttural sound outside the front door. Mrs Jones
got up, and by the time she opened the door her three
children were beside her. A strange Indian was there,
standing a little to one side of the doorway. As the door
opened wider he moved farther to the side. Johnny King
looked past him, toward the one-room log house, and saw
another Indian. The Indian was partly behind a corner of
the log house, with his musket pointed out between the
end of the logs. The child stared at the face pressed against
the musket stock, and he looked, frozen, into the big-bore
muzzle of the weapon. Then he and the smaller children
were hurled from the doorway. The door crashed shut,

and the mother barred it. That all happened in the twinkling of an eye, and the little boy's chief amazement was at
the explosive power and speed of his gentle mother.

He heard yells and the banging of muskets and the crash
of glass while he was still sprawled on the floor. When he
got up and looked out of the front window he saw a dozen
Indians charging on the house, waving hatchets and muskets. He saw his mother, with the father's five-shooter,
aiming through the shattered window. He saw her white
face and heard the sharp explosions of the revolver as the
room dimmed with blue powder smoke. Outside there was
the yelling of the Indians and the heavy, sickening explosions of muskets.

Johnny saw his mother lay the empty pistol on the table.
She looked outside and around the smoky room and at
the whimpering children, deciding what she was going to
do. Then she gathered the children together and took
them to the back bedroom. She had them lie down in the
northwest corner, which was farthest from the point of
attack, and covered them with a feather bed.

It was dark and stuffy under the feather bed, and
Johnny could not see what was going on, though he could
hear the banging of muskets and bullets crashing into the
house. He looked from under the bed and saw holes burst
in the partition between the bedrooms and big splinters
flying off the wood. The bullets were piercing the partition above the stepfather's bed on the other side. They
went out of the opposite wall, making clean, round holes
higher up, as if fired from near the ground. When the
boy saw that the musket balls were passing well above the

bed where the children were hiding, he crept along the floor, into the big room. He saw his stepfather come to the door of the other room and lean against the door frame. He was dressed but looked white and ill. The mother did not seem to notice him there. While the boy watched there was the splintering sound of a musket ball coming through the front door, and the stepfather staggered and leaned more heavily against the door frame. He called, "Oh, God, I am shot!"

The mother ran to him saying, "Oh, Harvey, don't say so!" She supported him in her arms while he unbuttoned his shirt. There was a huge wound near his right nipple. She helped him back to bed and Johnny crawled back to the other children. From the other side of the partition he heard the parting of his mother and stepfather; the man's advice broken by the woman's sobbing, and the voices of both broken by the sound of firing and the crash of musket balls through the partition. Then the man's voice changed to moaning, which stopped in a little while.

After that the boy heard his mother telling Cooper that it was hopeless to try to defend the house; he had better look out for himself and try to escape. The boy did not hear what the neighbor said, but in a little while he heard footsteps in the room. Looking from under the feather bed he saw Cooper pry off a window stop with his ax and take out the sash. He hesitated at the window, open to dubious freedom, looking to the east and to the west. Then he crouched, with one foot on the sill, and leaped out of the child's sight forever.

Soon the sound of firing stopped and the boy heard

unfamiliar steps in the big room. When he looked, light was coming into the room and an Indian was carrying loaves of bread in his arms. Another Indian came in and took the boy by the hand and led him out. The south wall of the big room looked flimsy and dead, riddled with holes, and its door and smashed window open to the raw November morning.

There were more Indians outside; Nelson was sitting on an upturned cut from a log in the yard, directing them. He was not silent and morose as he had been on his last visit to the house, and he seemed to know just what must be done. The boy was afraid of him now, and afraid of what would happen to the younger children in the house. But Nelson patted his shoulder and spoke kindly, "All right, Johnny. Nelson don't let them hurt you."

Johnny wasn't afraid any more, and when the other children were brought out of the house he told them everything would be all right because Nelson had said so. But the younger children still whimpered. They did not like what was going on and they knew the Indians had something to do with it. The Indians were carrying out the family's blankets and clothes and stuffing them under the house.

Nelson kept Johnny beside him, and when the other Indians were out of hearing he talked to him with guarded kindness and told him to take the little children to Mr Thomas's. While he talked, smoke came up from under the house, and the house began to burn. The small log house was also burning. The boy did not know any of the Indians except Nelson, whom he trusted completely.

When the house was blazing, Nelson sent all the Indians away except one. The remaining one, he said, would go with the children to the Thomases'.

Johnny watched the burning house for a while, and when he looked around for Nelson the chief was gone. The three children were alone with the strange Indian. The Indian was surly and he was in no hurry to go with the children. He stayed until the roof of the house fell in with a crash and an angry shower of sparks. Then he picked up his flintlock musket and started with the children. He took Johnny's hand, and Johnny took his sister's hand, and the sister took the little brother's hand.

The Thomas claim was to the northwest, and the Indian started to the southeast. Johnny objected that they were going the wrong way and held back. The sister saw that her brother had no faith in their guide and she objected and held back still more. The little brother knew that something was very wrong and he wailed and did not want to go at all. But the Indian insisted, leading and dragging the string of children after him. He got them almost as far as the fence near the barn. There was a low place in the fence, and he was going to take them over the fence into the woods. The children objected to crossing that boundary in the wrong direction and they held back with all their combined weight. The Indian muttered impatiently and let go the boy's hand so suddenly that the string of children staggered back and nearly fell. Then he went away.

They stood there for a while and the boy tried to decide what he should do. Nelson had told him to go to the

Thomases' but that was a long way, and it would mean crossing the lonely clearing where the Indians had been. Johnny decided to go to the Brannans', which was much nearer and toward the south.

He could not go any faster than the four-year-old sister, and she could not go any faster than the two-year-old brother, who was hungry and did not care about walking at all. Johnny saw it would take a long time to get them even to the nearest neighbor's and he decided to leave them and go alone for help. Near the trail he found a hollow in the ground. He put the younger children in there and told them the Indians would kill them if they made any noise. Then he covered them over with brush and hurried along the trail alone.

He went cautiously after he was in sight of the Brannans' house, and when he came in better view he saw that the door was open and the windows broken. There did not seem to be anyone about, and he went still closer. Furniture was scattered in the yard, and feather beds and pillows were ripped open, their feathers drifting idly about the household wreckage. The boy walked around the house, but he did not find anyone, alive or dead. He went back to the other children.

The attack had come as they were beginning breakfast; it was now the middle of the day and all of them were hungry. Johnny led the children back to the ruins of their home. Everything had been burned, but in the remains of the log cabin they found a meal waiting for them. Potatoes and firkins of butter had been stored there. The potatoes were nicely roasted, and streams of melted butter ran from the charred firkins. The boy smeared butter on some of the roasted potatoes, and the three of them had a good meal.

With hot food inside of him, Johnny's resolution came back and he decided to take the children to Mr Thomas's, as Nelson had directed. He led them round about, circling the ruins of the house by way of the barn and woodshed, which had not been burned. Near the woodshed the children's half-grown puppy came bounding up to them. The younger children romped with him and were happy. They had been well fed and now they had their favorite pet. When Johnny said they must go on, they wanted to take the puppy with them. The boy thought it would be fine to have him for company. Then he decided it would not do at all because the noisy, playful fellow would be sure to attract the attention of any Indians within hearing. He took a stick and drove the puppy away, when he wanted to carry it in his arms.

A little farther along the boy was surprised to see his mother lying on the ground in the clearing, a hundred feet or so from the ruins of the house. She was alive and the boy did not see any sign of injury, but she did not try to get up. The mother was pleased to see the children still alive and unhurt, but she reproached Johnny for dawdling. He must go at once, she said, and take the children to Mr Thomas's. He wanted to stay with her, but she told him she could not live, but if he went at once he could save himself and the children. He did not want to leave her, but she said if the Indians came back they would kill everyone. He was responsible for the children now, she

said, and he must do his best to save them. He promised
and went on into the woods with the other children. He
never saw his mother again.

Because of what his mother had said, Johnny made up
his mind not to leave the others again. But it was two miles
to the neighbor's house, and he had to lug the two-year-
old in his arms most of the way.

The Thomases' house had not been disturbed, but the
family was gone and the door locked. Nelson and the
boy's mother could not have known that when they told
him to take the children there. There was another neighbor a quarter of a mile farther to the north. Johnny set out
for there, lugging the heavy two-year-old and letting his
little sister get along as best she could. Sometimes he put
the baby down to catch his breath and rest his breaking
arms, but the baby would do so little walking and so much
crying that as soon as he could the boy would pick him up
and stagger on with him. Sometimes the four-year-old,
stumbling along the trail, would whimper and start to cry.
Then Johnny would say warningly, "Indians kill!" But
it did not help any with the two-year-old, who did not
understand the meaning of the words or of their dismal
journey through the forest.

Coming into the last clearing they heard the barking
of a dog. The house looked shut up and the boy did not
see anyone about. As the children approached, the dog
ran out and barked at them, crossly, and would not let
them come any closer. The baby cried that he was hungry,
and the little sister whimpered, and the boy who was not
quite seven stood there, trying to decide what he should

do next. Most of the day he and the younger children had been wandering in the dark forest and about ransacked or deserted houses. The only white person they had seen was their mother, dying in the clearing near their burned house. Now they were at the end of the world the boy knew, with a cross dog guarding the empty house where they might have stopped to rest.

He could not go any farther, so he started back. When the children complained more of hunger, he dug an edible root that his mother had once showed him, and later he got some bark for himself and the others, stripping it off the branches with his teeth. The bark and roots helped a little, but they were still hungry and they were exhausted.

In the Thomases' deserted clearing a feeling of overwhelming desolation and helplessness came over the boy. It was near the end of the late autumn day, and everything he had been told to do, or tried by himself, had failed. Everyone in the settlement was dead or gone—everyone but himself and the exhausted and hungry little children—and night was coming on. He did not know what to do, but he had to do something; so he started back, mechanically, toward the ruins of home.

After a time, looking ahead, Johnny saw an Indian coming toward them along the dusk of the trail. The younger children were being quiet for once, and he did not think the Indian saw or heard them. He carried the baby into the woods, with the little sister following. Before she had time to notice that they were off the trail he was hiding the children in the underbrush and whispering for them to stay where they were and keep quiet or "Indians kill." Then he ran back, diagonally, to the trail.

Most of the day Johnny had been in fear of meeting an Indian. Now an Indian seemed their only hope of being saved. He thought that even if the Indian killed him, the others would be no worse off. He could do no more for them without help. When the Indian came closer, the boy recognized him. He was Tom, whom the boy had often seen at the Thomases' when he was attending school. He was not afraid any more and hurried forward to meet the Indian.

Tom was not surprised when the boy told him of the attack. He had heard *hiyu* shooting that morning. He said it was not a good time for Boston children to be wandering in the woods. Johnny must get the *tenas men* and take them to Tom's house. When the moon was high he would take them to Seattle.

Tom's house was beside the White River, a few hundred yards away, but without a guide the children would never have found it. It was a hut of poles and mats, with a hole in the top by way of a chimney. It had fleas and smelled vividly of fish, but it was a fine, secure house with a fire in it, and orphaned children were never made more welcome. Tom's squaw set out high-smelling smoked salmon and berries that had been smoked, to discourage insects, and dried. It was tough, strong-smelling food, but even the baby ate with relish.

By the time the children had finished eating they were falling asleep. Tom's squaw spread the skin of a big black bear on the ground in the hut. The children fell on it as if they had been shot and slept like the dead.

Johnny was awakened from the sleep of exhaustion by someone shaking him by the shoulder. When he opened his unwilling eyes the moon was shining brightly through the circular hole at the top of the hut. His little brother and sister were sleeping beside him on the black bearskin in the moonlight, and Indian Tom was bending over him. "It is time," Tom said. "We go now."

Half asleep, the boy helped rouse the smaller children, who cried bitterly and fought against being disturbed. In a sleepwalking state he got them to the river. Tom steadied his dugout canoe while Johnny got the children into the light, nervous craft. Then he and Tom got in and they started for Seattle, down the moonlit river that wound through the black forest.

The late November night was frosty cold, and the children were dressed as they had been when they sat down to breakfast that morning—which seemed ages ago. When they were no longer disturbed they fell asleep in the bottom of the canoe, huddled against their older brother. They woke, crying with the cold. Johnny did his best to hold them in his arms for mutual warmth; but he, too, was shaking with the cold and he did not give or receive much warmth. While he was trying to comfort the shivering children and quiet the chattering of his own teeth a blanket was pushed forward beside him. He spread it over and around the three of them, with only his head looking out. Warmth began to grow under the tent of the blanket, and the little children quieted while the canoe pushed on faster down the cold river of moonlight. Johnny looked at Tom; he was naked to the waist and paddling vigorously to keep from freezing. Later, when the children woke and cried with hunger, he handed them four cold boiled potatoes, all the food he had in the canoe.

Early in the morning they came to where the broadened river was split by an island. The dugout followed the right fork, with Tom paddling harder and the canoe going more slowly. "Salt chuck," he grunted. The river fork met; luminous gray waters that seemed to open away forever from the one remaining shore ahead. The shore went up rapidly to high hills, and beyond the forest, on the hills, the morning was breaking gray and somber. A mile or two ahead a ship was lying at anchor off a little peninsula. It was a great black ship with the muzzles of many cannons poking out of the gun ports in her sides. Above there were three towering masts, with black yards, like crosses, against the somber sky of morning. The peninsula off which the ship was lying was like a high island, connected with the mainland by a strip of beach. On the high part of the peninsula and on the mainland were the houses of a village.

"Seattle," Tom said. He was paddling easily, with the canoe standing still in the mouth of the river, as if he were waiting for something. Then Johnny saw another canoe, paddled by an Indian, coming toward them. Tom and the stranger exchanged a few words, and the canoes drifted together.

In the boy's nostrils there was the strange, exciting smell of salt water. The breeze of dawn was fresh and stinging cold, and the water danced as if every little sharp wave were tingling with life. The canoes lay alongside each other and the strange Indian lifted the sleeping children into his canoe. Johnny followed them, and while he was getting settled the canoes drifted apart; Tom was paddling back into the mouth of the river, with his regained blanket about him. Johnny never saw him again.

Their new guide was named Dave, and he was good natured and at home on the *salt chuck,* and not at all afraid. He paddled directly for the warship.

The morning the three children were brought to the *Decatur* an expedition started for the White River valley. There were forty Seattle volunteers and four Northern Indians under Captain Hewitt. Traveling through the woods it took them two days to reach the settlement from which Tom had brought the children in one night.

At the Cox claim they found the house broken into and robbed. Farther up the river they found the Jones house burned to the ground and Harvey Jones cremated with it. The body of Mrs Jones was lying near the ashes of the house, where she had given Johnny his final instructions. She had been shot through the lungs at the time. Later, as she had feared, the Indians had come back and dispatched her with an ax. Enos Cooper was lying in the field, a hundred and fifty yards from where he had jumped out of the window, with a musket ball through his heart.

A mile or so from the Jones claim the volunteers came to the Brannan house, round which Johnny had wandered in search of help without finding anyone dead or alive. The volunteers did not find anyone alive, but they found Brannan hacked to pieces in the house, where he had put up a desperate fight, and they found the body of Mrs

The Massacre

Brannan in the well with her ten-month-old baby. Farther on they found the King house burned to ashes and three of the family butchered; and, to the confusion of history, a five-year-old boy, George King, had been carried away by the Indians. He was not related to Johnny King.

The volunteers buried the dead and went back to Seattle without meeting any Indians, hostile or friendly. But on the river they met a mysterious black man who told them that the night before their camp had been surrounded by a hundred and fifty Indians. Hewitt was pleased that they had not attacked his forty-four men, partly because fifteen of the volunteers' rifles were disabled relics carried for moral effect.

CHAPTER VIII

The Siege of Seattle

SEATTLE WAS ATTACKED by the Indians on the morning of January twenty-sixth, 1856.

Many participated in the battle, but only one participant left a written account. That was Lieutenant T. Stowell Phelps, navigating officer of the sloop-of-war *Decatur*. His account, written seventeen years later from notes made at the time, does not fall entirely into the category of history. History is fiction agreed upon, and while much of the lieutenant's account is fiction, the disagreement has been violent.

Lieutenant Phelps is extravagant in his charges of cowardice against the Seattle volunteers; and he makes much of their insubordination. Insubordination there was. All of the volunteers were rugged individualists; many of them afterward became capitalists and some of them millionaires. The company talked back to its officers and, in effect, voted on whether or not an order should be carried out. But Phelps's blanket charge of cowardice against the company does not fit the handful of men, a third of them with defunct rifles, who went into the heart of the Indians' stronghold to bury the dead of the White River massacre. It does not fit the company that held the junction of the Green and White rivers, on the battlefield which the Indians had chosen, until Lieutenant Slaughter was killed and his regulars forced to retreat to Seattle with their dead and wounded.

The Battle of Seattle has somewhat the sound of a comic opera title, and it had its comic opera touches, despite the anguish it caused at the time and the ruin it left in its wake.

The *Decatur* saved Seattle from destruction, and she managed it by the narrowest margin. On December seventh, while cruising, she struck an unsuspected reef off Bainbridge Island, across the Sound from Seattle. She hogged as the tide went out and left her draped over a ledge. On the next tide she was kedged off and worked to Seattle, with six feet of water in her hold. There she was beached beside Yesler's wharf for repairs.

On December tenth Captain Sterrett's place was taken by Captain Guert Gansevoort, who was a remarkably capable and unassuming commander. Ironically, he is chiefly remembered in connection with the most bizarre incident of the American Navy. He was executive officer of the brig *Somers* on her Caribbean cruise when the son of the Secretary of the Navy had a dime-novel dream about seizing the brig and going pirating on the Spanish Main—and was hung for it. The young man confessed the juvenile plot before he was strung up to the yardarm, but members of his college fraternity maintain to this day that the incriminating paper found on his person contained the secrets of the Sigma Nu fraternity and that he died rather than reveal their meaning. Along with him there died another confessed plotter and a sailor who was unquestionably innocent of being either a mutineer or a Sigma Nu.

In the *Decatur*, Captain Gansevoort found a dubious command. The sloop-of-war, built in 1838, was hove down on the Seattle beach beside Yesler's wharf, with her topmasts and yards sent ashore, her dismounted battery useless on the wharf, and a large section of her bottom stove in. A survey showed that she was only the ghost of a ship: a fabric of dry rot held together by an inch of sound outside planking that had been preserved by the sea. Gansevoort and his crew worked day and night, jacking broken frames into their original shape and covering rotten planking with new fir lumber from Yesler's mill.

While repairs were rushed on the old sloop-of-war the Indians rushed their preparations to rub out the village and capture the *Decatur's* munitions while she lay on the beach like a stranded whale. Until that time the Indians had defeated all the regular and volunteer troops sent against them, but they had got no comfort from their victories. All winter the guerrilla warriors, with their wives and children, had been starving in the swamps of the White River country while they sued, unsuccessfully, for peace. The only one who could make peace was angry Territorial Governor Stevens; and he was for hanging all the hostile Indians first and talking peace afterward.

So the war went on. By January the game was almost

up. The attack on Seattle was a farewell gesture or a last, desperate attempt to replenish their commissary from the stores of the village and their powder from the magazines of the *Decatur*.

While the Indians gathered the last of their strength for the attack the men of the *Decatur* worked desperately on their beached and helpless ship, and the people of Seattle passed anxious days and nights. The nights were the worst, in the village that was a sprinkling of candle-lit windows along the edge of the tremendous darkness of the forest, where it was easy to hear things. There were false alarms, sometimes three in one night, when candle lights were pinched out and everyone ran pell-mell for the blockhouse on the mound of the peninsula.

On the night of January eighteenth there was a woman's scream and the unmistakable explosion of a gun. The citizens, in their nightclothes, ran to the fort; the marines who had been sleeping there tumbled out of their hammocks and grabbed up their stacked muskets.

It was a false alarm so far as Indians were concerned. The shot had been fired by a boy of fifteen who was saving his sister from a sailor. The sailor, John Drew, was a deserter from the beached *Decatur*. He had tried to enter a house at the edge of the village and had awakened a young lady with the noise he made opening the window. She had tried to close the window when he was halfway through, pinning him down with the sash and screaming for help. In response her young brother had come in with a fowling piece and shot the intruder through the head.

That was the first defensive shot fired in the Battle of

Seattle, and it killed a man who was supposed to be there
to help defend the place. But then, as always, not everyone behaved splendidly. That night was a turning point
in the defense of the village. Working by lantern light the
officers and men of the *Decatur* finished the outboard repairs on the ship. In the morning, when she was afloat,
they laid her alongside Yesler's wharf and hoisted her guns
and spars on board. Then they hauled her out into Elliott
Bay and began the job of putting her back in fighting trim.
Whatever chance the Indians had had of capturing the
sloop-of war vanished during the night that John Drew
played his villainous role.

On January twenty-fifth affairs at Seattle took on the
full proportions of comic opera. During the day the survey steamer *Active* came into the bay and let her anchor
go near the *Decatur*, which was being feverishly tuned up
for trouble. On board the *Active* was Governor Stevens
and his staff, with Captain Keyes of the regular army and
Indian Agent Mike Simmons, the "Daniel Boone" of the
territory.

The swarthy, headstrong little Governor had been inclined to make the most of the Indian War and exaggerate
rather than belittle the danger of the settlers. But for
reasons that remain obscure, he ridiculed the idea of an
attack on Seattle. He went ashore and made a speech to
the citizens, ending with the words: "I tell you there are
not fifty hostile Indians in the territory, and I believe that
the cities of New York and San Francisco will as soon be
attacked by the Indians as the town of Seattle."

The Governor then went on board the *Decatur* and

tried to persuade Captain Gansevoort to give up his unnecessary watch over Seattle and accompany him on a cruise to Bellingham Bay. Gansevoort could not be persuaded, and the *Active* departed with the displeased Governor and his staff.

While the *Active* was still in the bay, showing her stern to the village, Indians began coming into town. They were peaceful Lake Indians under Chief Tecumseh, and they brought their women and children with them, asking for protection; but friendly Indians moving out of the woods suggested hostiles moving in. Tecumseh and his tribe were given a camp site inside the stockade, behind Madame Damnable's place. While they were getting settled Captain Gansevoort's Indian scout returned from an expedition in the woods. He reported that a large number of Indians had crossed Lake Washington for an attack on Seattle and that they might come in that night.

The same afternoon seventy-odd Seattle volunteers landed on the beach from canoes and straggled into the village. They had not come to defend Seattle but to lead a civilian life. Their three months' term of enlistment had expired on that inconvenient day. They had left the Duwamish blockhouse punctually at the hour of expiration, and that evening they were mustered out in front of Yesler's log cookhouse and the company disbanded.

By then Captain Gansevoort knew the storm was about to break and he ordered his fighting divisions ashore. The First Division, under Lieutenant Drake, was stationed at the south part of town. The Second Division, under Lieutenant Hughes, armed with rifles and carbines, occupied a store to the north of Drake's position. The Third Division, under Lieutenant Phelps, armed with muskets held the head of Yesler's wharf where the boats landed. The Fourth Division, under Lieutenant Dallas, armed with muskets, rifles and pistols occupied Mr Plummer's house at the southeastern part of town. The variety of arms suggests that each man carried an arsenal, but the suggestion is misleading. The *Decatur* had been almost stripped of small arms for the defense of other parts of the Sound, and her fighters had to get along with the miscellaneous weapons that were left. The Adjutant General had even attempted to borrow the *Decatur's* howitzer, but Captain Gansevoort had declined to give it up. The prized brass howitzer was now taken ashore in the launch and was posted in the rear of Lieutenant Hughes's position, where it could fire over the heads of the Second Division. The howitzer was under the command of Lieutenant Morris, with a crew of nine and marines to guard it. The remainder of the marines, under Sergeant Corbine, were posted at the north blockhouse, which mounted two nine-pound guns. Sentries were posted and the *Decatur's* men were ready for the defense of Seattle.

The position of the volunteers was now embarrassing. The men had just received their discharges, and technically the war was over as far as they were concerned; and on that very day the war seemed to be beginning in earnest. The village where they had just been disbanded was about to be attacked. The principles of patriotism involved were not too abstract for men who would have been fighting to save scalps that included their own; but some of the men responded to the new call for volunteers and some did not. The men who were citizens of Seattle and had wives and children and property to protect took up their arms again. Others from the outside, who had nothing more than their lives at stake, declined to see that the impending·attack had anything to do with themselves.

Some of the citizens went to the blockhouse that night, but most of them spent the night in their own houses, re-assured by the dim lights and dark bulk of the *Decatur* in the bay, and by the quiet footsteps of the sentries and officers making their rounds. In the village the black night passed quietly at the edge of the blacker forest. But in legend, at least, more was going on than met the eye, and it was a night of dramatic activity. Some of the things that almost certainly never happened have their own charm and they are included, in italics, along with doubt-ful and conflicting statements.

It was a windless, misty night ashore, but:

On the Sound a wild storm was raging. Through the storm there battled a big canoe, manned with friendly squaws of Chief Seattle's tribe. In the canoe there was a white woman, Mrs Maynard, the sister of Indian Agent Mike Simmons, and the wife of Doctor Maynard, who was temporarily in charge of the reservation at Port Madi-son. Mrs Maynard had been warned that Seattle would be attacked in the morning and she was on her way to give the alarm. The canoe was almost swamped many times, and once the wild storm drove it ashore on West Point. There it was surrounded by hostile Indians, and it seemed

[131]

that all was lost. But the squaws were loyal and undaunted. In the nick of time they had Mrs Maynard lie down in the bottom of the canoe, where they covered her with a wet blanket. When the hostile warriors demanded to know what they had in the canoe, Chief Seattle's Amazon's said it was clams. Mrs Maynard kept perfectly still, aiding the deception. The hostiles accepted the explanation and allowed the party to push off into the storm. The canoe reached the Decatur *safely and Mrs Maynard delivered the message that saved Seattle. Captain Gansevoort urged Mrs Maynard to stay on board and not venture out into the storm, but the brave woman insisted it was her duty to return to the reservation before the Indians discovered her absence and made trouble. The big canoe pushed off from the* Decatur, *into the storm, and landed her at Port Madison before daybreak.*

The story of the canoe journey through the storm is true, but the woman was not Mrs Maynard. It was Princess Angeline, daughter of Chief Seattle. She made the journey through the storm in a little dugout and delivered the message directly to citizens in the village. The exploit was a proof of her undying loyalty to the white race.

The Indians and whites at Port Madison were on the opposite side of the Sound from hostilities. They knew less of what was brewing than the people of Seattle. No woman or man, Indian or white, made a canoe journey across the Sound, through a storm that did not exist, to warn the village.

The Siege of Seattle

Meanwhile, in the calm and misty night ashore, there were strange sounds and mysterious figures moved.

That night the defenders heard what seemed to be the hooting of owls in the woods, and they knew it was the gathering hostiles signaling to one another. Captain Gansevoort's Indian spy, sub-chief Curley, was sent to investigate. He was gone a long time, and when he returned he reported nothing but owls in the woods. Some sixth sense warned Lieutenant Phelps that Curley had passed beyond the pale of being trusted. He followed Curley secretly. When the Indian thought he was no longer being observed he made an angry gesture, muttering something unintelligible, and started toward his own camp at a rapid pace.

In the darkness of that same night, two Indians, muffled in blankets, appeared at the sector guarded by Phelps's division. When they were challenged they explained that they were Lake Indians on the way back to their camp after visiting Curley. Phelps believed them and they were allowed to pass. They were Owhi and Leschi, the commanders-in-chief of the attacking forces, who had walked into the village to persuade the friendly Lake Indians to attack the settlement from within.

The daring spies were not Owhi and Leschi: they were Owhi and Coquilton, and they were on their way to a council of war with other hostile chiefs.

They were two other Indians, and the incident never happened.

[133]

There is disagreement even as to who guarded the village:

Later that night, on his rounds of inspection, Lieutenant Phelps visited the sector guarded by the Seattle volunteers. He found the sector deserted except for the volunteers' rifles, which they had left to represent themselves while they went home to bed.

The fighting divisions of the Decatur *were asleep in their hammocks in the blockhouse, and the citizens alone guarded the town that night.*

Whatever happened, the night passed without alarms. Daybreak saw the village unattacked, with blue uniformed sentries standing guard in the morning mist, and light blue woodsmoke going up sluggishly from the chimneys of cabins and frame houses at the edge of the forest.

On the sloop-of-war in the bay, and on the lumber bark *Brontes,* lying a cable's length to the south, brown coal smoke went up from the "Charlie Nobles" of the galleys, and there was a smell of coffee and breakfast cooking. The weather was not cold for January, and there was no snow on deck or on the ground ashore; but the morning had its sting of cold and it was a good time to think of breakfast.

At a few minutes after six Captain Gansevoort ordered the fighting divisions to fall back, one on the other, commencing at the outermost post, and move toward the boats at the head of Yesler's wharf. They embarked and returned to the *Decatur* at about seven-thirty.

The Siege of Seattle

Yarkekeeman Jim, the only Indian trusted by the officers of the Decatur, *held the fate of Seattle in his tied hands. He had been present at the council of war held in the lodge of the treacherous Tecumseh, back of Madame Damnable's. Jim had persuaded the chiefs to wait until daylight and make their attack while the marines were on board ship. It was now daylight, and the marines presumably were at breakfast. The attack might come at any moment, and Jim was being shadowed by his father, the suspicious Curley. Somehow he eluded that chief and slipped into Doctor Williamson's house, where he told the doctor that the village was about to be attacked. Hardly had he whispered the words when Curley entered the front door, demanding insolently where Jim was. Doctor Williamson answered by thrusting him into a convenient room and turning the key in the lock. He then hastened to inform Mr Yesler.*

The incident is true, only it was an Indian named William, not Jim, who notified Doctor Williamson, who notified Mr Yesler.

No Indian council of war was held in the village, and neither Jim nor William had anything to do with the warning, which Curley delivered to Mr Yesler.

Duly warned, the massive Yesler paddled out to the *Decatur* in a dugout and interviewed Captain Gansevoort. In Gansevoort's report to the Secretary of the Navy he states that "Mr Gesler" informed him that he had learned

[135]

from a private source, which was worthy of attention, that the Indians were just in the edge of the woods, close to the town. And Mr Gesler pointed out the positions they had taken up. They were in three parts, extending over a space of about two miles, just in rear of the town, the largest portion being at the extreme southeast, with a marsh of about 125 yards intervening.

Captain Gansevoort immediately had the long roll sounded. The marines, half through breakfast, were ordered ashore. Gansevoort went with them, leaving Executive Officer Middleton in command of the ship's battery. The four fighting divisions, numbering ninety men, landed at Yesler's wharf and went ashore at the double-quick to their assigned positions. The first three divisions formed a line from the head of the wharf diagonally across the neck of the peninsula to the blockhouse, and the Fourth Division continued the line south. As before, the rest of the marines were stationed at the blockhouse. Lieutenant Morris, with his howitzer crew, was stationed between the First Division and the Fourth, on the mound of the peninsula.

With his forces in order Captain Gansevoort had the howitzer trained on Indian Tom Pepper's house on the slope across the lagoon. According to Mr Yesler's information the main body of Indians had gathered in the neighborhood of that house.

At this point fat Nancy, Curley's squaw, waddled about the beach proclaiming: "Hiu Klickitat copa Tom Pepper's house!" She then leaped into a canoe and paddled off across the Sound in a shower of spray. Acting on this piece of feminine intuition Captain Gansevoort ordered the howitzer to be fired.

Whether the information came from Curley or from Nancy, or from Jim who was their son, it seems to have come from somewhere in the family. Gansevoort gave the order, "Fire!" and the sharp report of the howitzer rang out. A second later a ball of smoke blossomed from the side of the *Decatur* in the bay. A big gun boomed and a shell came screeching over the peninsula. Both shells fell near Tom Pepper's house. There was a yell from the woods beyond the village, and a crash of musketry, answered by the small arms of the marines.

By oversight, or otherwise, the citizens of Seattle were the last to know that the moment of attack had come. Most of them were in their cabins at breakfast when they heard the report of the howitzer and the dull boom of the *Decatur's* gun, the yell of Indians from the near-by forest and the rolling crash of musketry.

Seattle forgot all about breakfast and stampeded to the blockhouse. Mrs Blaine, the minister's wife, and her new-born baby were carried in a rocking chair. Mr Hanford ran with a small child in each arm, while his oldest son carried his rifle. Cornelius, who was seven, had to get along under his own power. He later became a judge and a historian, but his good upbringing nearly cost him dear that day. When he had run a few steps he remembered what boys should do upon entering or leaving a house, and he turned back to close the door. Ready to resume his flight, he was startled by the heads of Indians rising from behind a fir log.

Farther north in the village Louisa Denny, wife of David, was alone in the cabin with her two-year-old baby and her baking. Throughout her life she was the archetype of pioneer women, and her presence of mind was not upset by the bang and roar of big guns, the crackle of musketry and the yell of Indians. She dumped the biscuits from the oven into her apron, snatched up the baby in her free arm and was on her way without a wasted motion or lost second.

Hillory Butler, Esquire, late of Virginia, rose late that morning, but suddenly. By the sounds of battle, he judged there was no time to put on trousers. So he jumped into his wife's red flannel petticoat and ran like a Lady from Hell. According to one story he called after the Widow McConaha, "Wait for me, Mrs McConaha!" And according to another a woman called after him, "Wait for me, Hillory!" But Hillory neither waited nor was waited for. Little Virginia Bell dived into the blockhouse between the legs of a marine whom she brought down with a crash.

In the rout of settlers coming in there were Miss Kirkland and Louisa Denny, with her baby and her apronful of hot biscuits. Her husband, on watch at the blockhouse, ran out to meet her. As he ran, an excited volunteer inside fired off his rifle. Miss Kirkland fell beside the young mother and lay still, her face dead white. They carried her inside, thinking she had been killed. But she had only fainted, and the bullet that missed her head had cut off a lock of her thick black hair.

Indian War of 1856.

Looking south on Third Avenue, Seattle, 1868.

The Siege of Seattle

The Indians had emptied their rifles and Hudson's Bay muskets in a haphazard volley, replying to the howitzer and the *Decatur's* gun. In the time it took them to reload the citizens were out of effective range. On the way to the blockhouse none of them was hit, either by the Indians or by the volunteers. The Indians had now reloaded, and spent bullets pattered against the squared timbers of the building. Lieutenant Piexotto of the volunteers stood in the doorway, with one hand against the frame, watching for a sight of the Indians. Among the crowd in the blockhouse was Milton Holgate, aged fifteen, carrying the fowling piece with which he had killed the drunken intruder from the sloop-of-war. The boy had run to the blockhouse because everyone else was doing that, but he did not want to stay there to be protected along with the women and children: he wanted to take part in the fighting. He started out, under the horizontal arm of Lieutenant Piexotto in the doorway, and received a bullet between the eyes. He was the youngest and the first to fall, and they laid him under the stairway where the flag-wrapped body of Lieutenant Slaughter had lain in state after they brought him out from his defeat in the valley of the White River.

In the first phase of the attack the heaviest exchange of fire was between the divisions on the peninsula, in the southern part of town, and the Indians across the lagoon in the neighborhood of Tom Pepper's house. The distance was roughly two hundred yards—beyond the range of effective rifle fire—and the Indians had the protection of the dense woods. Now and then some of them showed themselves, and were driven to cover by grapeshot and time shells from the howitzer and the ship's battery. Lieutenant George Morris, in charge of the howitzer, was praised for delivering quick and accurate fire and for his cool efficiency in the battle.

Actually Morris had much the better of the argument, firing a smart howitzer at Indians armed with old muskets, who were learning about shellfire for the first time. But Morris did a good job that day. And when the changing art of killing placed him in the position of the outclassed Indians, his coolness did not desert him. That was six years later, when the Confederate Navy tried out something new on wooden ships of war. The ugly *Merrimac* was the experiment, and the futile shells of the rammed *Cumberland* bounced off her ironclad sides. Morris, in command of the *Cumberland,* fought on with the last gun left in action until his outmoded ship sank under the waters of Hampton Roads.

After the war the Indians admitted that they were disturbed by the time shells that lay still for a few seconds and then shot for a second time. They called them "the shells that *mox poohed*." Lieutenant Phelps describes a group of them who joined hands in a war dance around one of these trophies—and were blown to perdition. Phelps saw a great deal that day, and legends have played variations on his themes:

During this part of the battle Chief Curley came out on the neck of the peninsula, with his face painted black and a long rifle in one hand and a bow almost as long as him-

self in the other. He performed a war dance on the saw-dust and ended his display of bravado by leaping high into the air and disappearing with a fiendish yell.

It was Chief Seattle, not Curley, and he performed the dance on the sandspit.

It was Chief Seattle, but he did not do a war dance. He wrung his hands in distress at the sight of his own people and his white friends battling with each other.

It was Chief Seattle, but he was not between the opposing forces. He was at the Port Madison reservation, fourteen miles away, and he showed great distress at the distant thunder of the Decatur's *guns which announced that a battle was being fought.*

The Felker House, run by Mother Damnable, was the most pretentious building in town. Across its white-painted front there was a porch whose roof made a railed balcony for the second-floor rooms. The balcony was reached from a door at the end of the centered hall, and it was something like stepping out on deck from the passenger quarters of a ship. The house was the farthest point in town from the attack, and the second-story balcony was a promising place from which to watch the battle. A young man named Wilson stepped out there and had his neck broken by a bullet.

At the blockhouse there was a young man who knew what an Indian attack meant, and he did not want to see anything of it. His name was Johnny King, and he had had his seventh birthday since he saved his little sister and brother from the White River massacre. On that occasion he had been as resourceful as an old scout; but at the attack on Seattle he had no responsibilities to take his mind off himself. He was his seven years, neither more nor less, and the banging of the muskets and the sound of bullets thudding into the wall of the blockhouse reminded him of terrifying things. He pleaded and demanded to be taken on board the *Decatur*, which had been his refuge after his earlier experience. Physically he was safer in the blockhouse than in the open on the way to the ship, but he made a great deal of noise, and the sergeant of marines was his friend. Corbine saw it would be better for the child to risk a few bullets than to go mad in the noisy shelter where the air was blue with powder smoke and a young man lay dead under the stairs. The only door of the blockhouse faced the woods, under direct fire, but there were axes and saws inside, and Johnny wanted to be elsewhere. So the marines cut out a section of a timber at the back of the blockhouse, and one of them semaphored the *Decatur*. A gig was sent ashore, and as it neared the beach they turned the boy loose through the hole in the timbered wall; from there he did not need any instruction. Bullets whanged past him on the beach, and spent bullets dropped in the water about the gig as the sailors rowed the boy out to the sloop-of-war; but Johnny was not terrified any more because that was the way to the *Decatur*, and the only safety for him was safety as he saw it.

The Indians had no luck against the south of town, where Morris' howitzer and the guns of the *Decatur*

battered the woods about them with solid shot and grapeshot and explosive shells. After an hour or so the main
part of the attackers circled through the woods and
warmed up the attack on the north end of town. From
the woods a hundred yards away they poured a sharp and
steady fire down upon the head of Yesler's wharf. Captain
Gansevoort observed that their fire was returned most
spiritedly by Lieutenant Phelps's Division. If the captain
had seen the deeds that Phelps described for posterity, his
praise would have been greater:

*The Indians charged to within twenty feet of Phelps's
Division before they were stopped by the marshy sawdust
fill. There they took cover in the chaparral, behind logs
and stumps, and rained bullets on Phelps and his division.
The bullets were as thick as bees from a hive, and Lieutenant Phelps was in the gravest peril of all. Chief Kakum
of the treacherous Lake tribe had recognized Phelps as an
officer and marked him for death. Resting his rifle in
crotched branches, or shooting from behind a tree, the Indian sharpshooter devoted his morning to getting rid of
the young lieutenant. Kakum kept up his sniping until the
batteries of the* Decatur *came to the rescue, and a grapeshot took off a lock of his hair while he was hiding behind
a tree. The chief then observed that he could not compete
with a gun that shot around a corner and he retired.*

Phelps observes that during this phase of the engage-
ment his clothing and that of his men were riddled with
bullet holes. He explains the fact that none of them was
hit by saying it was a miracle. He does not, however, ex-

plain the greater miracle of how none of them suffered from powder burns at the point-blank range of twenty feet.

Meanwhile the squaws of the attackers had butchered the citizens' milk cows and oxen and set them roasting. The barbecue was ready at about three o'clock in the afternoon, and the squaws called to their braves to come and get it. The response was so nearly unanimous that Captain Gansevoort observed the enemy's fire reduced to a few scattering shots. Accordingly he ordered his divisions to fall back to the boat landing at Yesler's wharf and return to the ship for lunch. The retreating Indians paused to fire at the retreating marines, and the marines replied with a running fire of musketry and two shots from the howitzer. Then the Indians saw that they were only spoiling things for themselves and delaying dinner. They ceased firing, and the hungry armies retreated in opposite directions.

On their way to the boats the fighting divisions stopped at the blockhouse and took the women and children with them. Seattle was cleared of noncombatants along with the four divisions and the howitzer, but the marines and volunteers were still on guard at the blockhouse, and the village was commanded by the guns of the *Decatur*. Also, the Indians had shot away most of their ammunition and gone to dinner.

The men who had been left at the blockhouse were hungry too, and some of the volunteers crept out to the Boren house, which was a block to the northeast, at the edge of the woods, and brought in food. One of the Graham boys demonstrated a volunteer's accomplishments by baking a batch of biscuits within easy range of the Indians' barbecue, and taking them, hot, to the fort. The other food brought in was pork and flour and potatoes, but there was no fuel for cooking, and the fort was unpleasantly cold that January afternoon.

According to tradition "Uncle Tommy" Mercer solved the fuel problem. He went to Dexter Horton's barn, where he kept his horses, hitched up the black mare and the pale stallion, and drove into the forest. Mercer had always been kind and helpful to the Indians, and when they saw who it was they said "It's only Old Tom Mercer minding his own business" and they did not interfere with him while he loaded his wagon with wood and drove back to the fort.

The pause for dinner was an armistice in a battle that was never really renewed. Later in the afternoon the Indians delivered a few face-saving volleys of musket fire, and the batteries of the sloop-of-war answered with round shot; but the battle had grown cold and could not be brought to life again.

Under cover of darkness the Indians plundered some of the houses in the village of food and clothing. They burned all of the houses on the outlying claims, with two exceptions, and retreated south along the Duwamish River, burning unoccupied buildings as they went. The Battle of Seattle was over, but at the time the citizens could not be sure of that. All of them expected a renewal of the attack, and some of them a siege of two or three months.

The number of attacking Indians has been estimated as

high as three thousand, and according to tradition a thousand Klickitats came over Snoqualmie Pass to join the attack. The tradition disregards the condition of the pass. There had been three weeks of mild weather with rain that fell as soft, deep snow in the mountains. It is doubtful if any number of Indians could have got over, or if any of them tried. The attack on Seattle was the work of probably two hundred local Indians.

The outlying claims that were not burned were those of Thomas Mercer and David Denny, both of them known for their considerate treatment of the Indians. Afterward, when asked why they had spared Mercer's house, the Indians explained, "Old Tom might need it some time."

CHAPTER IX

Repercussions

FROM A MILITARY POINT OF VIEW the attack on Seattle was a case of "some dirt, not much hurt." Among the whites two rash young men were killed and none wounded. The most accurate estimate of the Indians' casualties seems to be none killed and none wounded. But it was a noisy battle, and the booming of the *Decatur's* guns was heard as far as the Strait of Juan de Fuca. On the evening of the day of battle the survey steamer *Active* came plowing back into the harbor under forced draft. On board was the fiery and stiff-necked little Governor who had declared, eighteen hours earlier, that the cities of New York and San Francisco would as soon be attacked by Indians as Seattle.

Since then there had been six hours of heavy gunfire. Ashore, at the edge of town, buildings were burning. To the south, along the Duwamish, flames were going up against the night sky; and when the Governor boarded the *Decatur* the cabin and wardroom were crowded with rescued women and children.

[147]

The people of Seattle buried young Holgate and young Wilson beside the White Church and prepared for another attack, which they all expected. The volunteers and marines put up a second blockhouse and began building a stockade around the town. Yesler, who had already provided so much, contributed seventy thousand board feet of lumber. The stockade consisted of two parallel walls, a foot and a half apart, with the space between packed with earth. It was twelve hundred yards long and gave protection on the north, east and south to the houses on the peninsula. The west side of the enclosure was open to the civilized salt water of the bay.

To give the pet howitzer mobility and scope, a road was built around the stockade, stumps in the village were grubbed out and brush cut down and burned. Lieutenant Phelps remarks with pride that soon the place had the look of a well-laid-out town.

While this work was going on, the weather remained raw, with deluges of rain. Officers and men alike wore the costume they found most suited for the job ashore: warm underwear, heavy marine trousers tucked into high cowhide boots, five blue flannel shirts, a folded blanket around the neck, crossed in front and secured with a cartridge belt, and a slouch hat. Whenever the rain let up a little the wearer took off four of his five flannel shirts and dried them in Yesler's log cookhouse or before some other friendly fire.

With two blockhouses, a stockade and a howitzer road Seattle was prepared for the second Indian attack—which never came. The marines' last skirmish in Seattle was fought with Madame Damnable. According to Phelps these men had survived where bullets flew thick as bees from a hive, and while their clothes had been riddled, no lead ever touched their skin. But in the action at the Felker House no miracles preserved them. Division after division fled in disorder, with stone bruises and dog bites.

The howitzer road was laid out to pass close to the Felker House, and for some reason Madame Damnable hated the crew of the *Decatur*. The first division that started work in front of her house was paralyzed by the sudden blast of her approach. Out she came, like a red-faced fury: a woman of coarse and masculine build, with her apron full of rocks and three savage dogs running with her. The fighting division stared anxiously, not being sure that she meant them. Then they broke and ran under her barrage of rocks, with the dogs tearing at their protecting clothes. While Madame Damnable pelted them she emptied the English language of its profane and obscene accumulations.

The next division laughed at the first for being routed by a woman. They took over the Felker House sector and lasted for two blows of their picks, which brought the cursing Jezebel with her man-eating dogs and a fresh apronful of rocks. The other divisions tried, but none of them made out any better than earlier sailors had on the shore of the man-eating and rock-throwing Cyclops. After that they shunned the place and worked elsewhere until the howitzer road was complete except for that one piece.

Captain Gansevoort inspected the job, and he was puzzled to see the fine road broken by a patch of stumps and salal. What was the meaning of this? The shamefaced young lieutenants explained the difficulty, and Gansevoort said, "Tut, tut! Why didn't you tell me before? I shall explain that the road is a military necessity." He walked confidently up to the door of the Felker House— and came back in disorder, with rocks and curses flying, and the great-voiced harridan and her dogs in hot pursuit.

Captain Gansevoort did not go back to the Felker House, but he was a commander and he explained to his lieutenants, who listened more attentively than Madame Damnable, that the road was a military necessity and it must be completed.

After that the lieutenants tried strategy. One party created a diversion while the other tried to work. But Madame Damnable showed them that the two parties could be stoned as easily as one, and it was a field day for her dogs. Then they tried surprise sorties: the assigned division would creep up on the job at odd hours, praying the harridan was asleep or busy in the other wing of the house. But Madame Damnable was never caught napping, and every childish and transparent strategy was met by a sudden blast of rocks and curses and vicious dogs.

Days passed while work on the road stood still, and it was the Fourth Division's turn to be under fire. Lieutenant Dallas did not have any ingenious plan left, and the morale of his division was low with memories of earlier defeats. When the door of the Felker House flew open for the Fury and her dogs, the Fourth Division broke and ran. All of them ran except Quartermaster Sam Silk. Sam stood his ground, with memories and recognition glimmering in his mind. The dogs, used to pursuing running men, passed him by. And Madame Damnable, reaching into her bumpy apron for a rock, paused in astonishment.

Sam took the aggressive and roared at the harridan: "What do you mean, you d - - - - d old so-an'-so? Many's the time I've seen you howling thunder around Fell's Point, Baltimore! You're a d - - - - d pretty one, ain't you?"

Madame Damnable was taken completely aback by the reference to her past. In shame she let go her apron with its load of rocks and bolted back into the Felker House. The thunderclap of the closing door was the last the *Decatur's* men heard from her. In peace they finished the howitzer road, which was never used for war.

The Indians never came back to raze the village of Seattle. Some of the warriors had dropped out of the fighting after the failure of the first attack. Six weeks later the remainder started on a desperate retreat over the Cascade Mountains.

Without the distracting presence of the Indians the Indian War was able to really get under way, and in that action the Seattle volunteers played an important part.

Governor Stevens declared martial law in Pierce County, in order that settlers suspected of giving aid and comfort to the enemy could be held without trial. When the time arrived for the regular term of court in the county under martial law, the only judge available was Chief Justice Lander, captain of the Seattle volunteers. He turned the volunteer company over to Arthur Denny, who was next in command, put his black robe in his carpet bag and paddled south in an Indian dugout. After two attempts to hold court Lander was arrested and held a prisoner until martial law was broken.

The next battle of the Indian War without Indians was fought at Seattle. The volunteer company, formed while Governor Stevens was in town, had been sworn in with the understanding that their company would be used for the defense of Seattle and not sent elsewhere. Unfortunately the understanding was with the Governor, but the company received its orders from Adjutant General Tilton.

In early June the Adjutant General issued an order that seemed to violate the company's understanding with the Governor. Lieutenant Denny was to leave eight men as a garrison for the blockhouse at the mouth of the Duwamish. He was to march with the remainder of the company to Fort Hays and begin cutting a military road through Snoqualmie Pass.

Respectfully, Lieutenant Denny wrote back that to carry out the order he and his men would have to take a heavy freight of tools and supplies with them; that they would have to pack everything on their backs through the unbroken forest. He also stated that eight men were not enough to protect Seattle and the Duwamish valley farmers on whom the town was depending for food.

The Adjutant General proceeded to issue new orders for the lieutenant to leave a garrison of twenty men instead of eight. He was then to go with the remainder of the company, in canoes, to Camp Montgomery. From that point the company was to proceed to its road making.

Repercussions

If Lieutenant Denny had been the kind of soldier who does and dies without asking what or why, he would have managed somehow to get his company and their canoes across the twelve miles of high, gravel prairie that separated Camp Montgomery from the nearest water; and he would have found himself farther from his destination than when he started. But Denny was a serious-minded merchant and he wanted to get back to business. He again informed Adjutant General Tilton that it would be unwise, with the *Decatur* gone, for Company A to leave the vicinity of Seattle. He suggested that if he did have to go to Fort Hays he might at least be left the privilege of taking the shortest and most practical route.

Tilton replied with an order removing Denny from command of the company. Second Lieutenant Neely was awarded the precarious honor and ordered to report to Camp Montgomery with his company for the road-making job.

With two of their officers already picked off, and the third presented with a ridiculous order, Company A went into action. They had named the blockhouse at the mouth of the Duwamish River "Fort Lander," in honor of their chief justice-captain who had been the first to fall in the war with the Governor. From Fort Lander the company wrote the Governor as follows:

SIR: With the enclosed you will find a set of resolutions to which are appended the signatures of the entire company—the origin and intention of which are as follows:

On the 9th of June, the Adjutant General issued orders to Lieutenant Denny, of Company A, to detail eight men to hold the blockhouse above Seattle, and to march his company to Fort Hays, there to perform certain duties. Lieutenant Denny, for reasons given in his note of the 13th of June, awaited further instructions. The Adjutant General, in his order bearing the date 16th June, says: "Your reasons are satisfactory. You will, therefore, proceed to, etc.,"—giving orders which at once show a lamentable, not to say criminal, degree of ignorance with regard to the country and its various avenues of communication over which he was moving men and materials of war every day. Lieutenant Denny, seeing that he was certainly in the dark, asked leave to take the most direct and easiest route to the point designated as the rendezvous; whereupon, the Adjutant General issued orders bearing the date of 24th June, in which he says, "You will turn over the command of Company A to Lieutenant Neely and await further orders," which order he obeyed, much to the dissatisfaction of the company. The order was read to the company on parade, and the command resigned to the officer designated. Immediately after which, the company held a meeting, and adopted the enclosed resolutions. In the proceedings had in this matter, we have intended to do nothing more nor less than they show on their face. To give a full, free and decided expression of our opinions and feelings on the subject.

With sentiments of due respect,

COMPANY A.

W. T. Volunteers

The undersigned members of Co. A, Washington Territory volunteers, do, by the following resolutions, express their undivided sentiment with regard to the matter herein alluded to:

Resolved, that we individually and as a company, do fully endorse and approve the course pursued by Lieutenant Denny, of Company A, in his recent correspondence with the Adjutant General, in regard to certain orders by him issued.

Resolved, that we do not approve of the course of the

Repercussions

Commander-in-chief in suspending Lieutenant Denny from his command. But on the contrary consider it an act of injustice, and an insult to the company, wholly unjustifiable and uncalled for.

Resolved, that in justice to Lieutenant Denny and to this company, the Commander-in-chief should reinstate Lieutenant Denny in his command immediately.

Fort Lander, June 28, 1856.

The letter and resolution burst in the Governor's office at Olympia like one of the *Decatur's* shells. If only Neely had defied the order, he could have been removed and the command passed to the next in rank, and so on down the line. But now the whole company had spoken.

A month later Lieutenant Colonel Fitzhugh arrived in Seattle, wearing a cocked hat and epaulets and a sword, and bearing Adjutant General Tilton's instructions.

At Fort Lander, Fitzhugh solemnly disbanded Company A. Then he retired to town and sent for the men, a few at a time, and talked to them about grave matters of military discipline and etiquette.

When Fitzhugh considered the men's resistance somewhat broken he made the final assault. Lieutenant Neely was directed to muster the company in front of Yesler's log cookhouse, where it had been sworn in. The company was called to attention, and Lieutenant Colonel Fitzhugh, in cocked hat, epaulets and sword, showed the men the resolution they had signed. He explained to them that it was not the thing for soldiers to rebuke their Commander-in-chief and brand an order of his "an act of injustice, and an insult to the company, wholly unjustifi-

[155]

able and uncalled for." That was insubordination, he said. It was also insubordination for them to sustain their former officer, Lieutenant Denny, in his refusal to obey orders. Insubordination was a serious matter, and its consequences were unpleasant. Among other things it precluded the possibility of an honorable discharge. In his final appeal he tempted the men with honorable discharge and full pay; he tried to shame them with the thought that they were the only company that had disobeyed orders; he tried to soften their hearts by telling them of the Governor's kind feelings toward them. When he had done all that could be done in the line of persuasion he held up the offending paper and gave the command: *"All who wish to rescind these resolutions, step forward."*

There was a great silence on Front Street. Across the way, in front of his little white-painted house, the massive, heavy-featured Henry Yesler sat whittling a pine stick that looked like gold in the last of the July sunshine. Near the edge of the young orchard, deep in grass, a few of Curley's Indians, naked with summer, paused to watch one of the last battles of the Indian War, which no longer had anything to do with them. A sea gull drifted overhead, with the underside of its body and one wing warm with the light of sunset, which was going from the land. A flunkey came out of the cookhouse with a pail that made a bright, empty sound. The wooden pump creaked and water gushed, and there was a slopping sound as the flunkey carried the pail back into the cookhouse.

Lieutenant Colonel Fitzhugh waited, with the resolutions in his hand. The Seattle volunteers waited, in untidy

Repercussions

but unbroken ranks: slouch hats over bearded young faces, patched hickory shirts and blue flannel shirts and red flannel shirts, and fading blue jeans tucked into cowhide boots, "California style," or coming down to soft-footed Indian moccasins. The young men looked with cold irreverence at the Lieutenant Colonel's breathtaking epaulets and cocked hat and sword—unseduced by the pomp and glory of the military world. None of them recanted and stepped forward.

A wagon creaked and rattled in the slow-falling summer dusk. Tom Mercer drove along the street, on the way to Horton's stable, with his docile black mare, Tib, and the white stallion with a mind of his own. As they passed Yesler's cookhouse and the military deadlock out in front the stallion raised his head and split the silence with a significant trumpet whinnying.

Lieutenant Colonel Fitzhugh sighed and addressed the disobedient company. "Men, my duty is at an end. I can do nothing more." He dismissed the men, and at the official end of the Indian War, Adjutant General Tilton would not accept the final muster roll of Company A, Second Regiment, Washington Territory Volunteers.

Tilton won that round. But Arthur Denny was speaker of the Territorial Legislature. The day before that body recessed for Christmas it passed a joint resolution instructing James Tilton, no longer Adjutant General, to receive the muster roll of Company A. And when the Legislature met in January it resolved that Company A was entitled to full pay for its term of service and equality with other companies of volunteers.

The final battle of that phase of the war was fought in 1865, when Arthur Denny and James Tilton opposed each other for congress. The territory was normally Democratic, and Denny was a Republican. But the Civil War helped, and Arthur Denny won by a large majority. That was the last battle of the Indian War, but the last shot was not fired until long afterward.

If any one thing had saved Seattle it was the *Decatur's* explosive shells, which made the Indians keep to the cover of the woods. They were the shells that "mox poohed," or shot twice, but there were also some duds.

One shell had screamed over the village into the wilderness beyond and disappeared in the earth. Years passed, and Seattle pushed up the hill. Digging a foundation, Gardner Kellogg found the unexploded shell and saved it as something that might come in handy some day. The day turned out to be a gloomy Sunday in autumn, cold with drizzling rain. Kellogg and his wife were having dinner with the Shoreys. The women were sisters, and while they were doing the dishes and talking, the brothers-in-law visited Kellogg's place at Fifth and Columbia. The stumpy clearing ended against a wilderness of young fir trees, but it was already laid out in town lots; the property was being improved and stump fires smoked in the misty rain. While Gardner was chunking up one of the fires he had an idea. "She'd come out in a minute," he said, "if we put the old shell under her."

Shorey had qualms, but it was Gard's idea, and his stump and his shell and his responsibility. They lugged the heavy shell from the woodshed, dug a hole under the stump, and slipped it in. Then they chunked the fire over it and went back to Shorey's house, feeling sure that no one would be out for amusement on such a day.

No one was out for fun. But Dexter Horton's cow had not come home at milking time, and the banker was out looking for her. It was a dismal cow hunt, along the muddy trails and through the wet brush of uptown Seattle. The only bright spot on his journey was a stump fire in a clearing. Horton stood as close as he could to the fire and warmed his front; then he turned his back and raised his coattails to warm his rear.

While the fire warmed the grateful banker it heated the iron of the *Decatur's* shell and warmed the cockles of its forgetful heart. It was a shell created to "mox pooh" and it let go with a roar! Dexter Horton landed in a heap, yards away, covered with rubbish. After his first, pure astonishment he was very angry! But in later years he was able to see that the incident would have been very funny if it had happened to someone else.

CHAPTER X

Kidnaping the University

THE INDIAN WAR is remembered for its small number of casualties and large amount of damage. In the fall of 1855 building lots were $250 and citizens confidently believed that they would presently find themselves in a western New York or London. A few months later they woke in a howling village surrounded by Indians. Many of them could not recover from the shock and moved away. Few emigrants came to the territory, and still fewer came to the recently besieged village. By 1860, only twenty families were left.

One of the discouraged ones was Doctor Maynard, who had given Seattle its name and been first in so many things. Now the forward motion of life had stopped and he was lost. He traded half of his Seattle claim for Charles Terry's claim at Alki Point. Seattle did not seem promising, but at least it had a harbor. Alki was only one of the breakwaters, with a desolate jumble of stumps and logs and a few deserted cabins. Presently, when Maynard realized he had made a bad bargain, he was able to console himself with the thought that he still had the other half of his Seattle property. But he did not have that either. He had filed on half his claim in the name of his eastern wife, whom he divorced soon afterward. The remaining half of the property was claimed by her, and Maynard was out. He was the first of the great Seattle pioneers to be lost in the counter-attack of a depression.

Maynard's loss was Terry's gain. Because of the war he got the stake in Seattle that he might have had from the beginning. The others who won something by the war were the Puyallup, Nisqually and Muckleshoot Indians, who got the reservations they fought for.

The rest were losers. The Indians who had stayed at peace suffered the most. The moment the last treaty had been signed their title to a vast area from the Pacific to the Rocky Mountains was extinguished. But the treaties did not become binding on the Government until they were ratified.

In 1858 the Government decided to do something for its charges. The result was a mission headed by Michael Simmons, the Indian Agent. The mission visited the various reservations, where the Indians were called together and exhorted to lead good lives and not to lie or steal or drink whiskey.

In May 1858 the mission visited the Port Madison Reservation, where Chief Seattle was living in the Oleman House that had once been the headquarters of his little nation. The Indians listened patiently to the expert Government advice about not lying or stealing or drinking, and in reply Chief Seattle made his last recorded speech. He was then well past seventy, suffering from hunger and neglect, which was his reward for co-operation with the whites through peace and war. He said:

"I want you to understand what I say. I do not drink rum, neither does Now-e-ches, and we constantly advise our people not to do so. I am not a bad man. I am, and always have been, a friend. I listened to what Mr Page says to me, and I do not steal—nor do I or any of my people kill the whites. Oh! Mr Simmons! Why don't our papers come back to us? You always say you hope they will soon come back—but they *do* not. I fear we are forgotten—or that we are cheated out of our lands. I have been very poor and hungry all winter, and am very sick now. In a little while I will die. I should like to be paid for my land before I die. Many of my people died during the cold, scarce winter without getting their pay. When I die, my people will be very poor. They will have no property, no chief, no one to talk for them. You must not forget them, Mr Simmons, when I am gone. We are ashamed when we think that the Puyallups have their papers. They fought against the whites, whilst we who have never been angry with them, get nothing. When we get our pay we want it to be in money. The Indians are not bad, it is the mean white people who are bad to us. If any person writes that we do not want our papers concluded, they lie. Oh! Mr Simmons! You see that I am very sick. I want you to write quickly to your Great Chief what I say. I have done."

Possibly, within a few years, something might have been done for the Indians, but the Civil War was fast brewing; and the Indians who had fought and those who had stayed at peace were alike neglected and forgotten.

Chief Seattle died on June seventh, 1866, in the gloomy

ruin of the Oleman House, where he is said to have been born. He was buried in the reservation cemetery, and his grave was neglected for a quarter of a century. In 1890 Arthur Denny, Hillory Butler and others of his aging pioneer friends had a handsome monument erected over the grave. The monument is of Italian marble, with an ivy-twined cross that bears the legend, "I.H.S." Some say the letters stand for Latin words which mean, "By this sign thou shalt conquer." But friends would never have added anything so ironic to Chief Seattle's cross. Others say it is the Greek symbol for Jesus. But Catholic children say the letters stand for "I have suffered," which is undoubtedly correct.

The Civil War years brought no booming times to the village diminished by the Indian War. Real-estate prices were in the ground, and Yesler's mill no longer ran night and day, with half a dozen vessels waiting their turn at the loading pier. But there was an occasional schooner or bark or brig for lumber, and the mill ran enough to keep the remnants of the town together.

Only a handful of new settlers came to Seattle, but that handful included some remarkable men. One of them was John Denny, father of the fathers of Seattle and an incorrigible pioneer. He was born on the Kentucky frontier in 1793, volunteered for the War of 1812, and fought in the Battle of the Thames, where Tecumseh was killed and Proctor's British army surrendered. Ten years later John Denny had pioneered on the Indiana frontier, and in 1835 he moved farther west to Illinois where he took part in the rough-and-tumble of frontier politics. He was a man of the Lincoln style, homely and lanky-tall, with a dry humor. Politically he was a Whig, and he served with distinction in the Illinois Legislature. On one occasion the Democrats locked John Denny and themselves and a few other Whigs in a committee room and started to pass a piece of party legislation. They had a quorum and the key to the locked room, but before the vote John Denny and some other Whigs broke up the quorum and ruined the nefarious scheme by jumping out of a second-story window. One of those who jumped was Abraham Lincoln.

In 1851, with his sons, John Denny took the Overland Trail and settled in the Waldo Hills of Oregon. After eight years he found Oregon too civilized and moved north to Seattle. He was then sixty-six years old, and still a fighter. He immediately became a leader in Seattle civic affairs and was an irresistible lobbyist for legislative aid to the town. Arthur Denny was speaker of the house of the Territorial Legislature, and father and son, working in official and unofficial capacities, secured the Territorial University for Seattle in 1861. Seattle had had the hypothetical university once before, and once it had shared the honor with the village of Boisfort, a hundred miles away. Then the Cowlitz Farm was selected for the site. The university was a kind of political pin that was easily moved about the map of the territory. Since there seemed no danger of the university being built, almost any village could have it for a while. If they insisted, two widely separated places could share the honor. But when the Dennys got the political pin back in Seattle they had plans to make it stick.

Kidnaping the University

"Uncle Tommy" Mercer had done a great deal for Seattle in his own right. He had also brought Dexter Horton, who had brought a safe and become the town banker. The weaver had contributed a great deal toward the building of a city, but he had still other resources. From the wagon train in which he and the Hortons had crossed the plains he produced another energetic builder. That was Daniel Bagley, a Methodist-Protestant minister, who had stayed in Salem, Oregon, while Mercer and Horton went north to Puget Sound.

In the unpromising year of 1860 Bagley followed his Oregon Trail companions to Seattle. There he took over the parsonage and church the Blaines had built, and which they had vacated after the Indian War. But Daniel Bagley was more than a parson, and from the time of his arrival he had dreams of greatness for the half-deserted village. When the Legislature yielded to Denny's seemingly innocent whim of wanting the Territorial University in Seattle, Bagley was one of the men pledged to help make it stick.

At Arthur Denny's suggestion the Legislature named Daniel Bagley one of the university commissioners. The other commissioners chose him for president, and they were as willing to let him do the work as he was to undertake it. The Act of Congress that had created Washington Territory allowed two townships of land for the building and financing of a university. And the commission, which was now Doctor Bagley, was presumably empowered to select and sell the lands.

The joker was that the Legislature had fixed the price of the university land at a dollar and a half an acre, whereas other Government land was selling for a dollar and a quarter. The legislators counted on that difference to keep the university hypothetical, and they never would have let it go to Seattle if they had known that the village meant to keep it. Another reliable obstacle was the provision that ten acres of land in Seattle be donated for a campus. Even with real estate at a low ebb it was not believed that anyone would tie up ten acres of town property in behalf of an imaginary university. The legislators further required that the university be opened for instruction within one year; they confidently believed that when some other town made a sufficient outcry for the institution it would still be movable.

But Seattle was playing a different game, and the plans were laid to steal the political pin. When the Reverend Bagley asked who would be willing to give the land for a campus, Arthur Denny answered by getting out his surveying instruments. He had planned to give ten acres on the northern boundary of his claim, but when they got there the place was such a solid wilderness of underbrush that the surveyor threw down his instruments in defeat. He was in the position of a man willing to give away a porcupine but not knowing how to wrap it. Then he said, "Bagley, I'll give it on the knoll."

The knoll was a beautiful and central site on the southern boundary of Denny's claim, and although it was covered with great fir trees, there was little underbrush and surveying was possible. When the knoll was found to comprise only eight and a half acres, the balance was made up by Charles Terry and Judge Lander.

Kidnaping the University

Arthur Denny now went back to the Legislature in Olympia to handle matters from that end, and Bagley set about nailing the Territorial University to its new site. The first, formidable job was to clear the campus of its tremendous forest, without a dollar to finance the work. There were, however, the two townships, and Bagley offered contracts to be paid in land at the rate of about two acres for a day's work. The contracts were let one week after he became president of the commissioners of the hypothetical university. For weeks after that Seattle trembled with the almost continuous thunder of big trees coming down.

While the campus was being cleared the Reverend Bagley was arranging for building materials. Yesler's mill accepted Government land in return for timber and rough lumber that was needed first. While the buildings were being framed Meiggs' mill at Port Madison was turning Hood Canal white pine into finished lumber for the outside and inside of the buildings. The foundations were of Port Orchard granite, and the cornerstone was laid in May, permanently anchoring the university in Seattle.

Materials such as hardware and paints were unobtainable in Seattle and had to come from Victoria, British Columbia. They could not be paid for in land, and to meet such expenses and to provide an endowment fund, Bagley proceeded to sell land for cash. At first it had been considered impossible, with the university's townships priced at an advance over other Government land, but there was a joker in favor of the project. The two townships could be selected from any unoccupied part of the public do-

main, offered or unoffered, and it gave the buyer his pick
of locations. The land sold readily, and presently, after
paying all expenses, Bagley had an endowment fund of
$23,000 for Seattle's center of learning.

Nine months after Seattle had been humored with the
site of the university a startling advertisement appeared in
the newspapers of the territory, and Indians in dugouts
visited the sawmills on Puget Sound, passing out handbills.
The advertisements and handbills read:

Territorial University

———

The Territorial University Building will be so far completed that School will be commenced in it on Monday, the
4th of November next, under the supervision of the President
of the Board of Commissioners, Rev. Daniel Bagley, who has
secured the services of A. S. Mercer, late of Ohio, as Professor
and Teacher.

The term will continue twenty-two weeks, and will be
divided into two quarters of eleven weeks.

Tuition will be as follows:

Primary Department	per qtr	$5 00
Common English	" "	6 00
Common English with History,		
Algebra and Physiology	"	7 00
Algebra and Physiology	"	7 00
Higher English	" "	8 00
Latin and Greek	" "	10 00

Daily lessons in vocal music gratuitous. A dormitory building will be in readiness that will accommodate twenty-five or
thirty young men.

Kidnaping the University

It is recommended that all who desire to attend be with us at the opening of the term, as much is lost by not being present at the formation of classes.

Daniel Bagley
Pres't Board

Seattle, W.T., Sept. 16th, 1861.

There was consternation in Olympia, where the legislators said that they had not considered the location as final, and they believed the building of the university was premature. The Legislature went to Seattle to look into the whole disconcerting business.

The Reverend Bagley handled the investigation splendidly. He welcomed the legislators as pilgrims to a shrine of learning. Seattle was very proud of its Territorial University and expected everyone else to be proud also.

The visitors had to admit that the campus and buildings were fine. Everything seemed to have been done in accordance with the letter if not the intention of the law, and the university was an accomplished fact. There was very little the Legislature could do.

About all the investigators did was to provide Seattle with a good story. There was only one steamer a day, and the investigators stayed overnight at the Felker House. The steamer left early in the morning. When a shrill whistle sounded, the befuddled legislators dressed in the dark of early morning and stumbled out with their carpetbags to Yesler's wharf. There they dived into the engine room and watched the engineer stoke the furnace with slab wood. After a while, when nothing happened, one of the legislators asked, "When are we leaving for Olympia?"

The engineer replied with dignity, "Sir, this sawmill does not run to Olympia."

They had heard the whistle of Yesler's mill, and they were in the engine room of the mill of the gods: the birthplace of Seattle enterprise that had defeated them.

The Territorial University had to start with primary and grammar grades because there were no candidates for a university education, and its first class of one was graduated fifteen years later. There may have been something in the Legislature's thought that the building of the university was premature, but Seattle got and kept the university. It now has an enrollment of twelve thousand and, very properly, a Denny Hall and a Bagley Hall.

Daniel Bagley also had other ambitions for Seattle. After he had helped to obtain the university he took up the development of coal mines. Coal had been discovered near the Duwamish River in 1853, and new fields were discovered later on the Black River and near Lake Washington. Nothing had been done with it because of the lack of capital. Now the owners of the recently discovered and most promising fields were in a dilemma. Before they had perfected their titles, coal and other mineral lands were withdrawn from pre-emption. They feared they would have their coal only as long as they kept quiet about it. Bagley became their champion, and their cause happily fitted in with his schedule.

Rival towns had made some unpleasantness about the sale of the university's townships for financing the university, and Bagley had to go to Washington, D.C., to get a retroactive law that justified the sale. While he was there he secured legislation making the withdrawal of coal lands non-retroactive, and the titles of the owners were thereby confirmed. With retroactive and anti-retroactive legislation balancing the account in favor of Seattle, Daniel Bagley returned from the lions' den wearing two lionskin coats.

Bagley then became a leading spirit in the development of the Newcastle coal field, near the southern tip of Lake Washington. The Lake Washington Coal Company was formed and sample coal was packed out and submitted for tests, in one case with an encouraging adverse result. The officers of the revenue cutter *Lincoln* reported that the coal produced so much heat it nearly melted the cutter's smokestack and was therefore unsafe to use.

The promoters of the company properly used the report as proof that they had a quick and hot article. They began mining seriously and transported coal in wagons to Lake Washington, then by boat, and then in wagons again to Seattle. The difficulties of transportation defeated the company, which presently sold out to another with larger capital. The new Seattle Coal Company substituted a tramway for wagons, tugs and barges on Lake Washington, a second tramway to Lake Union, more tugs and barges on that lake, and a third tramway from the lake to its Seattle bunkers. Transportation defeated the second company, and it sold out to San Francisco interests with still larger capital. The third company sold out to a fourth, and it in time was swallowed by Henry Villard's railway empire.

The Seattle coal industry did not profit its founders, but as it grew larger and more dim in the distance Bagley and his associates at least had the satisfaction of knowing that they had been pioneers.

Daniel Bagley did a great deal toward the material building of Seattle, but he was a clergyman by calling and he did not neglect the pulpit. In 1866, the year that the first coal company was formed, he built the "Brown Church," as distinguished from the "White Church," which the Blaines had built. And he was a forceful preacher and skillful at prayer. One Wednesday evening at prayer meeting he announced: "Let us now pray for Henry Yesler and the Widow McNatt."

His fellow worshipers prayed, as it were, in the dark, and they never were enlightened. Perhaps it was only a nice thought of Bagley's to pray for the attractive widow and the lonely widower in their unsolaced lives.

Seattle's modest achievements in the Civil War years were all homemade. But one promise for the future rose on the eastern horizon. In 1864 President Lincoln approved the charter of the Northen Pacific for a railroad from Lake Superior to Puget Sound. Governor Stevens had surveyed the road in 1853, and he had predicted that the terminus would be Seattle and that trains would be running to Puget Sound by 1858.

At the time, the impetuous little Governor had not foreseen the Indian War or the Civil War. Eleven years had passed before the railroad was even chartered. In those eleven years the settlers had known sorrow and discouragement, and they had discovered that the forward motion of life can stop. Stevens had discovered it, too, as a delegate

to Congress, fighting for the railroad against the opposition
of the South and the growing apathy of the North. He
had gone back to his military profession and died a general.
The railroad was not even chartered until two years after
the Battle of Chantilly had been fought in the great thun-
derstorm. In the storm-dusk the little general had seized
the colors of his old regiment and was riding along the
wavering line of troops, trying to rally them. But the
thunder drowned his voice as he called on them to take up
the forward motion of life, and a bullet took him through
the head.

The citizens of Seattle learned that a railroad can take a
long time, and the rush of progress is blind in a miry world
where it is always getting bogged down. But the railroad
was chartered at last, and it was coming to Puget Sound.
That meant Seattle would be the terminus.

From the very beginning Seattle had the seed of greatness, with its harbor and the mountain pass through which
a railroad would have to come to the Sound. In 1864 it was
still a village, but at least it had the beginnings of a city. It
had more houses than its population could occupy; it
had a sawmill and stores and saloons and two hotels; a
livery stable and a blacksmith shop that Doctor Maynard
had built and presented to the first blacksmith who appeared in town; a bowling alley, two churches and a university.

As yet there was no bawdy house, but that was changed
the following year. A lumber bark brought Joseph Pennell
from the Barbary Coast of San Francisco, where business
was bad. Pennell saw possibilities in Seattle, and he built

his emporium on the beach near Yesler's mill. He took his pick of Indian girls from the disillusioned tribes about the Sound.

Pennell's establishment was not the first of its kind on Puget Sound. It was classed as a squaw dance house, but Pennell called it "Illihee," which is Chinook jargon for "home." Generally speaking it was patronized by impersonal classes of men, such as sailors and loggers, as such places are—generally speaking.

Seattle did not have much growth during the Civil War years, but there were changes, and a few men did a great deal. Uncle Tommy Mercer brought Daniel Bagley, who helped capture the university and open the coal mines. He also brought his much younger brother, Asa, to Seattle. And Asa, too, did a great deal. He almost immediately became president of the university and a member of the Legislature. And though he had never seen salt water until he reached Puget Sound, he performed the most famous maritime exploit in Seattle history and became a legend while he was still in his twenties.

And old landmarks were changed for new ones.

Mercer's black mare, Tib, died in 1864 and was commemorated by a monument on the Lake Union farm. The stallion disappears from Seattle's history into thin air, dead in disgrace or deathless, as you choose. But the spirits of the two are the guardian spirits of the city. Tib is never far away in peaceful times. And like an old fire horse the pale stallion always comes back to trouble. After the first alarm you can hear him kicking down the stable door or thundering through the streets. Ordinances have been passed and plans laid to abate him, but he is deathless and usually invisible, and his stamping grounds are undefined. He has been known to materialize in broad daylight at City Hall. He may gallop down from the hills or come snorting from the sea.

No attempts are made to abate Tib, whose patient spirit is often evoked. When the Chamber of Commerce wishes to encourage funds from Eastern capitalists, they lead out the gentle mare and show off her good points. Look at her, gentlemen: strong as a locomotive and docile as a lamb; never sick a day in her life and always amenable to conservative reasoning. This is Seattle.

That is part of Seattle.

Look on this horse of another color, gentlemen: strong as a locomotive and sometimes as fire snorting, with ideas of his own about who his master is. Do not try to look him in the mouth. He has not bitten anyone recently, but the sign is ominous. And stand clear of his roughshod heels, gentlemen. Unfortunate things have happened. Sparks have been struck and rocks have flown and apple carts upset. And the overconfident have been kicked severely.

CHAPTER XI

A Saga of Youth

SEATTLE'S most enduring maritime exploit, the Second Mercer Expedition, is a saga of youth. Asa Mercer volunteered afterward that the mistakes he made were the mistakes of youth and inexperience. An older man, more worldly wise, would not have made the same blunders; neither would he have attempted the expedition. And no one could have been more steadfast, dogged by fate and his own mistakes. To defeat Mercer the fates shook the whole nation, and they timed their blows to the day and minute when they would be most damaging. Even then Asa Mercer did pretty well. He got a ship and made a raid on the Civil War widows and orphans of the East and brought a hundred of them to Seattle by way of the treacherous Strait of Magellan and through the shoals of financial difficulties that remain uncharted to this day.

Asa Mercer, of Princeton, Illinois, was graduated from Franklin College, Ohio, in 1860; the year after graduation he went West. He arrived in Seattle in June, with nostalgia for his college days. The Territorial University was then being built on Denny Hill, and Asa got a job grubbing out stumps and carrying lumber for the university building. Later in the summer, when there was an opening on the survey gang, Asa was on the ground and got the job. As fall drew near and the finishing touches were put on the campus, the need for a university president became plain. Again Asa was on the ground and got the job.

As president and teacher of the university, twenty-three-year-old Asa learned the problems of the territory, and he was reminded of the problems of the nation, engaged in the Civil War. In Washington Territory there were nine men to every woman, most of them young men working alone, of necessity, on promising donation claims. In the eastern part of the United States hundreds of thousands of young men were engaged in killing one another, and the great cotton mills were silent, with nothing to feed them. Young women who would normally have had the choice of homes or jobs were faced with the blank prospect of neither.

The youthful college president was not the first to see that the two problems were, to some extent, mutually remediable. While Asa was still attending college in Ohio, Charlie Prosch, editor of the Steilacoom newspaper, wrote editorials on the subject and sponsored a meeting of the young bachelors of the neighborhood. It was a kind of indignation meeting—indignation against fate that denied them wives—but although the sentiments of the bachelors were unanimous, the immediate results were no greater than might have come from the soliloquy of a lone man.

Asa's older brother, Thomas, expounded to him the idea that some of the female surplus of New England should be brought to Washington Territory, where the air was far from desert.

Asa was not the first to see the problem and its solution, but it was his nature to act where others theorized. He went to Governor Pickering and members of the Legislature with a plan. Most of them approved of it and all of them turned it down because the young territory was as broke as the young college president. Youth without money is still youth, and it is no college president who cannot raise some funds. Mercer went about and collected enough money from individuals for a trip to Boston.

In Boston the young man who had grown up in the middle of the continent mediated between the East and the West. He met with groups of young women who had been left widows and orphans by the war, and he told them about the charms of Puget Sound and the opportunities for employment in that fabulous place where women were at a premium. He offered to lead the worthy to that promised land. From scores of applicants Mercer selected those who came up to rigid standards of family, education and morals. The group was way above average, and even among those the selective process went on. Puget Sound was approximately as far away as another planet, without much more chance of return. Going meant ending the life the young women had known and beginning a new one. It was a hurdle some could take and others could not; it depended upon whether they were pioneers at heart. Of those who finally went there were eleven, between the ages of fifteen and twenty-five. To the lofty standards that young Mercer had set they added courage above the average.

It was a modest expedition, successful within its limits. The eleven young women and their guide reached Seattle in the spring of 1864, with the aid of two steamers, a train, a bark, a brig and a sloop: a steamer from New York to Aspinwall, a train across the Isthmus, a steamer from Panama City to San Francisco, the limited accommodations of a lumber bark and a lumber brig from San Francisco to Port Gamble on Puget Sound, and a sloop from Port Gamble to Seattle.

The sloop *Kidder* arrived in Seattle at midnight in the month of May. The village was expecting the party, and it was awake to see them come in at the end of their seven-thousand-mile journey, like young women born out of darkness and the sea. Lights were burning in the houses that were open to welcome them. On Yesler's wharf the women of Seattle crowded forward in welcome as lantern light shone on young New England faces; and in the background there was a forest of respectful young bachelors, washed and combed and in clean clothes.

The next day there was a reception in the town hall, and for many days after that the village was bright with a holiday spirit.

On the other side of the continent Mercer had promised the young women that they would find careers in the new territory. He had said nothing about the possibility of marriage. Now he made good his promise and found teaching positions for them in Seattle and surrounding towns.

Northwest Gateway

It sounded like a quietly prosaic ending to a romantic journey. But a year later Asa observed with satisfaction that all but two of the girls were married, and those two were preparing their trousseaux. And Asa had been elected to the Territorial Legislature as a reward.

The expedition had been a complete success; but when Asa looked about him the woods were fuller than ever of hopeful young bachelors, and there was not an unmarried young woman on Puget Sound.

What Asa had done once he could do again, and conditions in the East were more favorable than ever. The last year of the Civil War had ebbed away, with its bloody tide stranding more thousands of young women, and the pinch of hunger and commercial depression reminded them that they were waiting for dead men, in an uncomfortable spot. In the East there were the young women; in the West there was a life and a future for them; and in the Atlantic harbors the necessary transportation was waiting: hundreds of Government vessels, manned and coaled and lying idle, with no place to go.

Mercer's plan was simple common sense. He would take several hundred young women (A) from the New England states where there was nothing for them, embark them on a Government ship (B), which would otherwise be rusting in idleness, and bring them to Seattle (C), where instead of being a drug on the market they would be useful and desired, and where they would have a life.

Asa Mercer was still in his twenties, but he had lived long enough to know that not everyone is willing to sanction a course of action merely because it is the only humane and sensible one. In his own territory there were citizens who thought it just and natural that hundreds of thousands of young men should die in battle—and opposed doing anything for the girls they would have married, on the grounds that it was interfering with the course of nature and romance. But the young man was not worried by such objections. He knew a man in Washington who would see eye-to-eye with him and place human happiness and well-being above hypocrisies. The man was Abraham Lincoln. As a child in Illinois Asa Mercer had sat on his lap while he told stories that made people roar with laughter. Asa had not seen him since. He was not even sure that Lincoln would remember him, and it did not seem important. He remembered Lincoln and, in memory, the sound of his voice and the touch of his hand were assurance enough. Asa's plan was to go directly to Washington from New York and ask the President for a Government ship large enough to carry five hundred young women to Seattle.

He arrived in New York April seventeenth, 1865, after a long wait at Aspinwall for a steamer. He got a hotel room, wrote to his brother Tom of his safe arrival, and bought a ticket for the morning train to Washington. The only delay he anticipated was in getting an interview with President Lincoln, who was overwhelmed with the demands of a people racked by war and uneasily hollow with victory. He might have to wait days to see the President, but when he did there would be no question about the outcome. Tired with travel, and having to be up early in the morning, he went to bed early and slept like the dead.

At six next morning he came downstairs ready to have breakfast and be off to Washington. The hotel office was somber with crape, and on the wall there was a bulletin announcing the assassination of President Lincoln at Ford's Theater the night before.

The days of delay at the Isthmus had cheated Mercer out of seeing the President. All he had was the childhood memory of young Abe Lincoln, and the sound of his voice and the touch of his hand.

As Asa Mercer said afterward, he was at sea without a compass. The nation, too, was at sea without a compass. Going to Washington then would have been a sad and useless business. Mercer went in the opposite direction, to Massachusetts. Governor Andrew was one of the most influential men of the day, and it was from his state that Mercer expected to bring most of his young women. Massachusetts, the mother colony of the East, was also to be the mother colony of the West.

Governor Andrew approved of young Mercer's plan. Gallantry would not say that the state had too many women, but honesty admitted that it had too few men. Andrew was helpful, and he introduced Mercer to Edward Everett Hale. Hale was even more helpful. And Mercer had already helped himself a great deal. The young women of his first expedition had written home that the Puget Sound country was all that he had represented it to be, he had kept every promise to them, and they were happy and prospering. Mercer was almost snowed in with applications from young women and girls who were eager to accompany him on his second expedition. The austere process of weeding out and selecting went on until Mercer had chosen five hundred of New England's best. Then he headed for the Capital to secure a ship.

In Washington he had the sensation of being in a rubber landscape peopled with rubber men. No one opposed him, no one denied that he had a fine plan—and no one helped him. There was nothing into which he could get his teeth. President Johnson approved of his scheme and Cabinet members approved and senators approved. Months passed with his plan being approved all over Washington, and every time Asa went away with the personal approval of someone important, the rubber bastions went back to their original shape without a dent. He got nowhere except back to the sweltering little hotel room from which he had started.

After he had been everywhere else in Washington, Mercer's wanderings led him to the War Department and the office of General Grant. There, through shifting layers of tobacco smoke, the shabby, hairy little General listened to Mercer's story of the lonely young men in Washington Territory; the young women in New England waiting for word that they could give up their vigil for dead men and go West to a new life; and the Government ships, with idle crews and overflowing bunkers, waiting to make justice out of two injustices by bringing them together. Asa Mercer had told the story so often that the words sounded threadbare to his own ears. It was like a wooden sword, worn and frayed with hacking at rubber bastions of indifference. But he had to go on hacking until someone saw that his story made sense; until someone saw that the worn sword was the sword that justice carries in one hand, with the scales in the other.

General Grant smoked in silence, and when Mercer had made his final plea he said, "You have a fine plan."

The young man said, "Yes."

"I approve of it," Grant said.

Mercer's heart sank. President Johnson had approved, and Vice-President Seward had approved, and Stanton. Everyone in Washington had approved. Mercer had been almost killed with approval, like a cat choked with butter. When anyone gave the plan his personal approval it seemed like the young man's cue to pick up his tall hat from beside his chair. And General Grant looked as if his thoughts were already a thousand miles away. . . .

Grant's thoughts were three thousand miles away. Through the haze of cigar smoke he saw the garrison at Fort Vancouver, on the other side of the continent. "Bachelors Hall" on a party night, with the Fourth Infantry Band blaring lancers, cotillions and polkas. General Adair's three daughters were there from Astoria; and Governor Abernathy's daughter from Oregon City; Delia, the girl wife of Sergeant Sheffield, and Miss Hamilton, the belle of Portland. . . . A precious handful of young women from two territories and scores of miles away. Polished young officers in dress uniform, dancing with the young women in the firelight and candlelight of the big, rough room. Captain Wallen and Lieutenant Scott and Captain McClellan—who was a good friend even though he didn't turn out to be much of a general—Captain Brent, and Eastman. . . . At the edge of that little world of warmth and light and music and beautiful young women and gallant officers, an officer who was less fortunate looked on: a shabby, silent quartermaster captain who never danced. He would watch for a while and then climb the stairs to his room. All night he would sit there alone, smoking. And while he smoked and the house throbbed with the music of the regimental band and the music of dancing feet he looked out of the window at the Columbia River in the moonlight, going to the Pacific. In the moonlight he saw the ruined, weed-grown fields where a young captain had plowed and planted and hoed and slaved; a captain whose Army pay was not enough to bring his lovely young wife and children from the East. The summer-flooding river had drowned his field of oats, and the potatoes had rotted in the ground because everyone else had planted potatoes that year and they could not be given away. . . . Grant, too, had been one of the lonely young men of Washington Territory.

In his plea Mercer had said that the young men had good claims and comfortable cabins and abundant food, but where, in God's name, was a man to find money to bring himself a wife? And Grant had thought, "Where, indeed?" He had tried everything, while he and his young wife grew older on opposite sides of the continent. . . .

Grant said, "Come back tomorrow. I'm going to help you, Mercer." And without knowing how it had happened, Asa Mercer knew that he was beyond the rubber bastions of indifference.

Mercer came back tomorrow and other tomorrows, but his project was no longer standing still. Grant was working on it, and he explained what Mercer might have known from the beginning: The bigwigs of Washington were really in sympathy with his plan, but they were afraid of being parties to a matrimonial expedition. It was accepted as tragedy that countless thousands of New England boys were rotting at Gettysburg and Spotsylvania and in the Wilderness. It was sad about the girls they would have married, doomed to spinsterhood. But if anything practical were done to help them, they and everyone concerned would become a fitting subject for ridicule. Grant was something of a god then, and he was not in politics. He could wade in where politicians, who were no angels, were afraid to tread.

One stifling morning in July, Mercer called at the War Department and found General Grant in a hurry, about to go out. "Sit down, Mercer," he said, "and read the morning paper while you wait for me. I'm going over to the White House to meet the President and his Cabinet. I'll bring your matter to a head one way or another."

Grant was back in half an hour, brisk with action. He did not even look at the young man clutching the morning paper. Coming in he said to his aide, "Captain Crosby, make out an order for a steamship, coaled and manned, with a capacity to carry five hundred women from New York to Seattle for A. S. Mercer, and I will sign the same."

Mercer had begun to feel old, with four months of waiting and disappointments. Now time dropped away and he was a young enthusiast, dashing out of Grant's office with the signed order. He caught the first train for Boston and points north and issued five hundred tickets for the voyage. It was then late July, and he set August nineteenth for the sailing date.

In Lowell, Massachusetts, the mills were waiting, silent, for the bales of cotton the Yankees had burned so gleefully a little while before. From that victory-stricken town Mercer wrote, in part, to the Seattle *Gazette* and the territorial papers in general: "I appeal to every true, warmhearted family to open wide the door and share your home comforts with those whose lot is about to be cast in your midst. Let every neighborhood appoint a committee of a lady and a gentleman to meet us in Seattle upon the arrival of the ocean steamer carrying the party, with instructions to welcome to their homes as many of the company as they can furnish homes and employment for. . . ."

The ocean steamer to which Mercer referred with pardonable pride was a nameless vessel that he carried with him in the form of General Grant's precious order. With his passengers notified and provided with tickets, Asa Mercer raced back to Washington.

In Washington he joined the long line that was shuffling through the office of Quartermaster-General Meigs. The assorted humanity and the snail's pace of the queue and the wretched heat of the Capital were lost on the young man who carried a steamship in his hand, with sea breezes blowing about him.

Time and the line crept on until there was only one man between Mercer and the brusque, efficient Quartermaster-General. The man had provided a horse for the Army and been given a receipt, and he was there to collect. It was a small business that would take only a minute. Then it would be Mercer's turn. . . .

Quartermaster-General Meigs took the receipt with one hand and dipped his pen with the other, looking up sharply at the one-horse merchant. Then his face went apoplectic and the sweltering office exploded and burned blue with curses. Between ragings General Meigs shouted for a sentry to arrest the one-horse merchant, whom he recognized. The man had already been paid twice for his horse, and he was trying to collect for the third time. The Quartermaster-General had seen enough of the shoddy aftermath of war to sicken him. And he revolted volcanically at injustice that allows a man only one life to give for his country while another who has risked nothing can sell the same horse three times.

It was not the day or minute to have dealings with the Quartermaster-General. Asa started to draw back, but Meigs reached out and took his order brusquely, with a look of woe-betide-anyone-else-who-comes-here-on-any-funny-business. Still shaking with rage he glared at the order for a Government ship to take one A. S. Mercer on a Pacific voyage with five hundred women. He spoke quietly, after all, as he shoved the order back at the young man who had presented it. "There is no law justifying this order and I will not honor it. Next!"

Mercer could not have felt more crushed if he had been arrested and hauled off to jail with the shoddy little profiteer who had changed a splendid steamship into a scrap of paper and ruined the mission of his life. He saw General Grant again, and Grant was sorry for the way things had turned out, but he had already done what he could, and on any other day except that fatal one it would have been enough. Meigs was right about the law, and having leaned over backwards to be correct he was not inclined to unbend.

Washington having failed him, Mercer retreated to New York, where he took a room in the Merchants' Hotel. From there he carried on the unequal fight by mail. Weeks passed and he was ready to give up when he received a letter from Meigs. The Quartermaster-General had unbent part way. He even showed that he was willing to overlook the law in a good cause. For Mercer's benefit he had secured a special appraisement of the steamer *Continental*, although the law required that she be sold at public auction. The *Continental* was a fine and almost new propeller steamship of sixteen hundred tons, built of oak and hickory, with accommodations for five hundred passengers. She had cost the Government three hundred and fifty thousand, and Mercer could have her at the appraisement price of eighty thousand, cash.

The steamer was a bargain at the price, but Asa Mercer had never seen eighty thousand dollars and he was not exactly traveling in the right direction, embarked on the career of a philanthropist without money. One day when he was sitting in his hotel room, trying to imagine ways of raising eighty thousand dollars, he had a caller whose card proclaimed him to be Ben Holladay. Holladay was a total stranger, but he was not irrelevant. He said, like a mindreader or Satan tempting a young prophet, "Mr Mercer, you're in a jam. You want the *Continental* and you haven't the money to buy her. Let me have her and I'll fit her out for the voyage and take your party to Seattle for a song."

Mercer shook hands, fervently, on the life-saving deal, and Holladay brought in two thoroughgoing lawyers to draw up the agreement, by which their client got the ship and Mercer got transportation for five hundred passengers from New York to Seattle at a nominal rate. Again he set a sailing date and issued tickets. Some of the girls got free tickets and many more paid their own way, but there was no trouble obtaining the five hundred passengers called for in the agreement.

The sailing date was less than a week off when Gordon Bennett's *Herald* felt the need of something snappy for its readers. In the morning paper Mercer read a long, malicious article on his expedition and himself. According to the article all the men of Puget Sound were rotten profligates. And the most sinister of them all was a young Satan by the name of Asa Mercer who was collecting the flower of New England womanhood for the brothels of Seattle. The *Herald* appealed to them to spurn the tempter who would lure them to their fate, and stay at home. The article was copied everywhere, and while Mercer was getting his credentials printed, the table in his room at the Merchants' Hotel piled up with letters from the young women. There were hundreds of them, enclosing the *Herald* article and spurning Mercer in *Herald* style.

Proportionally the article could not have benefited the writer more than the sale of a horse three times had benefited the little profiteer; but again the damage was out of all proportion to the stakes. And it was irreparable, with the sailing date of the *Continental* a few days off. Four hundred young women had put Mercer and his expedition out of their lives. There were about a hundred faithful, influenced by the honorable success of the first expedition, and some families had joined the expedition. Mercer decided to do the only thing he could and settle with the fates for forty per cent.

He called on Ben Holladay with specimen letters of declination, and said that he would be able to muster no more than two hundred passengers on sailing day.

Then Mercer found the kind of contract he had signed in his young enthusiasm. Holladay had agreed to carry five hundred special passengers for not more than actual cost. He would have been better off with two hundred, but he declined to see it that way. The agreement called for five hundred, neither more nor less, and in failing to provide them Asa Mercer had broken the contract. Mr Holladay had obtained the *Continental* at a great bargain, and Mercer had gained valuable experience. But Mr Holladay had no hard feelings about Mercer's breach of contract. He was adding a fine steamer to his Pacific steamship line, and he offered to take Mercer's party at the regular passenger rate.

Asa would have been as well or better off taking passage in any other steamer, but he had set his heart on the *Continental*. Traveling with his expedition in that ship he would have at least the illusion that he had got something out of the efforts of General Grant and the unbending of Quartermaster-General Meigs. Mercer believed that Holladay had been able to keep his part of the agreement to the letter and that the *Continental* was ready to put to sea.

The *Continental* was not ready that fall; she was not ready that year. She was still to be overhauled and fitted out, and there were delays about everything. Months passed, and the young man who had grown older on his quest was growing wiser. He saw that no one helps the philanthropist, and that if he didn't do something for himself the expedition would absorb everything he had and he would arrive in his own country a prophet without honorarium.

Women were not the only thing that was a drug on the eastern market and in demand in the West. Asa's brother Tom had brought the first wagon to Seattle; he had prospered in the transfer business and had become a man of importance and a judge. There was still a dearth of wagons in the Territory, and they were selling cheap in New York. While Asa waited for the feminine *Continental* to get ready, he got together the last of his personal funds and bought two thousand dollars' worth of wagons and farm machinery. These he shipped home on a sailing vessel by way of Cape Horn and San Francisco. Had they waited for the *Continental* they might have been outmoded before they arrived.

Almost a year had passed since Asa Mercer started east to lay his plan before President Lincoln, and finally the *Continental* was ready. She cleared New York Harbor on January sixth, 1866, with about two hundred passengers.

January is not a pleasant month in the Atlantic. There were many seasick passengers before Sandy Hook; and there were more and sicker off Hatteras. But the *Conti-*

nental was able and she wallowed steadily south, through tremendous Hatteras seas, into more reasonable weather, with her big, slow engines stamping out the sea miles.

The girls got their sea legs, and on the rest of the voyage that lasted nearly a hundred days there was not one case of illness. One of the young women, who kept a diary, observed that the food was mostly parboiled beans. The owner had compromised between his first contract with Mercer and his second: the party paid the full rate and got the food intended for passengers carried as an accommodation. But the young women had good digestions and stout hearts; without them they would not have been there.

Asa Mercer observed afterward that it was a very pleasant voyage and remarkable in many ways. After his years' ordeal, it was truly restful to be at sea without an immediate worry other than a hundred young women.

The *Continental* visited the great harbor of Rio, and the lesser port, Lota. Gallant Spanish officers came on board and declared their passion for the New England girls, and spoke of villas and castles in Spain. Asa Mercer had said that most people on Puget Sound lived in log cabins. He had to be very firm, and he felt younger when the *Continental* trundled into the cold south. She rounded Cape Virgins, into the Strait of Magellan, through great tide races and squalls of sleet. She bore west and then southwest, then south through Broad Reach and Famine Reach; northwest through Froward Reach. In calms she trundled past the cold, wreck-strewn shores at the foot of the mountains, with mirages making great ships out of the wretched dugouts of piratical Fuegians. The smoke of signal fires rose as she passed, and fierce williwaws blasted down on her from raw granite mountains where no tree ever grew.

The *Continental* cleared Cape Pillar and Evangelistas and headed northwest into the Pacific, into warmer latitudes and more moderate seas. She touched at Charles Island in the Galapagos, at the end of the world. From there she went on five thousand miles farther north and entered the Golden Gate as spring was coming to California. She docked at San Francisco, ninety-six days out of New York, and the party was met by a rescue mission inspired by Gordon Bennett's malicious *Herald*. When the mission was convinced of the mistake Asa Mercer's troubles had only begun. The *Continental* was going no farther, and the young man's funds were gone.

The situation was nothing new. Before then and since a young woman's escort has found himself short on cash. But Mercer had the embarrassment multiplied a hundred times. The young women needed at least one floor of a hotel, and three hundred meals a day. They had good sea appetites, and Asa Mercer had three dollars in his pocket. And rescue mission or no, he and his virginal pilgrims were stranded in San Francisco, which answered cheerfully to the name of the "Wicked City." He would have to find or invent money to get his party out of there.

He remembered Bill Pickering, the Territorial Governor, who had been one of the enthusiastic supporters of what he termed the "raid on the widows and orphans of the East." When Mercer was leaving, Pickering had shaken his hand and said, "God bless you, Mercer, and make it a success. And if you need money, don't hesitate to wire me."

Mercer wired, "Arrived here broke. Send $2000 quick to get party to Seattle." Next day he was notified to call at the telegraph office for a message. Worries fell from him and he was once more an enthusiastic young man, racing to the telegraph office on Market Street. There he was temporarily stalled. The Governor had sent his telegram collect, and the charge was seven dollars and a half. Mercer had spent two dollars and a half on his telegram, which left him fifty cents. But he was not going to lose two thousand dollars for the lack of seven, and he was in a gambling town. He talked to the superintendent and explained how things were, and he suggested that the superintendent open the message. If it was an order for money, Mercer would be able to pay. If it was not, the company would be no worse off.

The superintendent was a good fellow. He opened the envelope and read the long message, and burst out laughing. Still laughing, he handed the dispatch over to Mercer free of charge. The Governor's telegram read like a political speech, broad with generalities and long with seven-cent words of welcome and congratulation. And like a political speech, words were used freely to draw attention from the issue. There was no mention of money.

Once more Mercer was on his own resources, rummaging in his overexercised brain. Again he found something that might be a way out of embarrassment—at his own expense: the wagons and farm machinery he had bought in New York with the idea of doing something for himself.

They had been sent by way of Cape Horn and San Francisco, from where they would have to be reshipped to Seattle. There was a chance they might still be in town. He spent his last fifty cents on a cab, racing to Coleman and Company, the shipping office.

The wagons and machinery were there, in the warehouse, and he had no trouble selling them for what they had cost, including freight. They saved the day for everything except his hopeful plan of doing a stroke of business for himself. Mercer was now an unalloyed philanthropist, with two thousand dollars in his hand. He sent the girls north in small batches on the lumber vessels trading between San Francisco and Puget Sound.

Seattle never saw the ocean steamer of which Mercer had written so proudly. While the brig *Tanner* was being warped in to Yesler's wharf with the first lot of girls, Asa Mercer was still in San Francisco, finding transportation for the remainder of his party. But the *Tanner* and the successive vessels got a fine reception. The University bell rang and the town was on the wharf, dressed in its best, to welcome the young women. Every man who could afford it bought a new suit of clothes, and those who could not had bought new overalls.

Once it got started, the expedition had been fortunate. All the girls arrived safely in Seattle and were welcomed into private homes, where they stayed until jobs were found for them. They became dressmakers and milliners and schoolteachers, and some of them taught in the University, where they did themselves credit. From start to finish it was an honorable and decorous expedition. Mercer has been ridiculed because it was too decorous, but he was no fool. His plan was bold and realistic, and with enough people to misunderstand, it is a question if its execution could have been too decorous. And the expedition accomplished its purpose. Within a year most of the young women were married. They became the mothers of Seattle and thousands trace their descent to the "Mercer Girls."

Within the limits set by fate the Mercer expeditions were a great success. But still the woods were pitted with the lonely claims of young men without women, and the eastern states were full of young women whom war and propriety had doomed to wait for dead men. With some help, and the cumulative success of his earlier expeditions, Asa Mercer might have gone back on a third and greater expedition and brought a thousand young women to Puget Sound, where there was plenty of need for them and where they would have had a life.

Asa Mercer was still young, but not so young as when he had gone east to lay his plan before President Lincoln. And there are some efforts one makes only once, in the first flush of youth. Mercer went on no more expeditions. Eventually he drifted away from his adopted territory and owned a big cattle ranch near the Bad Lands of Wyoming. The last mention of him in recorded history leaves him there in his eighties, far from the World War that was creating a new generation of widows and orphans, and a long way from the sea that had inspired the expeditions of his youth.

CHAPTER XII

The Railroad Turns Aside

SEATTLE was a naïve young town in 1864, with the smell of stump fires in its hair and sawdust in the cuffs of its trousers. When the citizens heard that President Lincoln had approved the charter of the Northern Pacific Railroad they believed that the path of progress was straight again and that it led through Snoqualmie Pass to their back door, where it would deliver wealth and a fabulous city.

The Northern Pacific had a substantial-sounding name, and it had also been granted alternate sections of land twenty-four miles on each side of the right of way. The amount was fifty million acres, and the directors of the company quickly figured on paper that they would clear half a billion dollars for their stockholders. But the railroad had to be built to carry prospective buyers to the company's lands. The railroad would cost around a hundred million dollars, and the company had two hundred thousand. So the Northern Pacific petitioned the Government to subsidize the building of the road or guarantee its bonds

[198]

in addition to the land grant. But Congress refused. Regretfully, the directors saw that they could never hope to take their profit of half a billion dollars on a capital of two hundred thousand. The presidents of some established eastern railroads were brought in on the enterprise, and they brought in still others.

By 1870 the Northern Pacific had induced Jay Cook and Company to finance the road. Cook had gained great wealth and reputation selling bonds for the Government during the Civil War, and he was now the leading banker of the United States. On his advice the charter of the railroad was amended to permit the issue of mortgage bonds for a hundred million dollars and to change the western course of the road. The original charter called for a railroad and telegraph line over the Cascades to Puget Sound and a branch to Portland, Oregon, with no land grants on the branch line. The amendment read: "A railroad to Puget Sound, via the valley of the Columbia." The new arrangement steered the road in a U-shaped course near the boundaries of Idaho and Oregon and the Pacific Ocean, and thereby left most of Washington Territory without a railroad and virtually without east and west communication. It also greatly lengthened the road, but that was not altogether to the bad. For every hundred miles the road was lengthened in avoiding the territory it was intended to serve, the company gained an additional two and a half million acres of Government land. By using steamers on the Columbia River and calling it a railroad the Company saved the laying of two hundred miles of track; and by serving Puget Sound with a branch line from near

Portland, and calling it the main line, the company gained four million acres of rich timberland in western Washington where it originally would have had nothing.

In March 1870 the Northern Pacific road was begun from the eastern end near Duluth, Minnesota; and in May the branch line to the Sound was started from the company's new town of Kalama on the Columbia River.

While the first ground was being broken Jay Cook and Company were raising funds. Bonds were offered in denominations of from $50 to $50,000, calculated to suit every purse. Newspapers and magazines and religious periodicals carried Cook's message to America. For the first time the advertising-reading public saw the West in colors that glowed; and they glowed most brightly in alternate sections of the uninhabited lands through which the railroad would pass: The lands were of remarkable fertility and beauty, the climate surprisingly mild, and opportunity was unlimited. The railroad was to be more than a railroad. It was to be a path of civilization, forty-eight miles wide, and as it advanced through the fruitful wilderness it would leave a broad wake of cities and prospering towns and smiling farms, and smiling purchasers.

The building of the road also had its patriotic angle. In Republican circles the colonization scheme was represented as a ganging-up on the defeated South. The development of northern territory and its swift growth of population would be a guaranty that the Democrats could never again hold power. Congress was altogether Republican, and Congress was uncommonly kind to the Northern Pacific.

The Railroad Turns Aside

The ribbon of empire across the continent was a great dream. Jay Cook announced that he intended to devote his life to it. But he was also selling bonds in the hope of bettering his already excellent condition. His commission on the sales was thirty-two per cent in cash and stocks. Payments were accepted in bank notes worth less than eighty cents on the dollar, and from what remained the railroad company had to pay seven and three tenths per cent interest in gold on the full amount. The railroad was climbing, hopefully, toward great profits, but the percentage of slip was also great.

While the main line of the Northern Pacific pushed west across the continent the branch line crept north from the Columbia River toward Puget Sound—at the rate of twenty-five miles a year. At the same speed the transcontinental line would not have been in operation for upward of a hundred years. One reason for the snail's pace of the branch line was that it would not be of much use to anyone until it had its transcontinental connection. As originally planned the completed branch would have given useful service between the substantial city of Portland and Puget Sound. But the railroad was financed by land and dominated by its subsidiary land company to the extent that the tail sometimes wagged the dog. Instead of serving Portland as its Columbia terminus the railroad had gone twenty-five miles down the river on the other side and made a terminus in the wilderness. There it was selling real estate and booming its private town of Kalama as a rival of Portland.

There had never been a hint from the railroad about its

choice of a western terminus, and the towns of Puget Sound might have learned something from Kalama. But every town on the east side of the Sound, and some towns on islands, had reasons why it would be chosen; and each one watched the road's slow advance north with the eagerness of a man watching a favorite in a race. And all of them were betting on the same iron horse.

By the middle of 1872 the Northern Pacific had made some progress toward giving service to Puget Sound. It had bought out the Oregon Railway and Navigation Company, which had the monopoly on Columbia River and Puget Sound steamboat service. And the branch line had crept to within thirty miles of the Sound.

That summer the selection of the western terminus assumed the nature of an auction. Five directors of the road arrived and cruised about the Sound in the company's *North Pacific*. The steamer visited each aspiring town, and the directors asked the citizens how much they would pay for the western terminus of the railroad.

The citizens of Seattle had expected their town to win the terminus on its merits, but they were ready to make sure. Seattle had outgrown Yesler's log cookhouse as a meeting place; but Yesler had built a pavilion, and the citizens gathered there to pledge everything they could scrape together. Their bid was $250,000 in cash and bonds, 7500 town lots, 3000 acres of land, and the use of half the town's water front for tracks and a depot. The total value of the pledge was over $700,000, and the population of the town was only 1142.

The five voyagers on the *North Pacific* did not decide

on the terminus, but they narrowed the choice to Tacoma, Seattle and Muckilteo. Tacoma, on Commencement Bay, was a few cabins and a sawmill in the wilderness, and Muckilteo was still less. Olympia was the only rival Seattle had feared, and Olympia was ruled out. Seattle waited confidently, and Tacoma and Muckilteo waited.

The Northern Pacific kept them in suspense another year, and then Arthur Denny received a telegram from the company's town on the Columbia:

Kalama, July 14, 1873

A. A. DENNY, SEATTLE

We have located the terminus on Commencement Bay

R. D. RICE

J. C. AINSWORTH

Commissioners

It was then twenty years since Governor Stevens had predicted that within five years the transcontinental railroad would be running to Seattle through Snoqualmie Pass; and Seattle was not even to have the aborted railroad that was finally coming. Two wars had been fought since then, and the impetuous Governor who had made the prediction had been dead ten years at Chantilly; and the enthusiastic young city builders who had heard him were no longer young: Arthur Denny and Carson Boren were in their fifties. David Denny, the youngest of them, was in his forties. Henry Yesler was growing grayer and more massive as he neared his seventies; and Maynard had gone pioneering again. . . .

[203]

Earlier in that year of disillusionment, time and the East had caught up with the convivial Doctor and had found him a threadbare, aging man, shadowed by poverty. In the old days he had worn his black hair cut short and brushed back from his great, bold forehead, and his octagonal steel-rimmed spectacles were usually pushed up clear of his eager, forward-looking eyes. Now he did not have much to look forward to, and his white hair came down to his shoulders. But he was still as dapper as he could be, and he kept up a bold front and was always cheerful and joked with his friends. He was distinguished looking, like an old actor dead and gone to hell for everything but pride.

Maynard had gone on the theory that whatever helped the town helped everyone, including himself, but somehow he had not been included. As he had been first in so many things, he was the first to fail. He still had his devoted second wife, Catherine, and the log cabin home and office where he used to give land away by the acre to encourage the growth of the town. But he did not have anything left to give away.

Early in 1872 the Doctor heard from his eastern wife, who still claimed half of his original claim; she was coming out to Seattle to look after her property and to see him. According to eastern reckoning his legislative divorce was not valid and he was still married to her. Doctor Maynard and Catherine took the news more quietly than the town. People knew the Maynards were devoted to each other, and the Doctor was a gallant and resourceful man. They wondered how he would manage, confronted by his two lawfully wedded wives.

When the steamer from Olympia came into Yesler's wharf, most of the town was there to see the reunion. And the Doctor managed handsomely. He and the second Mrs Maynard greeted the first affectionately, and Doctor Maynard gave an arm to each. With the two women of his life he walked ashore between the rows of spectators. He was old and frail, but unbowed, and he managed that summing up of his life with genial gallantry; the men of Seattle took off their hats to the Doctor and his wives.

It was quite simple, after all. The three Maynards walked the short distance home to the log cabin that had once been the largest and finest house in town. There they lived in harmony until the first Mrs Maynard returned East.

Doctor Maynard died in Seattle on March thirteenth, 1873. The funeral was at Yesler's Pavilion, and from there the procession moved north to the Denny Park cemetery near Lake Union. But Doctor Maynard was still a little ahead of his time. The city fathers had voted to use the land as a park, and there were to be no more burials. The Masonic Cemetery had been laid out farther north, but there was no road by which it could be reached. So Maynard's coffin was stored in the tool house of the old cemetery. A few days later a trail was cut through the woods, and Maynard went pioneering again.

Doctor Maynard was first to sleep in the new cemetery. The pioneers who were then living, and those who were dead, followed him in time. In 1884 Seattle's park commissioners had the bodies moved from Denny Park to the Masonic Cemetery, where the Doctor had led the way.

One of the bodies moved was that of Mary Ann Conklin, otherwise Mother Damnable or Madame Damnable, the profane and rock throwing, who had routed all the fighting divisions of the *Decatur*. The workmen were of another generation and they were not afraid of Madame Damnable. She was quiet enough now. But when they tried to lift the coffin, it was so heavy it could not be stirred. Aging wags suggested that she had been up to her old trick of gathering her apron full of stones. The contractor had to build a derrick over the grave to lift the coffin, which was estimated to weigh nearly half a ton. When it was opened, out of pardonable curiosity, it was found that Madame Damnable had been gathering stone unto herself. Her body was petrified into a ponderous stone effigy that gave her material immortality.

It took Seattle time to find out that the Northern Pacific, for which it had prayed, was not bringing public service but a blackjack. The promise of steel rails, and the rails themselves when necessary, were a means to the end of securing and exploiting public lands. Seattle was ruled out as a terminus for the very reason that it was an established town. It had offered more than two thirds the value of the entire county, but by going into the wilderness and building its own city the Northern Pacific would not have to share with anyone. And Seattle had to be destroyed in order that the company's town could live and be the metropolis of Puget Sound.

The Railroad Turns Aside

The contest has been described as unequal, and it was. On one side there was a transcontinental railroad, with half a billion dollars of profit within reach, promoted by America's greatest financier and backed to the shameless limit by Congress. On the other side there were the aging and monumental Henry Yesler, sitting outside his small sawmill, whittling a pine stick; Arthur Denny, the sharp-featured surveyor and legislator and town proprietor; David Denny, the earnest and religious citizen, interested in temperance and in providing for his eight children; Carson Boren, who was called "Uncle Dobbin," and who disliked city building so much that he had sold the town half of his claim cheap and devoted himself to hunting; Thomas Mercer, the weaver, a gentle man who had dreams—and approximately eleven hundred other people. Those and a village of frame houses and a few thousand acres of real estate were the tangible assets of the town the Northern Pacific had set out to destroy.

The things they overlooked were Seattle's intangible assets. Among those were Madame Damnable and Mercer's horses that had come out of the sea: Madame Damnable for stubbornness, the docile mare for patience and the pale stallion for the unbroken spirit.

The selection of the terminus tested the citizens' attachment to Seattle. Those who were shaken off dusted themselves and moved to Tacoma, and a few firms went too. All the old-timers stayed to fight, and most of the others stayed with them. They had come to better their condition, and there had been occasional discord in the process. Now they all had to fight to save their town from destruction. The common cause of survival brought unity and a fighting spirit. The younger and more naïve suggested that the village build its own transcontinental railway. Oddly, the more responsible citizens were having somewhat the same thought.

Less than a week after Seattle had received its death warrant from the railroad a mass meeting was held in Yesler's Pavilion. The chief speaker was Selucius Garfielde, the golden-throated orator. Garfielde had twice represented Washington Territory in Congress, and he had been one of the earliest boosters. In the age of innocence when Governor Stevens had first arrived, Selucius had joined with him in stirring up the settlers' enthusiasm for their territory. When Stevens had envisioned the rich caravans of Asia marching through the forests of Snoqualmie Pass, Selucius had kept up with him and predicted other things as glamorous.

Seattle had its heart set on a railroad, and Selucius explained how it could be done. He admitted it was too early for Seattle to think of building its own railway across the continent. But east of the mountains there was the inland empire with its golden grain. Seattle must build its own railroad through Snoqualmie Pass to Walla Walla and bring the grain harvest and the grain fleet to Puget Sound.

Selucius had figures to show that river traffic on the Columbia, with its two portages, could never compete with a direct railroad to Puget Sound. The transcontinental line of the Great Northern was still years short of completion, and when it was completed Seattle's direct railroad to the grain fields would have the business and the advantage over its rival's devious road.

It was a fine speech, and Yesler's Pavilion shook with cheers as the citizens of Seattle voted to build a railroad of their own. The Seattle and Walla Walla Railroad and Transportation Company was organized, and within two months half a million dollars of its stock subscribed. Arthur Denny and Judge McGilvra then went to Walla Walla to stir up interest at that end.

Judge McGilvra was a New York and Chicago lawyer whom President Lincoln had appointed United States Attorney for Washington Territory in 1861. He was a man of great ability and fighting spirit, and at Yesler's Pavilion he had urged the citizens to "Carry the war to Africa" by building their own railroad; he was ready to help them do it. Since then he had drawn up the papers of the company, handled its legal matters, secured the necessary legislation and canvassed for subscriptions to stock.

While Seattle was working hopefully for a railroad the Northern Pacific was having troubles with its own. The westward progress of the road had been delayed while the company exploited the Red River country with branch lines. Its transcontinental progress was years behind schedule, and the sale of bonds had fallen off. Construction progress became still slower while the company concentrated on securing more land. With its blank check from Congress the Northern Pacific rewrote its charter and added new flourishes to the course of its road. It was now continued north from Tacoma through the length of

Puget Sound, where there would be steamer service instead of rails. At Bellingham, twenty miles from the Canadian border, the railroad took to the land again and headed east to near the border of Idaho. There it turned south and met itself, completing a steel noose about Washington Territory. The original charter had called for a direct road to Puget Sound and a branch to Portland, Oregon. But the noose had the advantage of snaring twenty million acres of public lands in one territory alone; and it was designed to strangle Portland and Seattle—towns which the railroad had been intended to serve.

The fever of land grabbing was a symptom of illness. Two months after the railroad had announced Tacoma as its western terminus Jay Cook and Company failed with a great crash. The nation became panicky, and the railroad was mired down in troubles and profoundly embarrassed. There was no hope of finishing the transcontinental line for years. And it was doubtful if they would be able to finish the branch line.

The Northern Pacific made it.

At three o'clock on the afternoon of December sixteenth, 1873, the two hundred citizens of Tacoma and a few railroad officials stood in the rain and watched General McCarver, the town proprietor, drive the last spike. Across the railroad tracks Chinese and Irish and American tracklayers stood in the rain and looked on, glumly. They did not join in the cheers when McCarver had finished driving the common iron spike.

It was not much of a ceremony, and in some ways it was a pity, because General McCarver was an historic figure. He had come from Kentucky to Chicago when it was a small town. From there he had gone west to found a town of his own, which was Burlington, Iowa. He had crossed the plains in 1843, at the dawn of western history, and joined with Captain Sutter in building the town of Sacramento, California. Afterward he had pioneered in Oregon, and now he had just driven the last spike in the railroad that linked the Columbia River with Puget Sound.

The citizens cheered and Director Ainsworth of the Northern Pacific wiped his forehead, nervously. Across the tracks the tracklayers waited in ominous silence.

The younger people of Tacoma had never seen a railroad train, and it was a twenty-year-old memory to some of the others. Their hearts leaped in answer to the sound of a great whistle. To the south a locomotive loomed up out of rain and smoke and steam. It grew in size and slowed in speed as it rolled into the new station, pulling a few cars, with clanging bell and hissing steam. The first railroad train had reached tidewater on Puget Sound.

The citizens cheered in the rain, General McCarver shook hands with Director Ainsworth, and on the other side of the railroad tracks the workmen finally raised their voices. In Chinese and pidgin English and in English they yelled: "Where's our money? When do we get paid?" And two mobs of them flowed across the railroad tracks, around the stopped train. "Where's that money, Ainsworth?"

The sweating director had been afraid of just such an embarrassing moment. A week before the same men had built a barricade across the unfinished tracks and demanded the five thousand dollars due them in wages. If it was not paid on the spot they were going to take it out in trade and tear up five thousand dollars' worth of rails. Ainsworth had been embarrassed then. The company had failed to send money for wages, the contractor had disappeared, and there was not enough cash to buy a gold spike for the coming ceremony.

Ainsworth had persuaded the men to wait while he tried to raise the five thousand on his personal credit. Five hundred was all he had been able to manage. He had divided that among the construction hands and promised the rest within a few days. The men tore down their barricades and went to work again, but no funds arrived from the company and Ainsworth could not borrow any more. The line had been completed at the personal expense of the construction hands, and now they wanted their money.

There was no money, and the men were already well off for promises. They piled up ties and rolled logs across the track and started to tear up the rails. Their ribald calculations showed that the Northern Pacific also owed them two bridges, which they were about to collect.

The spike-driving ceremony ended on a loud, sour note. Children who had been promised a ride on the new railroad were disappointed by evasive elders. Their elders, too, were disappointed in the coming of the railroad, which seemed about to go away again. There were rumors that unpaid crews, farther south, had already torn up the rails and wrecked bridges. People were warned, on their lives, not to travel on the railroad for which they had waited twenty years.

CHAPTER XIII

The Steel Noose

SEATTLE'S FIGHT with the Northern Pacific turned out to be a Seventeen Years' War. It was fought on the moving stream of time that carried the village far from the starting place. When it began, railroad partisans predicted that Seattle would shortly be deserted, and its business moved to Tacoma. When it ended, Seattle was still on Elliott Bay and it had grown bigger and tougher.

On May Day 1874 Seattle was a deserted village, as the railroad had predicted, but the population had not moved to Tacoma. They were at Steele's Landing on the Duwamish, starting to build a railroad with their own hands. It was simple, if improbable. Walla Walla would not give much help with the railroad to the grain fields, and the Government would not give any help. Seattle did not possess enough wealth to pay for building the road, and there was no way of raising the money. Therefore the citizens would have to grade the road and lay the narrow-gauge tracks themselves.

Northwest Gateway

At dawn on May Day all the steamer whistles and the whistle of Yesler's mill had blown endlessly; the bells of the Blaines' White Church and Daniel Bagley's Brown Church clanged with pagan enthusiasm. They were answered by the clamoring of the school bell and the big bell of the Territorial University on Denny Hill. The two nine-pounders, left over from the blockhouse and the Indian War, thundered and were re-echoed from Duwamish Head. Those were the opening guns of Seattle's war with the railroad. Then the entire population of the town started for Steele's Landing, in steamers and in barges and in wagons.

All morning the citizens worked with picks and shovels and wheelbarrows, grading a piece of road. Men who had grown soft on their way to being capitalists recalled that they had once been good with the pick and shovel and did their best to prove the fact.

At noon the women served a great picnic dinner, and after that there were speeches. John Denny, the father of the fathers of Seattle and veteran of 1812, made a fighting speech from a wagon. And Henry Yesler, of the mill of the gods, made his famous seven-word speech. When he was called on he turned his massive face toward the afternoon sun and said, "Let's quit fooling and get to work."

Seattle's attempt to build a railroad with citizen labor was the impossible dream of a young city. Commenting on it an Oregon paper observed that it would take them two hundred years to reach Walla Walla.

It was a foolish attempt. It was also profoundly wise. All the people of the town had worked together in the earth, and they were all bound together by the same dream of youth. The May Day picnic was also good copy. On the other side of the continent people heard that Seattle, on Puget Sound, had been denied a railroad and that the citizens were working with their own hands to build a railroad over the mountains. Through that story many of them heard of Seattle for the first time, and the name was linked with the spirit of undefeated youth. Somewhere beyond the mountains of the far West there was a little band of the undefeated, and the odds against them were great. The story was a spark to the imagination, and young men from as far away as New York headed west to join the fight.

The Northern Pacific was fighting too: a personal fight to crush Seattle and build up Tacoma. Tacoma was only thirty miles south, and Portland was only a hundred miles farther. But people going from Seattle to Portland could go only as far as Tacoma the first day. The railroad had its monopoly of steamboats on the Sound, and the steamer schedule was synchronized with its trains. When the Seattle steamer arrived in Tacoma, the Portland train had left, and passengers had to stay overnight in the company's town. When the train from Portland pulled into Tacoma, the steamer for Seattle had left, and again passengers had to spend the night in the company's town.

At the mass meeting in Yesler's Pavilion, Judge McGilvra had raised his battle cry of "Carry the war to Africa!" In 1877 he carried the war to Washington, D.C. There he worked with the Territorial Delegate, Orange Jacobs, for Government aid to Seattle's railroad, and forfeiture of their enemy's lands which were already forfeit. There was no help for Seattle's railroad because, for some reason, railroad monopolies were being publicly criticized; and Congress extended the time for the completion of the Northern Pacific Railroad into the future, making the company's grants secure.

Jacobs and McGilvra failed in their two aims, but Judge McGilvra discovered something that might embarrass the enemy. The Northern Pacific had amended its charter again, and the steel noose about the territory had contracted. In the process the upper edge of the noose had been drawn toward the south, away from Skagit Pass and the Canadian border. It now went east across the territory through Naches Pass, and an additional five million acres of public land were set aside for the Northern Pacific. The company still had its forty-eight mile checkerboard along the original noose; altogether, one half of Washington Territory was closed to settlers and reserved for the railroad, and in return the company had provided a hundred miles of track between two of its own land-speculation towns in the western part of the territory, and a hundred and fifty miles in the eastern part, with a few hundred miles of Columbia River between.

Judge McGilvra went back to the Capital for another shot at the enemy. Before the Senate and the House he argued that since the railroad had decided not to build through Skagit Pass its land along the discarded right of way was forfeited and should be thrown open to settlement.

The Steel Noose

The railroad lobby was almost all-powerful, and it fought bitterly, but Judge McGilvra had a good case and he made the most of it. And Congress could not quite explain why the railroad should have five million acres of valuable land for every pencil mark it drew across the map. So the land along the Skagit line was thrown open for settlement, and Judge McGilvra went back to Seattle with five million acres of the Northern Pacific's hide. That was part of Seattle's retaliation for having to spend the night in Tacoma every time it wanted to go somewhere else.

Since the May Day picnic two years before, Seattle citizens had worked at their railroad on and off. The result was a dozen miles of graded road pieced out by four miles of track, which the owners of the Renton Coal Company had laid from their mine. The wheat fields of the inland empire were still hundreds of miles away and, at the citizens' rate of construction, a hundred years. If the road could be completed to the mines it would reach productive traffic a dozen miles from home. But the town couldn't build a full-time railroad in its spare time. Someone would have to take charge and put it on a more practical footing. That someone was James Colman.

James Colman had come to America from Dunfermline, Scotland, and gravitated to Puget Sound, where he earned the reputation of being the best millwright and engineer in the lumber industry. He was a man of great piety and business tact and reticence. He has been described as "studiously avoiding every form of public display and showing a profound distaste for newspaper commendation or any notoriety attending his business affairs or public work." When he arrived in Seattle in 1872 he leased Yesler's mill for a San Francisco partnership, and by 1875 he was in sole control.

Soon after Colman came to Seattle the clipper bark *Windward* was driven ashore on Whidbey Island and dismasted. He bought the hulk and had her towed to Seattle. There she was beached near Yesler's mill and Colman established his residence on board. The following year he bought the mill, which later burned down and was a total loss. With some of the machinery saved from the wreck he built another mill.

When the tide flats were filled in, the hull of the *Windward* was buried intact under solid earth; and Colman built the Colman Building over the grave of the clipper ship that had been his residence.

Colman was a director of Seattle's unborn railroad, and in the spring of 1876 he took charge of the construction. Within a year fifteen miles of Seattle's railroad had been built to the coal mines and were operating at a profit. The construction included two and a half miles of trestle over the mud flats, and wharves to deep water where the largest ocean-going vessels could load at any stage of the tide. The equipment included two locomotives, twenty coal cars, a dozen flatcars and a first-class passenger car seating thirty-six, with room for ten more in the baggage-smoking compartment.

There was an official opening in March, with a free excursion. Riding to the end of the fifteen-mile line, the citizens of Seattle were very proud of their homemade railroad. Everything but the locomotive and the rails had been made on the ground; even the car wheels and the castings for the passenger car had been made under the supervision of the remarkable man from Dunfermline who later became a millionaire.

The little road was a big success. Ships and barks and big iron steamers from San Francisco loaded coal at its piers. Former skeptics declared that Seattle would have its railroad over the mountains; it had the man to do it and it would presently have the means. But the Northern Pacific was still smarting from the loss of five million acres of its hide, and Seattle must be destroyed. Citizens were defiant but somewhat grim when they heard that the Northern Pacific was rushing a rival coal line from Tacoma to Wilkeson.

Then Seattle had a romance.

It harked back to Asa Mercer's second expedition. In 1866 the young college president had sat in a New York hotel room, wondering. He had five hundred young women to transport from the East to Puget Sound, and he had the offer of a beautiful new steamship for a quarter of her value—but there was a gap he could not bridge. While he was searching for ways and means, someone had brought him a card with the name Ben Holladay. And Ben Holladay came in with two legal vultures and stripped the young man of the steamship *Continental* and charged his passengers first-class fare—and fed them on third-class parboiled beans. Ben Holladay, who was out to better his condition, added the *Continental* to his spreading steamer and stagecoach and railroad lines. And after a while his German bondholders sent a man out to California and Oregon to see what could be salvaged from the wreck.

The man they sent was Henry Villard, a journalist. Villard made a brilliant salvage job for the bondholders, and he also salvaged something for himself: Ben Holladay's dream of an empire. Villard saw that Holladay had lacked imagination; he had only fallen from one of the foothills of dizzy finance, and there were pinnacles a hundred times as high.

Henry Villard went back to New York with the dream that he had contracted. He won over the German bondholders and pyramided his successes until he had the backing of unlimited capital. The unknown journalist of one year became the financial wizard of the next, and suddenly Villard was in control of everything from Lake Superior to the Strait of Juan de Fuca. The Northern Pacific monster was one of his mouthfuls, and he was president of the unfinished road.

Henry Villard was a gentleman railroad president. He traveled in tasteful elegance and made companions of civilized minds like James Bryce, M.P., and Lord Russell of England, Baron Hertzog of Germany and Carl Schurz of New York. And he wooed Seattle instead of trying to strangle her. He predicted that the town would become a rival of San Francisco, and he proved himself a good spender by buying up the coal mines and the fleet that carried coal to California. He bought Seattle's homemade railroad for a quarter of a million dollars, and he began building a connection with the rest of America by extending the road through Stuck Junction to Tacoma.

The romantic financier was going to build the ship canal from Puget Sound to Lake Washington and do many other fine things. He was going to provide for Seattle handsomely. The inexperienced town was dazzled by the gilded cage, and she also was out to better her condition.

The great day came in September 1883. Henry Villard had driven the last spike of the transcontinental railroad at Missoula, Montana, in the presence of legislators and European titles and New York financiers and gentlemen of culture. Now he was making a triumphal journey to the Pacific through his possessions. He was coming to Seattle with his expensive retinue, and Seattle was waiting for him, dressed like a bride.

In a love note Henry Villard had promised Seattle that he would arrive in his private car. But the railroad connection was not complete, and Villard could not keep that graceful promise. More suitably, he was now going to approach Seattle from the sea. The new *Queen of the Pacific* would dock at the foot of Main Street, and the coal bunkers, which were now Villard's, were tied up with red, white and blue bunting. Over Main Street there were arches of evergreens set off by the red berry-clusters of mountain ash, and on each side, between the board sidewalk and the unpaved street, there was a continuous hedge of young evergreen trees. The buildings along the way were decorated with bunting and pennons and flags and evergreens; there were Chinese lanterns for illumination at night, and circles of gas jets on each side of the grand arch that spanned Commercial Street at Mill.

[221]

Northwest Gateway

The ceremony was to be on the campus. At the end of the enchanted street the square, cupola-topped university building stood on Denny Hill like a great white wedding cake festooned with green icing. In evergreen letters across the front were the words: WELCOME TO HENRY VILLARD AND HIS GUESTS. On the campus there was a pavilion, roofed with four thousand yards of new canvas and hung with Chinese lanterns; at the back of the pavilion was painted a rising sun with the motto: ALKI.

The *Queen of the Pacific* was due at four that afternoon. Elliott Bay was empty of traffic except under the lee of West Point, where a dozen decorated little steamers lay in wait.

The big black steamship slid into sight around the point, with the press steamer *Arrow* going out to meet her and drawing alongside. As the sea giant and the question-asking little one were passing, the rest of the mosquito fleet steamed out of the cove and fell into double column behind Villard's ship. All of them were dressed in flags and pennants and code flags: the revenue cutter *Oliver Wolcott*, the *Arrow, Messenger, Lucy* and *Lone Fisherman* were to port, and the *Favorite, Edna, Lilly, Tillie* and *Queen City* to starboard, with the odd-numbered *Augusta* bringing up the rear. The *Emma Haywood*, with visitors from Tacoma, ranged about farther off, hoping Seattle wouldn't be too good to Mr Villard.

The *Queen of the Pacific* was escorted to her pier, and from there carriages took the great man and his party to the campus. Under the four-thousand-yard canopy of the pavilion there were flattering and hopeful speeches of welcome, and a young lady read an address "replete with graceful compliments."

Villard answered charmingly, but he was under strain. He regretted that he had to treat Seattle so shamefully, among such extensive and expensive preparations, but he was under the pressure of time, and. . . .

While it was still daylight the *Queen of the Pacific* was standing out of Elliott Bay with urgent black smoke rolling from her stack. The romantic financier could not even stay to see the illumination. Seattle was left standing in the pavilion, before the painted rising sun with its motto, ALKI, meaning by-and-by.

Seattle was saved from the gilded cage although, God knows, she had been willing enough. Henry Villard's empire blew away like smoke, and the Northern Pacific went back to Seattle's enemies. And the battle went on from where it had left off, except for a shift in holds. When the Villard-Seattle romance interrupted the fight, Seattle had the beginning of its own railroad, which the company was trying to block. When the fight was resumed the company had a branch line to Seattle which Seattle was trying to make it operate. It was actually the citizens' narrow-gauge coal line with Villard's extension to Stuck Junction, and a spur to the main line.

The rails rusted for a year, with no wheel turning over them. The company's stand was that the line did not belong to it, and it would not touch anything which it did not rightfully own.

Men who had been children when Governor Stevens first promised the railroad were now in the fight. One of them was Cornelius Hanford, who was now a judge. At a meeting of the White River valley farmers who lived along the rusting "Orphan Line," he gave the judicial opinion that since the road was built on land condemned for public use and was not serving the public, the people could condemn the line and run it themselves. The farmers decided they were the public; they condemned the line by extending their fences across the tracks, and they started to tear up the rails.

The rails were the road's nervous system and crowbars under them always brought a response. The company suddenly decided that it owned the orphaned line it had been disclaiming, and it promised to give Seattle railroad service.

The service was something of a technicality. Once a day a locomotive pulling one car went to Seattle. It then returned, backing all the way to Stuck Junction near Tacoma, where it never connected with any other train. Merchants were refused freight except in carload lots, and the rates were discriminatory. Travelers from eastern points could not buy tickets to Seattle, and the name did not appear on the company's printed matter.

Seattle, however, was staying on the map and it had new champions in the fight. One of them was Daniel Hunt Gilman, who arrived in 1883, just as Villard's reign was wavering to its end. Gilman was a Penobscot, Maine, man of thirty-eight, strongly built, with a soft voice and deep-set eyes and a softly turned face of iron. He was gentle voiced and quiet because he saved all his energies for fighting. And he was a veteran of an earlier fight with a railroad. That had been in 1864, at the Battle of Roanoke

The Steel Noose

Station, when Gilman and his cavalry troop charged the Richmond and Danville railroad bridge across the Staunton River. Gilman had hit the bridge so hard that he went clear through the defending infantry, into enemy territory, alive but with a bullet through his body. He rode for a week behind the enemy's line before he escaped to his own, where he had to spend four months in a hospital.

Another man in the fight was Judge Thomas Burke, who was thirty-four when Gilman came to town. Judge Burke was a square and stubby lawyer, under medium height, with a great and well-filled cranial dome and one of the most Irish of all faces. He was working his way through law school in Michigan when his imagination was caught by a story in the newspaper. It was the May Day picnic story about the people of the village of Seattle who were trying to build a railroad over the mountains with their own hands. Burke passed his bar examinations and arrived in Seattle the following May. There he became a probate judge when he was twenty-eight, took an enthusiastic part in civic battles, and married Judge McGilvra's daughter.

Judge Burke was related by temperament and marriage to the battle cry of "Carry the war to Africa!" But when the two fighters talked it over, Daniel Gilman had the plan of attack. Here was Seattle's transportation position: She was blocked to the south by the Northern Pacific's monopoly. She had been blocked in the attempt to cut her way out east over the Cascade Mountains. To the west there was water and the railroad's steamboat monopoly, which took people to spend the night in Tacoma whenever they wanted to go somewhere else. The way to the north was still open, and the Canadian Pacific Railroad was in operation. *Seattle would cut her way out of the United States and have transcontinental service across Canada.*

Burke admitted it was the only hope, but Seattle had already learned that financing a railroad is expensive.

Gilman had thought about the financial end. He had good connections in New York, and Seattle had a reputation for vitality. Investors wouldn't be afraid of finding the town dead on their hands. If Burke could raise the money for the trip, Gilman would go to New York and see about raising the money to build the railroad.

Judge Burke raised $500, and Gilman went east and interested New York capital. Burke went to close the deal, and the new Lake Shore and Eastern Railroad started with half a million dollars of capital, which was mostly eastern.

The first division of the new railroad was to open the coal field at Issaquah and provide paying traffic while the next section was being built. It was like the plan for the first railroad, only it went much faster and more smoothly, not having to depend upon citizens working in their spare time. The road was for public service, so there were no grants of public land; but the first half million dollars was expected to build the road across the Snohomish River and after that, if things went well, there would be more capital.

Everything went very well. There was only one cloud on the horizon toward Canada, and that was Eugene Canfield, of Fairhaven, on Bellingham Bay. Canfield had a dream of building a railroad from Fairhaven to Seattle. Except for starting twenty miles short of the Canadian border, Canfield's road was the one the Lake Shore and Eastern was building; and if his had been built it would have saved Seattle the trouble. But Canfield's road was still a dream. All he had done was to secure from Congress the right to build bridges across the rivers that Seattle's road would have to bridge. Canfield maintained that the permit constituted a monopoly on crossing those rivers, and the Northern Pacific backed him up.

The Canfield cloud grew darker as the Seattle company began building its bridge over the Snohomish, and some of the cloud drifted as far as New York, where Gilman had gone to raise more money. When he called on the bankers they showed him a Canfield pamphlet with heavy legal opinions to the effect that Canfield of Fairhaven had a monopoly on crossing rivers and Seattle would have to stay on the other side.

In Seattle, Judge Burke saw the cloud, and he wondered if there wasn't some Northern Pacific smoke in it. Then he had a message which said that a judge in Tacoma had issued an injunction against the building of the Snohomish bridge. Burke had been a judge and he didn't have too much faith in writs, but this one made it awkward because there wouldn't be any more money available until the bridge was built. It was a pity that Gilman was in New York, because there was going to be a battle at the Snohomish, and Gilman had experience in fighting at railroad bridges.

The Lake Shore and Eastern trains were running as

far as Snohomish on the unbridged river, and a train was leaving in a quarter of an hour. The judge walked down to the little wooden depot on the water front at Columbia Street. The train was in the station, filling up with passengers, and in one of the seats was Canfield's lawyer, sitting primly with the brief case that held the writ. Judge Burke went on to the next car, where he found John Leary. Leary was a member of the Company; the judge told him what was up and said they must reach Snohomish City ahead of the writ. The best thing they could do was to crawl into the cab of the locomotive, which would get there ahead of the passenger cars.

The stubby little judge told the engineer, "Let her out for all she'll do, and don't stop this side of Snohomish!"

It was irregular, and there were passengers to deliver at Ballard and Issaquah and other points along the line; but Burke took the responsibility. The engineer let her out and they went rocketing north at forty miles an hour.

In the second car Canfield's lawyer sat primly with the brief case that held the writ, and he wondered why the train hadn't started. . . .

At Snohomish, Judge Burke sent the locomotive back for the cars, which had been uncoupled and left sitting in the station at Seattle. Leary got all the men he could find to work on the bridge and Burke found Sheriff Whitfield and told him how things were. The sheriff was a reasonable man and he wanted Snohomish City to have through railroad service. So he took both his deputies and disappeared in the direction of Mount Baker, looking for bandits.

The Steel Noose

When the passenger cars arrived later with Canfield's lawyer and his brief case there was a hitch, because he couldn't find anyone to serve the injunction. The lawyer pursued the sheriff and his deputies while they pursued imaginary bandits. But no one caught up with anyone else until Judge Burke sent the sheriff word that he could come home. When the injunction was served it was meaningless, because the railroad bridge which it forbade was completed.

That was the Battle of Snohomish Bridge, and Gilman, who had experience in such things, was away in New York, trying to raise more money. But the little Irish judge had won the battle in his own way. Gilman had also been successful and he came back with money to build the next division. Seattle's railroad pushed on toward the Canadian frontier and transcontinental service.

The Battle of Snohomish Bridge was the deciding battle in Seattle's fight for a railroad. It had begun with the Northern Pacific trying to strangle a village of eleven hundred people. After seventeen years the monopoly found itself fighting with a city of forty thousand that was as tough as Madame Damnable turned to stone, as good at hard pulls as the black mare, Tib, and as independent as the white stallion with a mind of its own.

The Northern Pacific bought the unfinished Lake Shore and Eastern line and gave Seattle everything she asked for in railroad service.

CHAPTER XIV

"The Chinese Must Go!"

THE *Queen of the Pacific* had an expansive name for an expansive age. No one as yet had managed to control the Pacific Ocean. But the name of the steamship suggested that her christener had ambitions, and some of the men who had traveled in the *Queen* did well for themselves up to a certain point. When Henry Villard had nailed down the Northern Pacific with a gold spike and embarked on the new steamship for a tour of his western possessions he had cut himself a pie-wedge of the United States from Lake Superior to the Columbia River and the Strait of Juan de Fuca. And he was about to better his condition when he suddenly lost out.

The *Queen* had been a new ship then, fresh from the builder's yard in Philadelphia. On February seventh, 1886, she was only four years old; but that Sunday, as she lay at the Seattle dock, the view up Main Street was not so enchanting. The wooden city sprawled over its steep hills without a sign of Christmas tree hedges or bridal arches or Chinese lanterns: the Chinese lanterns were particularly absent. The green icing of garlands was gone from the white wedding cake of the university building on Denny Hill, and they had taken down the great evergreen letters: WELCOME TO HENRY VILLARD AND HIS GUESTS.

Seattle, like many other places, was suffering from the collapse of the Villard boom, and the West was also suffering from one of the left-over materials of railroad building. That was why the Chinese lanterns were particularly absent.

The Chinese had already discovered that Americans are an inscrutable people. They had first been attracted to the Pacific Coast because California's male population was up the Sacramento, digging for gold, and someone had to do the menial work. Then the Central Pacific Railroad had to be built to meet the Union Pacific, and the need for labor was so great that shiploads of coolies had to be brought across the Pacific, often without being consulted. There was work to be done in America, and it was the destiny of Chinese coolies to do the work. After the Central Pacific, the Northern Pacific Railroad had to be built. Up in Canada there was the Canadian Pacific, and the "amazing Chinese" dangled from ropes over precipices in the Canadian Rockies, with the Frazer River going mad a few thousand feet below them. With hammers and chisels they cut the first foothold of the new railroad. When the railroads were finished they looked round to see what other work was to be done. They went to work in mines and mills and on large farms and wherever there was work to do, and they worked hard and faithfully and did not haggle about wages.

Then the Americans showed themselves to be inscrutable. They were no longer thrilled by the sight of the "wonderful Chinese" doing their work. In San Francisco, Kearney's sand lotters kicked them and said they were taking food out of American mouths.

By 1885 the same thing was being said farther north. On September fourth of that year the population of Rock Springs, Wyoming, turned on five hundred Chinese coal miners and drove all of them out of town except eleven who were killed in the process.

In the Squawk Valley, twenty miles north of Seattle, some Chinese had come to pick hops along with the Indians. The night after the Rock Springs massacre there was an Indian uprising at Squawk. Indians fired into the tents of the sleeping Chinese, killing three and wounding three more. The others escaped by throwing themselves into the river and working their way downstream, where they hid in the willows along the shore. It was an American tradition that Indians should be punished for massacring people while they were asleep; but instead of punishing the Indians the inscrutable Americans protected them, and they also protected the whites who had taken part in the massacre.

The Chinese had understood it was a peculiarity of Americans to get excited about outrages and condemn them publicly. Instead, public meetings were held all over the territory, approving the massacres and declaring "The Chinese must go," although it was the Indians and white men and not the Chinese who had broken the law.

Two thirds of the men who had built the western division of the Northern Pacific were Chinese. The railroad owned Tacoma and it had leased land to the Chinese for a Chinatown. But at a mass meeting on October third the people of Tacoma appointed a committee of fifteen to deal with the Chinese; the committee gave them thirty days to get out of town.

When the time was up, about three hundred men and a string of wagons streamed into the Chinese quarter of Tacoma and began moving the Chinese out. The Chinese knew better than to resist and they got no help from the officers of the law or the town officials; and that was not surprising because Mayor Weisbach was president of the Anti-Chinese Congress, which had decreed that they must go.

The belongings of the Chinese were loaded into wagons in the rain, along with the few who were too old or sick to walk. Then the procession started for the Lake View station on the Northern Pacific, which the Chinese had helped build. It was eight miles to the station, and as they were herded along the muddy road, under the cold November rain, the Chinese pondered the inscrutable ways of Americans who had brought them to America to work and then were angry with them because they worked.

At the Lake View station on the prairie the Chinese and their belongings were dumped on the roofless platform, where they spent the rest of the day and night in a storm of wind and rain. In the morning they were loaded onto a train for Portland, along with the corpse of a man who had died of exposure.

Next day the Chinese quarter in Old Tacoma was

burned to discourage their return; and two days later, at New Tacoma, the torch was applied to the houses and stores that the Chinese had built on land leased from the railroad. It was called "peaceable expulsion."

Seattle was still without useful railroad service, but she shared in the railroad building by-products of depression: labor agitation and anti-Chinese agitation. When the *Queen of the Pacific* lay at the ocean dock that Sunday morning Seattle had already had six uncomfortable months. But they had been without violence and without forcible or "peaceable" expulsion of Chinese, and things had finally simmered down to comparative quiet.

During the summer there had been anti-Chinese speeches and small but noisy torchlight parades. On September nineteenth the miners at Black Diamond pelted the Chinese out of camp with lumps of coal, injuring nine of them, and the next day Seattle had a public meeting of approval. It was followed by a meeting in the interests of law and order presided over by Henry Yesler. Yesler was then serving one of his terms as Mayor of Seattle although he had been the unofficial mayor ever since he built his cookhouse in 1853.

At seventy-five Yesler was still vigorous, and he was comfortable and practical. And the meeting he presided over was comfortable and practical: resolutions were passed calling for citizens to abide by the law, and promises were made to get rid of the Chinese by all lawful means.

Two days later, on September twenty-fifth, the Anti-Chinese Congress met in Seattle to advocate dispensing

with the Chinese by lawful means and others. It decreed
the banishment of all Chinese from the western half of
the territory by November fifteenth. The congress, sponsored by the Knights of Labor, was attended by public
officials, socialists, delegates from labor organizations and
from fraternal orders, anarchists and businessmen; and it
was presided over by the mayor of Tacoma.

Hatred of the Chinese made strange bedfellows—if that
was the moving force. With many, persecution of the
Chinese was a phantasy that had nothing to do with that
race. Dennis Kearney, who launched the idea in San Francisco, had begun with the cry: "Down with the rich hell
hounds!" When the police caught up with him on Nob
Hill he was urging his mob to attack the mansion of
Charlie Crocker, the railroad builder who had been in
charge of importing coolies to build the Central Pacific.
Kearney did not shout "The Chinese must go!" until he
had been discouraged from attacking those who brought
them by the shipload.

Many of the agitators who appeared in Seattle pro-
gressed in the opposite direction. The more radical ones
who came to attack the Chinese stayed to advocate shooting the bankers and businessmen and burning the records
and redistributing property and wealth. The anti-Chinese
agitation was only a grindstone for their axes. It might
well be asked, "What were businessmen doing in such
company?"

If there ever had been a Chinese threat to Washington
Territory it was over before the agitation began. The Chinese Exclusion Act had been passed in 1880; by 1885,

when the threat was discovered, there were slightly more than three thousand Chinese in the entire territory. By the end of summer many of these had gone, and the larger employers of Chinese were replacing them with white labor. Nevertheless the hunt for dead lions was pushed with a great deal of vigor and a great deal of torchlight and noise.

Those who disapproved the hunt were also active. While the Chinese in Tacoma were being served notice to leave town the law-and-order faction in Seattle met on October third, and Sheriff McGraw swore in several hundred citizens as deputies to protect the Chinese. The meeting was at Frye's Opera House on Front Street, and thereafter that faction was known as the "Opera House Party."

Around the middle of the month the Anti-Chinese Party staged the largest torchlight parade Seattle had ever seen. Three thousand marchers filled the streets, carrying banners and placards that showed American women and children in chains because of Chinese competition; there were fierce demands for their expulsion and transparently concealed threats of violence.

The marching and shouting seemed to have a therapeutic effect on the crowd. Two weeks later, when the Chinese were driven out of Tacoma, Seattle was reasonably quiet and no attempt was made to duplicate the outrage. By November fifth the town was in such good humor that the leaders of the Opera House Party and the Anti-Chinese Party staged a joint harmony meeting.

The evening started pleasantly. George Venable Smith, of the Knights of Labor, proposed Henry Yesler as chairman. Politic speeches were made by both sides; then the aging, massive Yesler called on Judge Burke.

Burke was in a position to make or break the love feast. During his rise to prominence he had been the champion of the oppressed and the idol of the workingmen. But they had been disappointed when he sided with the Opera House Party for the protection of the Chinese. All of them felt he had gone too far in his championing of the oppressed, and they were beginning to wonder if their faith in him had not been misplaced.

With the right fence-walking speech Tom Burke might have ended the meeting in a tableau of harmony, with both factions cheering him. Instead the stubby little judge made a fighting speech. He was an able orator, and his voice crashed like volleys of musketry as he blasted at the enemies of law and order:

I am an American and I appeal to Americans. Of the two methods, the lawful and unlawful, I favor the American method. He is no true American, whether native or foreign born, who will not stand for law and order. He is unworthy of American citizenship wherever he comes from if he is willing to bring disgrace and dishonor to this Republic of ours by spurning and scouting the laws which we ourselves have helped to make. . . .

Judge Burke recalled his immigrant parents and the wrongs of Ireland, and he appealed to every Irishman in the audience to protect the law that found the Irishman a serf and made him a free man. In part the appeal was aimed at acting Chief of Police Murphy, who was one of the leaders of the anti-Chinese group. Burke continued more specifically:

And yet you have seen in an American city, where a foreigner hardly able to speak the English language holds sway as mayor, a mob in defiance and contempt of law and justice pillage and destroy their business houses and dwelling places and drive them out in midwinter to perish of cold, exposure and hunger. . . .

The "foreigner hardly able to speak the English language" was Mayor Weisbach of Tacoma, who had been active in the Anti-Chinese Congress and inactive about helping the Chinese when they were being driven out of his city. Weisbach was one of the heroes of the anti-Chinese element, and as the short-necked little judge blasted at him with all his oratory there were derisive shouts and hisses. The audience split as definitely as if Judge Burke had divided it with an ax; and Governor Squire ducked out of the love feast to telegraph the Secretary of War for United States troops.

Ten companies of infantry arrived from Fort Vancouver a few days later. Seattle was quiet again after having let off steam, and the Chinese problem had been solved without illegal or violent methods. The Chinese had been discharged from all the mills and mines and factories of the county. The only ones left with jobs were a few laborers and cooks and house servants. Both factions of the late disagreement hobnobbed with the troops, who had nothing to do. After a week they were sent back to their Vancouver barracks.

"The Chinese Must Go!"

That same month fifteen of the anti-Chinese ringleaders were indicted under the Ku-Klux Act for conspiring to deprive the Chinese of their rights. The case was still in the courts that Sunday morning when the *Queen of the Pacific* lay at the ocean dock. But everyone knew the men would be acquitted. There had been no violence, the Chinese had not been deprived of their rights, and it was hard to prove the intent. It was all legalistic now. The anti-Chinese craze had died away two months before, and the city was worrying along through the Villard depression.

Seattle was uadorned and damp that early Sunday morning, and as still as the thin, lonely fringe of fir trees that stitched the somber hills to the sky.

Suddenly the fire bell crashed the damp gray silence and hammered on and on. It sounded like a job for fire chief Kellogg, who had once blown up Dexter Horton with a shell from the *Decatur*.

The fire bell went on crashing its alarm, and men were blackening the streets, empty until a minute ago. Even in the rain the big wooden city on its hills looked like something made to burn; only there wasn't any column of smoke to prove a fire. The fire bell stopped, and still there was nothing but men blackening the street like coal poured into a chute and all sliding in the same direction.

Captain Ezekial Alexander thought of calling a hack and going to see the excitement, but he had a valuable steamship to think about. The city had been attacked by Indians not so very long ago, and it looked like a firetrap. Better to stay on board and be ready to pull out into the stream if need be.

Northwest Gateway

Presently Captain Alexander knew that he had a ring-side seat. The crowds were pouring into Main Street again in solid lumps, coming straight down toward the ship: a solid mass on each side, with a thinner column between. In the background loaded wagons were turning out of the side street, through the mob, with drivers standing up to lash their horses.

The captain sent the chief officer to find out how many of the crew were on board. Between the black mobs coming down Main Street the thinner line was made up of Chinese. Some of them carried bundles and twin baskets slung from poles across their shoulders; and those looked like baggage wagons bringing up the rear.

The bewildered Chinese were herded down the street toward the ocean dock, and the sound of the mob was a dull roar, like a tide rip coming nearer. The mob was two mobs, arguing in shouts: one for driving the Chinese out, the other for letting them go. In momentary, partial lulls the hysterical jabbering of the Chinese sounded like the twittering of lost birds in a storm.

The anti-Chinese mob had the upper hand; they herded the Chinese onto the dock and started to drive them on board the *Queen of the Pacific*. At the foot of the roped-off gangway they were stopped by quartermasters and officers, and Captain Alexander bellowed, "Where're your tickets? What d'ye think this is? A free excursion steamer?"

The mob was abashed by life growing unexpectedly complex. The committee of fifteen, who had done the planning, had overlooked the cost of transportation. They were going to herd the Chinese on board the steamship, which would take them to San Francisco. They were driving them out free, and they supposed the ship would take them free. Now the captain demanded tickets. They churned about and argued until one man with a great brown beard took off his hat and revealed a perfectly bald head. The man passed his hat among his close-packed neighbors, and the crowd expanded to make room for men reaching into their pockets. Other hats were being passed, and they filled up with silver and greenbacks.

Within five minutes the collectors were at the gangway, their sweaty hats loaded with paper and silver. The purser counted the money into canvas bags, and counted out a hundred-odd steerage tickets in return. The mob cheered its purchased victory. "Get 'em on board! There's more coming. Shove 'em along!" Tickets were pushed into the hands of the Chinese as they were shoved toward the gangway. A muscular quartermaster stopped each one and Captain Alexander asked, "You want to go to San Francisco?" They all wanted to go to San Francisco. One did not even want to wait for words and tried to bolt up the gangway. The quartermaster caught him by the queue and held him while the captain asked, "You want to go to San Francisco?" "Go like hellee!" was the answer.

By the time the Chinese had been questioned and taken on board, as many more were waiting alongside, and more were being herded into the warehouse on the dock. Captain Alexander again demanded tickets, but this time the rioters had trouble raising funds. They were still churning about and arguing when a sweating deputy sheriff strug-

[241]

gled out of the mob and presented Captain Alexander with a paper. It was a writ which charged that Chinese were being held illegally on board his vessel. The *Queen of the Pacific* was enjoined from sailing, and the captain was required to produce the Chinese in court at eight o'clock the following morning. It was then one o'clock on Sunday afternoon; the sailing hour of the *Queen* had already passed, and the weather threatened rain.

The Anti-Chinese Party had taken the city by surprise. They had waited until the Opera House Party thought the excitement was over and the danger passed; then, on Saturday night, they had made their final plans and appointed a committee of fifteen, at the Bijou Theater. The theater was a burlesque house in the district between Yesler Way and Jackson Street known as the "Lava Beds." And though concealment was novel to the place, the secret was strictly kept.

At daybreak on Sunday morning the committee of fifteen got to work, with acting Chief of Police Murphy at the head and a growing mob at their heels. They went from door to door in Chinatown, and while committee-men questioned the Chinese about cubic feet of air and sanitary ordinances the mob carried out their belongings. Sheriff McGraw and a posse tried to interfere, but while they were at one house the rioters started work on another. Territorial Governor Watson Squire lived in town, and he wrote a proclamation that was read to the rioters; but the rioters only jeered in defiance and went on evicting the Chinese.

After that they rang the fire bell for help. The eighty

Chinese riot, 1886.

Photograph by L. D. Lindsley

Ruins after the big fire of June 6, 1889.

A new city rises on the ashes of the old.

"The Chinese Must Go!"

Home Guards, under Captain George Kinnear, mobilized at the Columbus Street engine house; the Seattle Rifles turned out, under Captain Green; and Captain Haines's Company D, of the local militia, gathered at their armory in the Kenyon block. At noon printed copies of the Governor's proclamation were handed out. The Home Guards marched about town and were jeered, and marched back to their engine house. All the while the removal of the Chinese went on until all of them and their possessions were on the ocean dock or aboard the *Queen*. The Anti-Chinese Party had got them that far, and the forces of law and order had enjoined the ship from sailing.

Both parties settled down to wait for morning. The Home Guards and local militia guarded public buildings and patrolled streets, and Governor Squire telegraphed the Secretary of War for troops. The Anti-Chinese Party was reinforced by agitators from other towns; they moved the Chinese from the ocean dock to the adjoining warehouse and isolated the building and the steamship and the dock with massed thousands. In the interests of neutrality an icy February rain set in with the evening and fell alike on the Chinese-protecting and the anti-Chinese. But there were more of the rioters to get wet, and the mass outside the warehouse and dock thinned under hours of ordeal by water.

Toward morning the committee of fifteen worked a stratagem. They woke sixty of the Chinese and, under cover of darkness and deluging rain, marched them to the Northern Pacific Railroad station. Seattle's daily train of one car left for Tacoma at four o'clock in the morning; later

[243]

there was a train south. It was a means of getting some of the Chinese out of town before they had their day in court. A handful of men were left at the warehouse to guard the sleeping Chinese, and the mob accompanied the sixty to the railroad station. But some of the militia were on guard at the station and they had got wind of the move and had sent the train out ahead of time.

The committee of fifteen and the mob took their prisoners back to the warehouse at the ocean dock. There they found that Home Guards had arrested their guards and were now guarding the Chinese. They were armed with new breech-loading rifles, and the mob did not dispute with them. To some extent the Home Guards were doing their work for them. They turned over the remaining Chinese and went home to bed.

The ornate wooden courthouse was on Third Avenue between Jefferson Street and Yesler Way, at the edge of the "Lava Beds." It was only four blocks from the ocean dock. At eight o'clock on Monday morning Sheriff Mc-Graw and the Home Guards and the militia companies brought Captain Alexander and the Chinese from the *Queen* into court. For four blocks they marched between the thickening masses of the Anti-Chinese Party, through a storm of howls and jeers; and afterward the courthouse was surrounded by a mob of several thousand.

In the courtroom Judge Roger Green addressed the Chinese through an interpreter. He had been informed, he said, that they had been kept on board the *Queen of the Pacific* against their will. They had been brought there so the court could determine if that was true. The sentiment of the community was in favor of their leaving, but if they wished to stay they would receive all the protection the legal authorities could give them. Did they want to stay or go?

The Chinese heard the voices of the thousands who were being kept back by the armed guards at the doors, and all but sixteen of the hundred said they wanted to go. They were then marched back to the ocean dock with armed guards.

The rioters followed but did not interfere, and all but the sixteen were sent back on board the *Queen*. There were still about two hundred and fifty in the warehouse, guarded by the Seattle Rifles and the University Cadets. The Chinese in the warehouse were now given the same choice as those who had gone to court. The Opera House Party had raised money for their fares to San Francisco, but those who wished to stay would be protected if possible. The battle of the anti-Chinese group was won—if there ever had been occasion for battling. Both parties were in favor of the Chinese going; both had marched them about town for one reason and another; both had guarded them in the warehouse; and both had dug into their pockets to pay the one-way fares.

All but a handful of the Chinese voted to go to San Francisco. They knew it was no paradise, but it had its points. San Francisco was like the world: it let in any who wanted to come; and though it kicked and beat them while they were there, it let them stay as long as they could stand it.

Seattle's tension eased with every Chinese who shuffled up the gangplank.

Nearly two hundred went on board; then the gangplank was drawn in smartly and dock hands were casting off the hawsers. The forces of law and order protested, but big Captain Alexander had his laws and orders.

"A hundred and ninety-six!" he shouted from the deck above. "That's all the steerage passengers the law allows me! Sorry!"

A few minutes later the *Queen of the Pacific* was swinging out into the bay. She was a fine big steamship, and if she had been bigger she would have saved Seattle a great deal of trouble.

Captain Alexander was not the only one who was sorry. There was a mob in the street outside the dock and there were over a hundred Chinese on the dock, where they couldn't be kept indefinitely. The next steamer for San Francisco was the *George W. Elder*—universally known as the *George W. Roller* for her gyrations at sea—and the *Roller* would not sail until Saturday.

Sheriff McGraw and Captain Kinnear of the Home Guards decided grimly on the only course they could think of. They would take the Chinese back to Chinatown and guard them till the *Roller* came in. In the shelter of the dock, which they controlled, the companies loaded their weapons and formed the Chinese in a column with their belongings. The Home Guards took their place in front, the University Cadets in the rear; and the sheriff led the grim parade up Main Street, past shouting anti-Chinese partisans.

"The Chinese Must Go!"

Until then the temper of the mob had been reasonably good natured. There had been a great deal of noise but no physical violence, and none of the Chinese had been hurt while the rioters had them in their power. They preferred to have the Chinese go without getting hurt—but they had to go. The mob had got them all out of Chinatown and as far as the ocean dock, where they had one departing foot in the sea. They had thought their battle was won. Now they saw the Home Guards and the Cadets marching the Chinese back toward Chinatown. Ahead of the marching column the street was blackening with the mob, and its dull roar gave off higher and more deadly overtones.

With the Sheriff in the lead the Home Guards marched as far as the intersection of Commercial Street. There Main Street was blocked solidly, and another phalanx closed in from the north, trying to force the marchers down Commercial Street toward the depot. The Sheriff tried to get a hearing, but his voice was battered down by hoots and yells. The rioters would have gone home if they could have been made to understand that the fares of nearly all the Chinese had been paid and they were only waiting for the next steamer south; but they were in no mood to listen. The only one who could make himself heard was one of the leaders of the mob who was a stranger to the Home Guards. He was a young giant with a magnificent physique and a fair, curly beard. He also had a powerful voice and he was mad with excitement, cursing the Chinese and their guards and urging the mob to disarm them. Some of the rioters charged between the Home Guards and the Chinese, turning them back; but there they were met by the

[247]

protecting rifles of the University Cadets, and they could only mill around helplessly.

Urged on and led by the furious young giant some of the rioters closed in on the Home Guards and tried to disarm them while the guards tried to beat them off with the butts of their rifles. Through the struggle and shouting the voice of the big stranger was audible: *"Take their rifles; they're afraid to shoot!"* He had caught the barrel of Private Carr's weapon and was trying to wrench it away from him. Carr was a big man, but he was almost lifted off his feet in the struggle. *"They're afraid to shoot."*

Someone standing near the pair fired from the hip. Other rifles crashed and a shotgun roared, the mob recoiled and the powder smoke drifted away, and four men lay twisting in the muddy street. All the Chinese were also down, but unwounded, having thrown themselves flat on the ground.

The only man badly wounded was the young giant with the fair curly beard and the magnificent physique. He had been shot through the abdomen at close range and blood was pouring out of him in a steady stream. Even then his vitality was appalling. He raged on from where he had left off, cursing the Chinese and their protectors and calling on the mob to charge again and disarm the guards. He offered to lead them himself, and time after time he half rose and fell back in the mud. Never at any time did he pay any attention to his wound or think about himself.

The Home Guards looked at him, past their leveled rifles and shotguns, and they were apalled by the mystery of the magnificent human engine that had come to die in the mud at their feet. They were also apprehensive, because the broken giant was rallying the mob with his tremendous voice. The rioters had recoiled from the firing, but now they were pushing forward a little, shouting for vengeance and cursing members of the Home Guards by name: Private Carr, who had knocked down one of the attackers with his rifle butt, Judge Hanford and David Webster and the Methodist Minister, Banks. But most of their hatred was for stubby little Judge Burke, holding a shotgun with both hammers cocked. Burke had not fired, but he had wounded them all, and wounded them worst by siding with their enemies. He received all the hatred of a champion who betrays the cause.

The dying giant was still rallying the mob when the Seattle Rifles came up from the dock on the run. They formed a line beside the prostrate Chinese and faced the mob while they loaded with ball cartridges. Company D of the militia had heard the shooting from the courthouse, and now they pushed their way through the crowds and completed the hollow square about the Chinese, who had been forgotten by the rioters.

Two express wagons came for the wounded men, and the dying giant was quiet at last as he was lifted from his pool of blood in the muddy street. As the wagon rattled away toward the hospital the Home Guards saw his heroic body relaxed and shaking flabbily with the jolting of the vehicle. His presence and his passion and his death were all something of a mystery. None of them had ever seen him until he was in the act of trying to disarm them, and his anti-Chinese passion had consumed him before their eyes.

The next day, when he was dead, they learned that his name was Charles Stewart and that he had arrived in Seattle a few hours before he was shot. He had come from Mason County, a hundred miles away, to see the excitement in Seattle. It was not his fight and it was not even his country, because he was a Canadian citizen.

The mob held the Home Guards and the militia companies nearly an hour, threatening the men they blamed for the shooting and promising to lynch Judge Burke. Then they allowed them to go on. The Chinese had been forgotten in new hates, and they lived in Chinatown, unmolested, until the *George W. Roller* took most of them away.

The Home Guards returned from Chinatown to the courthouse through a mob of three thousand that ringed the building, and they were relieved to get through. But presently they found that the law-and-order faction did not have a monopoly on law. A constable arrived from the police court with a warrant for the arrest of five of the guardsmen. The five were Private Carr, Judge Burke, the Reverend Banks, David Webster and Frank Hanford, although his brother, Cornelius, was the one intended. The five were charged with shooting with the intent to kill.

The police building was beyond the maelstrom of the mob, but the constable was strong on law and order. He insisted that the five must go with him through the mob that was clamoring for their punishment and offering to lynch Judge Burke. The Home Guards were the backbone of law and order, but they were also armed, and they opposed the idea of having five of their number turned outdoors on such a wolfish day. And four of the five objected to going. The fifth was Thomas Burke, who was in danger of being pulled to pieces, but the stocky little judge was a resolute man. He submitted to arrest and said, "I have taken my stand in support of the law and I am therefore under greater obligation."

The arresting constable was determined to do a thorough job. He had one prisoner, but his warrant called for five. He found Judge Green, who was in conference with the Governor, and asked his services to secure the other four.

Judge Green was the Chief Justice of the Supreme Court of the territory, pledged to law and order. But he could hear the mob outside, and he reacted much as the Home Guards had done. He said, "These men are officers of my court, on duty here. I shall not allow them to be arrested in my presence." The constable departed for the police building for further instructions, and Judge Green returned to grooming the *deus ex machina* of Seattle's fierce drama.

The *deus ex machina* was the genial Territorial Governor Watson Squire. Squire had been the foremost munition merchant of his day. He had modernized the material of the armies of Denmark, Sweden, France, Spain, Egypt, Mexico, Colombia, Argentine and many other countries. He had put them all on a modern footing, and he had been honored for his services by the chamber of deputies at Versailles. Squire had made large investments in Seattle before he ever saw the place; when he retired from business in broken health he settled there, and President Arthur appointed him Governor.

When the arresting constable had appeared with his warrant Governor Squire was looking to Judge Green for advice. When the constable had been sent away Green said, "He'll be back in half an hour. We must act quickly. We can control the situation if you declare martial law; it can't be controlled otherwise."

History records: "Thereupon the governor, suddenly recovering from the painful perplexity into which the deplorable situation, his deep sense of personal supreme responsibility and the imperative necessity of instant decision had plunged him, said: *'We'll proclaim martial law!'*"

Judge Green immediately seated himself and wrote the proclamation, which the Governor signed.

The ink was still wet on the document when the arresting constable returned with his warrant. Judge Green read the proclamation to the constable in the presence of the Governor and the Home Guards. Then he read it from the courthouse porch to the crowds in the street.

Territorial Governor Squire did not have the right to proclaim or administer martial law, but he acted in good faith and martial law was a success. The Home Guards and the militia companies guarded the city for three days, without sleep, and then the United States troops arrived by steamer from the Columbia.

The troops stayed several months while the city quieted down, but the citizens of Seattle had handled the crisis and they had nothing to be ashamed of. At great inconvenience and risk of life they had protected the Chinese, whom they did not want, and had preserved law and order, even at the expense of straining the law somewhat.

"The Chinese Must Go!"

The final contest between the Anti-Chinese Party and the Opera House Party was fought by ballot at the general election in November. Under the name of the "People's Party" the anti-Chinese captured every office in the county. But the Chinese were gone; nothing alarming happened; and nothing came of the scheme to shoot the millionaires and burn the records and redistribute property and wealth.

CHAPTER XV

The Phoenix

THE CITY began with a single wooden cell implanted on the shore of Elliott Bay. In forty years the cells multiplied into a city and it was time to start all over. The multiplying cells had blocked out something that resembled a city, but it was only a wooden model, and it was not a very good model. It had grown without intelligent plan, and much of it had merely happened. Property owners were in possesion of ramshackle wooden buildings and shoddy wooden blocks that they would not think of erecting if they had it to do over, but they could not bring themselves to tear down those buildings because they brought in good rent. By 1889 a few men had started the inevitable replacement with brick, but most of the town was wood, with wood or sawdust underfoot.

There had been no rain in the last half of May, and none the first week of June. The weather was clear and warm, and wooden Seattle was tinder dry. The town was full of firetraps, and one of the likeliest was the building on Front and Madison owned by Mrs Pontius. It was a flimsy

The Phoenix

wooden affair with three dwelling floors. In the basement
Mr McGough had a paint store with the usual turpentine
and oils. The floor was littered with wood shavings, and in
the middle of the floor there was a lighted stove where a
handy man was boiling glue. The glue boiled over and
caught fire on the stove and dripped among the shavings.
The handy man threw a bucket of water at the flaming
mass and washed it over to some open turpentine, and the
building went up like a torch.

The fire bell clanged and Engine Company One galloped down the dry planked street to put out the fire.
They laid hoses from the nearest hydrant and played two
feeble streams on the cornices of the burning building.
Someone in the crowd said that anyone drinking beer
could do as well. The fire bell kept on clanging, and Engine Company Two galloped up with the polished steam
fire engine that was the pride of the town. The firemen
laid a hose to the bay and began pumping salt water. The
streams from the hydrant dwindled and the fire grew.
There was no longer any hope of saving Mrs Pontius's
building. Then the block was given up. Volunteers began
carrying goods from stores and furniture from houses into
the dry planked street, where sparks and firebrands show-
ered over them. Across the street a bucket brigade was
wetting down the roofs of low wooden buildings. Sparks
and embers fell, but the flames of the burning block arched
high above them, toward Frye's Opera House. Luckily, it
was of brick. Then spectators looking up saw a hand of
flame rise from the mansard roof and wave to the fire
demons over the Denny block.

Northwest Gateway

"The Opera House is on fire!" Not even the great brick building was sacred.

The bucket brigade was gone from the low roofs across the street from the roaring Denny block. The wooden shacks smoked and burst into flame. Volunteer firemen dragged their hoses between the two fires and turned dying streams of water on the Opera House. The streams stopped as the hoses melted, and the firemen retreated with their engines around to Second Street, some of the men with their clothes beginning to burn.

Seattle was in for a big fire. The city was like matchwood, the water was failing and the fire chief was out of town. His assistant had no ideas about handling such a fire. The practical young mayor, Robert Moran, took personal charge of his city.

Mayor Moran organized the crowds into work parties: some of them to carry goods out of threatened buildings, others to get them out of danger. They formed into long chains that reached to the water front or up the unthreatened hill. Small and more valuable objects were passed from hand to hand of the human conveyor belt, and they went up over the hill or down to the wharves in a steady stream. Another heavier stream of goods went to the water front in express wagons and drays.

The fire had started at the center of town, and in less than an hour and a half four solid blocks were a roaring furnace that rained fire down on the surrounding blocks. Even boards were carried up in the blast of heat, and they fell burning on furniture and goods in the street and set them afire. A pall of smoke hung over the city with a doomsday air; the fire bell clanged on and on as if the ringer supposed it was something that would help put out the fire, and the bells of the Episcopal and Catholic churches tolled steadily; there was the steady rumble of drays on planked streets and the hurricane roar of the fire. Then heavy explosions blasted through the other sounds of doom.

Mayor Moran had taken charge of the fire fighters, and they were dynamiting the wooden Colman Block. Beyond it stood the great brick San Francisco Building, with its iron shutters closed and barred. If it could be saved it would block the spread of the fire to the south. The blasts of dynamite shattered the wooden buildings into a kindling pile. Firebrands rained down and the pile roared as the fire spread south. The city jarred with the shock of other buildings being blown up, and the San Francisco Store stood in a pall of smoke with the flames beating against its side. A few men stood on the roof with a hose, waiting for the water to come on; but the pressure had died and no water came and the firemen went away. The building stood for a while, unfazed. Then the iron shutters jarred as the heat expanded and opened them; smoke rolled out of the windows, and the San Francisco Store became a part of the fire.

Across Commercial Street a human conveyor chain was passing goods that came from the streets above and went away to the wharf. The chain parted and opened a gap for a fire company that raced from the railroad station to the fire. The company of forty was from out of town, and on their new, four-wheeled hose wagon was painted: TACOMA FIRE DEPARTMENT.

Seattle cheered through explosions of dynamite and the distant crash of falling walls; and most of the bitterness of the Seattle-Tacoma feud went up in the smoke of the burning city.

The wharves were considered safe because the wind was blowing the fire the other way; but the wind changed or the fire made wind currents of its own. After a while the human conveyor chains dwindled and disappeared. The last few drays came through the smoke like shadows in a black rain of cinders, with a sunrise of fire in the gloom behind them. Sweating, black-faced draymen said the whole goddam town was burning up.

About that time it occurred to two captains that the wharves might also go. The *Ancon* and the *Mexico* were lying beside piles of goods that had seemed safe a few minutes before. Now nothing seemed safe but Elliott Bay. Captain Wallace of the *Ancon* began to load his ship with valuables passed down by hand from the burning city above. And the winches of the *Mexico* rumbled as she started loading a general cargo that had been the stocks of stores.

The *Ancon* took everything on her pier and pulled out into the bay. The *Mexico* loaded cargo until the roof of the warehouse beside her began to smoke, and then she backed out to safety.

From the bay they watched the water front burn. The fire had come down to the sea near University Avenue and from there it was roaring south, under piling and over warehouses and wharves. The Commercial Mills were

The Phoenix

blazing ruins in the wake of the fire. Wooden warehouses were smoking and flashing up into flame, and piling under the piers roared like a furnace. Even the street ashore was burning as fire ran under the planking and came up through the cracks like yellow grass. A corrugated iron warehouse blushed red and then went white. The iron sheeting dropped away like thin melting ice, and the building joined the great storm of fire that was driving south. At the foot of Yesler Way, in the path of the storm, shacks in the rear of Yesler's wharf convulsed and fell apart. The roar of dynamite blasted through the crackling roar of the burning city and water front. Black figures of men swarmed in and pulled at the wreckage of shacks. But they shrank back from the breath of the fire storm and dwindled south. The wooden wreckage blazed; warehouses smoked; Moran's machine shop caught fire, and Yesler's mill and wharf burned fiercely under the pall of smoke that hid the city.

In the wooden county courthouse at Third Avenue and Jackson Street a jury of twelve men and thirty murder witnesses underwent ordeal by fire. Judge Cornelius Hanford was presiding, and Hanford was a man who kept his form. As a little boy he had gone back to close the cabin door while his family was fleeing to the blockhouse. Now with the city burning and the fire roaring up the hill toward the wooden courthouse he sat, black-robed and correct, and presided with dignity.

The trial was an important one. A man named Evans had been indicted for a Seattle murder after he had returned to Ireland, and when he heard of the indictment he rushed back to meet the issue. Between them the prosecu-

tion and the defense had thirty witnesses. Cross-exam-
ination was lively, with Judge Hanford overruling or
sustaining objections. It was an interesting trial, but not interesting enough to hold the jury's attention. Outside a pall
of smoke hung over the city, with the orange light of fire
in its heart. Bells were tolling, and the courthouse jarred
with dynamite explosions and the crash of falling brick
walls. Merchants on the jury sweated in the growing heat
and wondered how their places of business were making
out. To judge from the sights and sounds everything was
burning or being blown up, and the old wooden building
where they fidgeted would be among the next to go.

Judge Hanford glanced from the inattentive jury to the
window. Diagonally across Third Avenue, a hundred feet
away, he saw the ugly wooden Trinity Church with its tall
bell tower clear cut against the gloom of smoke that was
growing livid with a hurricane glare. While he looked,
flames raced up the tower and waved for the fire to come
on. . . .

"Court is adjourned," Judge Hanford said. "Those who
can, please stay and help save the courthouse."

When the home-going stampede was over only four
young men were left for the new kind of court battle. One
of them found buckets, which he filled with water, and
another brought a ladder. The first need seemed to be for
wetting down the courthouse roof, which was already beginning to smoke. If the building went the wooden county
auditor's office would go with all the real-estate records of
the county and the murder trial defendant, who had been
returned to the basement jail.

The Phoenix

They put the ladder up against the side of the court-house, but it was too short to reach the overhanging eaves. A young man named Booth said, "Hold it straight up, near the eaves, and I can make it." The judge and a juror and a witness or two held the ladder upright while Booth scrambled to the top and pulled himself up on the smoking roof. The next need was water. A flag pole went up against the side of the building, with a grimy flag in the smoke. The judge and his assistants tied buckets to the flag halyards and hoisted them up to Booth, who dashed water on the smoking roof. Then he sent the buckets down to be filled again. Each time the buckets went up on the halyard the flag was automatically lowered to half-mast. Each time the buckets came down the flag rose to the top of the pole again.

The judge and his small cloud of witnesses were not alone in trying to keep the fire from crossing Third Avenue. Trinity Church and the rectory were flaming, but the house directly across from the courthouse had not started to burn. Volunteer firemen swarmed around it and tore it down and dragged the wreckage away. To the south, at Third and Yesler Way, the fire was kept back by the big fruit trees in Gardner's yard. There were apple and pear and cherry trees, with the cherries already ripe. Leaves shriveled on the trees to the west, but the trees did not burn. The Gardners' house was safe, and so were the hams and bacon that Mr Gardner had carted home from his burning meat market. The things not safe were the kegs of lard, which melted in the heat and ran over neighbors' goods piled under the trees. The Gardner girls had a bad

moment when they saw the Langshan chickens run under
the house with their tail feathers burned off. And one of
them had a worse moment when she remembered that all
her school dresses were at the laundry, which had burned.
Her sister consoled her with the news that the Central
School had also burned, and so had the Old South School.

The eastward spread of the fire was checked at Yesler
Way and Third by the trees in the Gardners' yard. A
bucket brigade kept the roof of the Catholic Church
doused and saved that building. And Yesler's mansion, at
Second Avenue and James, held out against the fire with its
roofs gaudily covered with blankets and carpets, which
amateur fire fighters wet down as fast as they dried. On
the east side of Second Avenue, at Columbia, the brick
Boston Block was being held against the fire by volunteers.
Volunteer bucket brigades extended from the street en-
trances to the second and fourth floors, and volunteers
with wet mops wiped out sparks and beat out the flames as
the window casings caught. The building was on fire re-
peatedly, but volunteers hung on in the smoking building
and blocked the fire from the residence quarter up the
street.

Up on Third, at Jackson Street, the judge and his handful of jurors and witnesses went on dousing the courthouse, which steamed in the heat of the burning church
and rectory. And the flag continued its journeying: to
half-mast as the buckets went up, and to the top of the pole
as the buckets came down. Finally the flag went up to the
top of the pole and stayed, grimy and riddled with sparks,

but blowing triumphantly in the smoke from the dying fire across the street.

Elliott Bay stopped the fire to the west. And its spread to the north, through the warehouses and piers, was stopped by a water lot at the foot of University Avenue. On the west side of Front Street the fire on land was blocked by a building foundation, and firemen made a stand to block it altogether. Shanties were torn down and dumped over the hill into the bay; burning sidewalks and street planking were torn up and thrown after them. Men with buckets on ropes worked on the Lake Shore and Eastern trestle, pulling up water from the bay and pouring it over the ties. And a bucket brigade of two hundred passed up water from the bay to Front Street. On the east side of the street another brigade brought water from Arthur Denny's house and disputed a little wooden building with the fire. Afterward those who should have known said it had caught fire at least fifty times, but at the end of the fight it was still standing, wet and charred.

To the south there was no stopping it. It roared across Yesler Way in a column that reached from Second Avenue to the warehouses and piers and flashed over the sawdust flats with their warehouses and mills, rooming houses and bawdy houses, cheap restaurants and saloons. The fire rushed down on them so fast that the citizens had only time to get out with their lives and what they had on. Even then it was close. Women fainted in the blast of heat or went into convulsions, and they had to be carried or dragged to safety. A boy yelled from the second-story window of a rooming house that had begun to burn. If he had a family or friends they had forgotten him; and the routed citizens of the sawdust flats streamed by the burning house: shabby businessmen, prostitutes in negligee, bartenders with black cash boxes under their arms and dirty white aprons whipping about their knees; dope fiends and procurers and twisted attempts at human shapes that were obviously mistakes. The boy yelled until a passing mill hand ran up the burning stairs and carried him down with the clothes of both on fire.

By evening the fire was under control, but the wharves and the business district and the sawdust flats were a thundering furnace that covered sixty blocks. The residence streets of the fortunate and respectable had been saved, but the shacks and brothels and rooming houses were gone.

That night on the bay anchored ships and barks and steamers stood out in the red glare of the city, sharper cut than vessels seen by day, with the tremendous darkness behind them. On the other side of the fire the homeless drifted aimlessly through the streets. The families of landlords saw their tenants for the first time, and a petty thief forgot his manners in the respectable part of town: he snatched a lady's purse and was caught by the crowd, but two of the special police saved him from being lynched.

Some of the homeless wandered all night; some of them drifted back to the edge of the fire to see if anything valuable could be picked up. Others were overtaken by exhaustion and they lay down in vacant lots and in fields at the edge of the woods: gamblers and cripples and prostitutes and the children of the poor. Exiles in a world of trees and ferns and sweet-smelling grass, they huddled together and slept through the warm June night under the fixed and wandering stars.

Seattle the city found she had friends. Her old rival Tacoma had been the first to respond with a company of fire fighters. Other companies with hose carts came down the Sound from Olympia and up from Port Townsend and Snohomish. At two-thirty in the morning Portland's steam fire engine, "Multnomah," came up by train with a full crew. At four-thirty the steamer *Potter,* from Victoria, plowed into the bay and docked at the unburned Canadian Pacific pier. She had been chartered by private subscription and she immediately put ashore a Canadian fire engine manned by the chief of Victoria's fire department and a company of twenty-two. Fire still threatened the docks, and the company went to work where it landed.

Half an hour later the stern-wheeler *Quickstep* came in loaded deep with provisions, which were a gift from Tacoma. Later in the morning she was followed by Captain Brown's *Clara Brown,* also from Tacoma, with another load of provisions. After the *Clara Brown* came the revenue cutter *Wolcott* with twenty tons of food and blankets from Port Townsend. Early in the afternoon a special train arrived from Tacoma, bringing the city's third contribution of food for the day as well as the Tacoma relief committee with a staff that included twenty cooks and ten dishwashers. They also brought tents and tables, cookstoves and silverware, a thousand blankets and the best quality of linen. While Seattle was without stores and restaurants Tacoma stayed and served three thousand free meals a day in the big tent at Third and University; she also put up tents with beds for the homeless. And on the evening of the first day the steamer *Quickstep* returned from Tacoma with yet another load of provisions.

Relief contributions came from all over the west. San Francisco sent ten thousand dollars and Virginia City, Nevada, sent four thousand. But Tacoma gave the most in money value and her contribution had the personal touch of devoted men and women. It also marked the end of a bitter rivalry that had lasted seventeen years. At the beginning the railroad had predicted that Seattle would be ruined and her population would move to Tacoma. When Seattle was in ruins Tacoma people moved in quietly and helped keep the city alive.

Tacoma's contributions were great and varied, and one of the most charming was that of Captain Brown of the stern-wheel steamer *Clara Brown*. After Captain Brown was no longer needed on the mercy run between Tacoma and Seattle he made a tour of Puget Sound at his own expense. He visited every town and village that had a dock and raised contributions for Seattle's destitute. When that field had been thoroughly worked the steamboat man had another thought. He ran an excursion for Tacoma people who wanted to see the ruins of Seattle, and he turned the proceeds over to the relief committee.

Seattle did not intend to be in ruins long. On the morning of June seventh the business district was still burning, with fire-fighting companies from British Columbia to Portland, Oregon, keeping the fire in bounds. But the big First Regiment armory was standing, and six hundred businessmen without businesses met to plan for the future. One of the items that came up had an irony of its own. Seattle had raised five thousand dollars for the sufferers of the Johnstown flood, and before the money could be forwarded Seattle burned up because of a drought. Mayor Moran asked the wishes of the meeting: should the fund be kept for Seattle's own emergency or should it be sent on?

The six hundred voted unanimously to send it on.

While the city and the merchants' enthusiasm were still hot the meeting voted to widen the streets and improve the grades and take out the worst jogs. The business district was to be rebuilt entirely of fireproof materials. And remembering how they had got used to firetraps in the past —and clung to them—the merchants voted against even temporary wooden buildings. When the ruins were cool enough to handle and the rubbish cleared away, the business district blossomed with streets of lily-white tents pitched on the ground of charcoal black. Familiar names appeared on signs, and business was carried on under canvas while work got started on modern buildings of brick and stone.

Most of what was lost was better gone, and much of what was left was good. Up at Third Avenue and Yesler Way the Gardner girls were very proud of the big orchard trees that had saved their house and kept the fire from spreading east. But presently the landlord's workmen arrived with axes and cut down the big cherry trees still loaded with ripe cherries and the big apple trees with little green apples forming. They cut down the whole orchard and burned the trees, and they filled the sad vacancy with tents. There was a housing shortage in Seattle; rooms were renting for fifty dollars a month, and the demand for tents was strong.

From the beginning Seattle seemed to have a genius for major excitement with minor personal injury. The village had fought a noisy and spectacular battle with the Indians at the cost of two lives; and the furious anti-Chinese riots had taken only one. The Seattle fire was the most spectacular of all, with sixty city blocks burned to the accompaniment of exploding dynamite and falling walls, and reckless fire fighting by volunteers. And no one is known to have been killed or severely hurt.

It was a thoroughly fortunate fire that released the city from its wooden cradle. And there was drawing power in the rapid and spirited building of a modern city out of the ashes of the old. While the city was still rebuilding new residents arrived at the rate of a thousand a month. When the glue boiled over on June sixth, 1889, Seattle had a population of twenty thousand. A year later, with building still in full swing, another census showed a population of forty-three thousand. That same year, the Northern Pacific settled its differences with Seattle.

Overnight the great fire had changed a wooden town into a city of brick and stone, and full-fledged railway service followed on its heels. Good fortune did not stop even there. Jim Hill's Great Northern Railroad was building through a northern pass, headed for Bellingham. Suddenly the Empire Builder changed his mind. Seattle would be the link in his transcontinental-transpacific dream. Hill headed his tracks south and hired Judge Burke to usher a second railroad into its surprised western terminus. He also planned a freight terminal at Smith's Cove and the largest freight-and-passenger ships in the world "to extend the Great Northern to Yokohama and Hong Kong." And presently the Nippon Yusen Kaisya steamship line made Seattle its eastern terminus. The railroad battle was won twice over and the city began realizing its old dream of the caravans of Asia streaming through its gates.

The Great Northern Railroad entered Seattle in 1893, and in that year of fulfillment Seattle went broke. The panic of 1893 and the following years of depression staggered the nation, but Puget Sound lacked resistance because of its swift, adolescent growth, and Puget Sound was hardest hit. In Seattle, men who thought they knew about storms and how to weather them went over like straw men. And when they picked themselves up they were empty handed. The enterprises they had started in the 'fifties were being carried away by men who had come in the 'eighties to turn the crown into the pound. The ones who survived were those who had been tough minded and saved their money. Those who had nothing to win or lose lived in a shacktown at the edge of Seattle's bluffs and, like the Indians before them, they kept from starving by digging clams.

CHAPTER XVI

Gateway to Gold

THE SENTIMENT IS THIS: you live only once at most, and if you are poor, only part of once. If you are comfortably fixed there is still inefficiency and loss, and this life is never wholly satisfactory. You live in the sometimes dull house, in the dull street, reconciled and sometimes compensated, and yet—part of you still waits for something great and splendid to happen. Part of you still listens for the blare of the master calliope and the roll of chariots that are not gilded but gold. Part of you still waits for some spark to fall and ignite this sodden life.

In the depression years, with the mighty fallen or gone away, Seattle was the dull house on the dull street. The house and the street had grown tremendously—so had the dissatisfaction with life. Those who had something were afraid of losing it, and those who had nothing were afraid of having even less; and great and splendid things were the impossible dreams of youth.

On July fifteenth, 1897, people in thousands of depressed towns heard the unexpected blare of the master calliope and the roll of golden chariots. The steamship *Excelsior* had reached San Francisco with prospectors from the Yukon; among them they had a fortune in gold from the new Golconda on Klondike Creek. A blacksmith had brought back $115,000; a fruit grower had $130,000, and he was offered $2,000,000 for his claim; a Y.M.C.A. secretary had cleaned up $85,000 in two months; another man had brought $96,000.

Two days afterward there was even greater news from Seattle. The steamer *Portland* had arrived with a ton and a half of gold, and she was racing back for more. Her prospectors had only a sample of the incredibly rich ore of the Klondike. A servant girl had cleaned up $50,000 in one week; a man had panned $24,000 on Bonanza Creek in one day; $800 in gold had been washed out of one pan of gravel; a man from Michigan had taken out $100,000 in the first half of the summer and then sold half his claim for $1,300,000. The placer gold of the Klondike was not the usual difficult dust; it was coarse gold and nuggets, easily picked up. Expeditions were already fitting out in Seattle, which was the jumping-off place for the new Eldorado. . . .

In dull streets all over the United States, and farther away, men heard the blaring of the master calliope and the roll of golden chariots. The great parade was happening at last and it was forming in Seattle; for those who joined it there was escape from all the ills that poverty and moderate circumstances are heir to. The chance for wealth had come, and for life without inefficiency and loss. Schoolteachers drew their savings from the bank and farmers left their farms; dry-goods clerks in New York pooled their savings and drew lots to choose the fortunate one who would go to the Klondike and bring back fortunes for them all; tin-horn gamblers packed their bags with sure-thing games; and ministers left their flocks. And all the time news dispatches and articles fanned the excitement and most of them spoke of Seattle as the fitting-out point. Some of them said, indignantly, that the fitting-out point was San Francisco, or Portland, or Tacoma, or Victoria, or Vancouver—but those did not ring true. The majority of dispatches came from Seattle, and they agreed over-whelmingly that Seattle was the place.

On any project as delicate as acquiring great and sudden wealth you can't afford not to be superstitious. If you fitted out at Portland or Tacoma how could you be sure of finding the gold of the Seattle dispatches?

The gold rush made up in Seattle. Gold seekers tumbled out of every Northern Pacific and Great Northern train and out of every Sound steamer: pale bookkeepers and brown farm hands and pursy businessmen; self-conscious young men with determined young wives who believed that wealth is as much a woman's business as a man's; un-successful lawyers, undertakers and prostitutes; boys who had never been away from home and men in their seventies —all with the gleam of gold-getting in their eyes. There were also miners among them.

They arrived by the thousand. Hotels put extra cots in rooms and in the corridors. Livery stables rented sleeping space, and strange bedfellows woke in the hay and looked at one another; then they remembered about the gold in the Yukon and they brushed off the hayseeds and began another day preparatory to glory.

The depression was over for Seattle. Swelling crowds squeezed through narrowing alleyways between store fronts and piled-up goods waiting for drays. Cooper and Levy were the largest Alaska outfitters. They advertised: *The bigger the party, the better,* and outfits they had sold were stacked up like cordwood for two blocks along First Avenue. The swelling parade to fortune buffeted between mountains of goods and the doors of restaurants and saloons that roared as unceasingly as waterfalls. Emancipated dry-goods clerks and Sunday-school superintendents and housewives fitted themselves out for the land of gold, and thereby scattered nuggets where they were. Newspapers and outfitters printed lists of necessities, which started with food and supplies for a year and a dog team. Single entrepreneurs invented and sold devices which they hoped would assist the innocents' gold gathering—or their own. Two brothers, susceptible to advice, spent ten thousand dollars outfitting themselves. New buildings went up in the city growing overnight, and discarded ships and prostitutes were reconditioned.

The city roared, and the water front roared. Every day good steamers and schooners and barkentines, and doubtful ones and deathtraps, sailed with their overloads of men and women and dogs and freight. And after each crowded sailing there were more passengers and freight than before. Vessels were on their way round the Horn from New York; and along the beach amateurs were building boats, syndicates were slapping steamers together, and the Moran Brothers shipyard, awakened from depression, was turning out an even dozen of identical stern-wheelers for the Yukon River.

Dawson was the capital of the Yukon gold country, and Dawson was the goal. There were two main ways of getting there: one was the long voyage around the Alaska Peninsula to the mouth of the Yukon River, then the long voyage up the Yukon by river steamer. All it required was patience and getting to St Michael at the right time. Parties that left Seattle later than July were in danger of being frozen in on their way up the river, and the ice did not go out until June. The other way to Dawson was by water to the head of Lynn Canal in southern Alaska. From there, at Dyea or Skagway, it was only six hundred miles to Dawson by way of Chilkoot Pass or White Pass and arctic lakes and rivers and the wild White Horse Rapids. That was the short cut to the coarse gold and nuggets on Klondike Creek. On the map it looked easier than going up the Yukon River in a steamer because it was shorter, and a gold seeker didn't have to wait until spring to start.

The gold rush was by way of the short cut, and on the first lap of the journey the tenderfeet were fortunate. Even the most unseaworthy, overloaded vessels held together in the inland passage, sheltered by islands. From the head of Lynn Canal the journey required more effort. The dry-goods clerk or housewife or runaway boy or bicycle mechanic had to begin by getting a half ton or so of equipment to Chilkoot Pass or White Pass. The moun-

Photograph by L. D. Lindsley

The gold rush brought boom days to Seattle; this shipyard is building twelve sternwheelers at once.

Photograph by L. D. Lindsley

Greenhorns went to school to learn how to pan gold.

Lake Union, Seattle's fresh-water harbor.

Seattle waterfront.

tain passes were thirty miles away, over frightful mountain trails, under almost continuous rain. The way was beset by deep crevices and boulders under soft snow, fallen trees and snowslides and landslides and slippery precipices. At the end of thirty miles of terrible labor and terror and suffering the tenderfoot was at Sheep Camp. From there he had to pack or drag his freight six miles to the foot of steep Chilkoot Pass, with its thousand steps hewn out of ice.

There were casual Indians who could be persuaded to pack outfits the first thirty-five miles for a dollar and a half a pound. But what bookkeeper or seamstress or young lawyer could afford to pay for everything at that rate? And why carry purchases that were probably mistakes, in spite of what the salesman or sidewalk merchant had said? The road to the gold seekers' Calvary was strewn with discarded six-shooters in new holsters, shotguns, fishing rods, gold-locating devices and preparations to drive away arctic mosquitoes. Overloaded men fell exhausted on the trail; determined young wives sat in the snow and cried; some of the tenderfeet started back; the litter of discarded equipment kept growing, and hardly anyone increased his burden from the free supply. Only now and then a broken and despairing gold seeker picked up a discarded revolver and shot himself.

Even for those who could afford it the Indian packers did not go beyond the thousand steps cut in the ice of Chilkoot. From there the tenderfoot had to go it alone, packing over the snow and ice to Lake Bennett. There it was necessary to cut down trees and build platforms and whipsaw logs into planks, and turn planks into boats big enough to carry a year's supplies, and seaworthy enough for the White Horse Rapids. Many a haberdasher and housewife and gambler among the tenderfeet had never cut down a tree in his or her life, or whipsawn lumber, or built a boat, or shot rapids in an arctic river.

There was also White Pass, which led from Lynn Canal to Lake Bennett, where its travelers were faced with the same problems. And White Pass was worse. Of the thousands who started in 1897 not one out of ten got over either pass to the lakes.

But there was gold in the Yukon, and in the States the fever went up, and in Seattle the rush grew. Even after the last ice-scarred steamer from St Michael limped into Elliott Bay the gold seekers kept pouring into Seattle to get outfitted and be ready for the opening of shipping. Enterprising men started schools of mining, with real sluice boxes and gold pans, and experienced miners for professors; and there were dog sleds, which the pupils learned to drive, although the mild winter of Seattle brought more rain than snow.

Those stirring times were an athletic field for popular emotion. At first there was only one emotion. The mad stampede for gold seemed to justify the cultivated European dictum that Americans are not concerned with anything else. But that was disproved wildly in the twinkling of an eye. As winter was shutting down over the arctic, word drifted out that the tenderfeet who had reached Dawson were starving. Some of them had not started with enough and others had lost everything through shipwreck in the White Horse Rapids; others had thrown their food away, thinking they could buy more. There was not enough food at Dawson for all the mouths that had come to feed, and no more supplies could be got in until spring.

The report was taken up by newspapers all over America. Magazines followed with articles about the plight of the miners in the Yukon; in the articles they were referred to as "pilgrims." The newspapers followed with editorials and the latest news about the pilgrims, and there was no news because the North was silent with winter. The public joined in the clamor, and countless theorists thought up countless ways in which the pilgrims could be rescued.

Secretary of War Alger had charge of such things, and while everyone had a different plan, opinion was agreed that Alger must *do something*. And Alger behaved splendidly.

Everyone who had an idea was allowed a War Department hearing, and the department bought some of the most promising inventions offered. One of them was a trackless locomotive with a battery of steam nozzles in front that melted a road through the arctic snow as the locomotive proceeded to the scene of distress. In the snow-free wake of the engine, suitable vehicles followed with victuals for the starving. The idea was ingenious, but difficulties must have cropped up, because the engine was never built.

The Reverend Sheldon Jackson spoke with authority, because he had spent years on the Alaska coast as a missionary. And there were no mercenary strings attached to his plan. He proposed that Uncle Sam throw off his thin disguise and reveal himself as Santa Claus by going to the rescue of the pilgrims with reindeer.

The plan suited the spirit of the day, and the earnest, bespectacled missionary departed for Norway by the first steamer he could catch. He sailed empowered by the War Department to purchase reindeer broken to harness and to hire Lapp drivers and bring them to Puget Sound with all speed.

In northern Norway, Jackson bought 534 draft reindeer and proceeded to hire drivers for the rescue expedition. There he had difficulties. Some of the Lapps had never heard of the Yukon, others were sure it must be a long way off, and all of them had settled down to a quiet winter and did not want to be disturbed. The Reverend Sheldon Jackson pleaded with them and offered all he dared. Then he cabled Secretary of War Alger and offered the Lapp teamsters more. Still they did not want to be disturbed; but the offer was handsome and Jackson persuasive. After a while the drivers agreed to go if they could take their wives with them. Nothing had been said about wives, and Jackson cabled again and was empowered to offer transportation and keep for such wives as the Lapps considered necessary.

Jackson received the cable joyfully and told the Lapp teamsters, through their interpreter, that all had been arranged. But there was still another hitch. The Lapps consulted among themselves and then they went to consult their wives, after which they reported that their wives did not want to go. They were sure the Yukon was a long way off, and they had settled down to a quiet winter at home and did not want to be disturbed. They were not tempted by the offer of keep because they had plenty of reindeer meat for the winter; and they were not interested in transportation because they did not want to go anywhere.

The Reverend Sheldon Jackson cabled the War Department that the Lapp women did not want to go. Without the women he could not get the teamsters, and without the teamsters the reindeer would be useless, and without the reindeer the pilgrims could not be rescued. He thought the Lapp wives might be persuaded if he could offer some inducement above transportation and keep.

American public opinion was demanding in a swelling chorus that something be done for the starving pilgrims in the Yukon, and Jackson was authorized to offer the Lapp women whatever was necessary to their welfare and happiness. It may have been intended that Jackson should find out what was necessary; but he took the instructions more literally. He told the Lapps' interpreter that he was empowered to offer the women anything they considered necessary to their welfare and happiness. The interpreter agreed the offer was generous, and he advised the women to sign the contract at once.

The earnest missionary and the hardy men and women of Lapland and the wondering reindeer crossed the Atlantic and the continent of North America and reached Seattle in the spring.

By that time the excitement over the starving pilgrims had died away. And the pilgrims, who hadn't actually been starving, had already rescued themselves. The Canadian mounted police at Dawson had sent most of the improvident down the Yukon by steamer before the river froze over for the year; others hiked to Fort Yukon and Circle City. All were safe except those who had died on the way.

Uncle Sam now had five-hundred-odd antlered draft animals, though the reason for them was gone. But the expedition had not been in vain, because it had done a great deal toward soothing an excited public bent on mercy.

The expedition was sent to Fort Worden, Port Townsend. The Lapp contingent was quartered in a vacant barracks and the reindeer turned loose in a big field of grass. They were to be kept there until Christmas, or such other time as there would be use for them.

The fort was under the command of Captain William S. Graves, a serious-minded and conscientious young officer who had grown up on a farm. Graves kept an eye on the reindeer herd and he was not satisfied with their progress. Instead of fattening after their trip, the beasts were growing thinner, and after a few days some of them were too weak to get up.

Captain Graves called the Lapp drivers and demanded an explanation. He had provided the reindeer with comfortable pasture and water and yet they were pining away. What ailed them?

The Lapps had been too polite to mention the fact, but since they had been asked they explained that the animals did not understand about grass and ate nothing but reindeer moss. There was no reindeer moss and they were starving to death.

The humane farm-boy captain was horrified and he

launched another campaign for the rescue of the starving. There were telegrams to Secretary of War Alger and cables to Norway, and presently a shipment of reindeer moss was rushed across the Atlantic and across the continent. It arrived in time to save the lives of most of the deer.

When the Reverend Jackson saw the reindeer moss he recalled having seen plenty of the same thing on the southern Alaska. coast. The reindeer and their drivers were shipped north and landed at Pyramid Harbor. There they would find their own forage while exploring army engineers used them for pack animals.

The reindeer were a failure as pack animals, and there was not enough moss in southern Alaska and the beasts began dying off again. Meanwhile at Fort Worden Captain Graves was having trouble with the Lapp women. It had begun over a weekly jug of whiskey that the interpreter was requisitioning for himself.

Graves ordered the whiskey discontinued, and the villainous interpreter took his revenge. He called the Lapp women together and explained their contract explicitly. The United States War Department had agreed in writing to provide everything they considered necessary to their welfare and happiness. The opportunities were unlimited, and the women need have no unsatisfied yearnings. . . . They called on the captain in a body, demanding new dresses that were necessary to their welfare and happiness. Some of the bolder ones spoke of pianos. . . .

The Laplanders were paid off and sent home; and Congress voted to have the reindeer shipped farther north, to abundant moss, there to be turned loose to increase and multiply and supply Alaska with reindeer meat for all time to come.

The solution was a triumph. Someone who understood about such things whispered that Uncle Sam's reindeer were Lapp draft animals and as such were all castrated males. But Congress turned the herd loose with its best wishes for fruitfulness and multiplication. Fortunately herds of wild Siberian reindeer were already in Alaska; they were fruitful and multiplied and covered the deficiencies of their emasculated cousins, who still get the credit.

The gold rush of 1897 had its embarrassing moments, and its cost in suffering and loss, and loss of life. It also proved that there was gold in the Yukon, and in the spring of 1898 the blare of the golden calliope was louder in the land. A war with Spain was going on, but it did not get in the way of the gold rush. In the Seattle papers even the news of Dewey's victory at Manila was somewhat cramped by Alaska steamship advertisements that shared the front page. The S.S. *Roanoke* was sailing "To the New El Dorado." The *Centennial* was sailing, and the *Queen of the Pacific*, with her name cut down to *Queen* in an age where time and breath were money. The *Utopia* was sailing, and the *Humboldt* and *Rosalie* and *City of Seattle;* the brigantine *Blakely;* the *Brixham* and *Skagit Chief;* and the new schooner *Mildred.*

With gold and war and sailings the newspapers were as full as life. And to make life fuller there were ads for ladies' complete Alaska outfits, including furs, and persistent ads for the restoration of manhood.

Gold seekers poured silver and currency into Seattle, and the city roared and grew as they passed through the mill and went north in seaworthy vessels and doubtful ones, and in deathtraps. The cranky whaling schooner *Jane Gray* sailed with a company of sixty-four, bent on exploration and discovery in the north. On deck she carried a steam launch and lumber for boat building. The expedition was led by a school superintendent. At night, hove to off Cape Flattery in a rough sea and baffling airs, the cranky craft was knocked down by a squall, and the sea poured through the cabin hatchway. Thirty-seven were drowned, but the school superintendent got on deck and cut the launch loose from the sinking schooner, and twenty-seven were saved.

The rush that spring was still by way of Lynn Canal and Chilkoot Pass and White Pass. White Pass was being boomed as suited to pack horses. Tenderfeet who did not know how to take care of themselves took horses without even knowing that they needed care. And White Pass was not fit for men or beasts. It was lower than Chilkoot and innocent looking, but under its mushy snow there was every treachery that nature could produce. Horses sank in quaking bogs and snapped their legs in hidden traps of rock and fell over unsuspected precipices, and they were killed by ignorance and abuse. Then there was an epidemic of spinal meningitis, and still the gold seekers kept crowding in. They did not stop until White Pass was blocked with dead horses and dead men and ownerless outfits and it was impossible to go on.

That was the big year of the Klondike rush, and before the end of spring forty-five thousand men had disembarked at the head of Lynn Canal. All of them were heading for Klondike Creek, which is not one of the great rivers of the earth, and the size of the gold field was limited.

But the golden tide had started, and the tide was fed. The last steamer out of St Michael in the fall brought the news of the strike at Nome.

Nome was a different proposition. There were no mountain passes and arctic lakes and rapids to plague the pilgrims. When they disembarked by the Arctic Circle they had only to walk up the beach to the tundra. The gold was under that, in the ruby sand. Afterward gold was found in the sand of the beach. But most of those who went were disappointed. During the winter, miners from the upper Yukon had got wind of the strike and hiked to the Arctic Circle diggings in blizzards at fifty below, and the best claims were already staked. And living was expensive for those who stayed. One man who brought a cow quickly sold a thousand dollars' worth of milk. But when he tried to get rich still faster and butchered her, the cow that gave the golden milk was worth only five hundred dollars as beef.

On the way to the founding of Seattle the schooner *Exact* had carried a gold rush for the Queen Charlotte Islands. It had also carried Charles Terry and his stock of goods for a store. Terry had been in the gold rush of 'forty-nine and he had learned wisdom. Gold prospecting has its romance, but if you are interested in the gold itself the best chance is to let it alone and keep a store.

Seattle kept store for Yukon and Alaska gold fields, and Seattle prospered. In 1898 a Government assay office was opened, and in the first ten years the purchase of bullion was more than $174,000,000. A generous share of that amount was spent near by. On First Avenue the Horseshoe Saloon opened with the mahogany bar and fixtures that had won first prize at the Centennial Exposition, and its sign was a solid silver horseshoe with nails and calks of gold. One bawdy house spent two hundred thousand dollars for tapestries and plush. A more decorous note was sounded by "Honest Kate," whose parlor house was a model of respectability. No naughty word was countenanced in the parlor, where customers and girls met and conversed like ladies and gentlemen. Honest Kate rated herself a friend of man and a substantial citizen, and her only touch of levity was a standing offer of free medical attention for any gentleman who could prove that he had come to grief in her estimable house. She drove about town in her own excellent dogcart; when automobiles came in, hers was the best and in the best of taste. In after years, when Honest Kate's chauffeur laid his duster and goggles aside he retired with a competence.

Northern gold did not build Seattle, which already had the facilities of greatness, but it was profitable grist for the city's big, waiting mill. It gave Seattle some of its activity and color of today: the big Alaska steamship piers, with their weekly sailings; the Alaska outfitters who still hold forth on the older, southern coast of the city; and the tradition of a totem pole in Pioneer Square.

In the summer of 1899 Seattle's jubilant Chamber of Commerce went on an excursion to Alaska. One of the souvenirs brought back by the party was a fifty-foot totem pole, carved by Thlinget Indians and painted in barbaric colors. The souvenir was set up in Pioneer Square, where Yesler's mill had run night and day in booming village times. Seattle had already made out well with a name adopted from an Indian chief, and the barbaric totem struck a responsive note. In the story told by the carvings a woman married a frog and had a frog child; thus the second generation was smaller than the first. But all the succeeding generations were much larger; and as a climax they went for a ride in a whale. Seattle partisans could have proved that the story symbolized the history of their city, which had started boldly and diminished and waxed great to emerge, gigantic, on the sea. But no one thought of that when Thlinget Indians made an unpleasantness by representing that the totem was theirs and had been removed unlawfully. According to Seattle the Indians were inspired by totem-pole-chasing Alaska lawyers. But a settlement was made and the totem pole remained in Pioneer Square until 1938, when it was destroyed by fire. Alaska Indians were then commissioned to carve the totem pole that now stands in the square. It is a replica of the original but somewhat larger—perhaps because of the human tendency to remember things as being greater and grander than they were.

Gateway to Gold

In 1909 Seattle paid more substantial tribute to northern gold. The Alaska-Yukon-Pacific Exposition began with a modest scheme to exhibit Alaska products in a Seattle building and ended in a World's Fair. It was an ambitious attempt for a young city, and it was a success. The fair paid its expenses, and none of the exhibiting countries withdrew or declared war on one another. The city was also on its good behavior. The fair was Seattle's debut among the cities of the earth, and Seattle cleaned house so thoroughly that it was never again the roaring city of gold-rush days. Afterward there was one experiment in running Seattle as an open town, but it was voted a failure; respectability had come to stay.

In retrospect only irrelevant details of the exposition stand out. The amusement area was called "Pay Streak," and one of the attractions was free souvenir rings. The victim stepped up to an open booth and had her finger measured for a ring. An assistant then rang a little bell. If the victim still waited for her ring, a larger bell was rung. If she continued to wait, a church-size bell announced her density to the howling spectators.

Somewhere on the grounds a gentleman in a silk hat and cutaway coat and striped trousers and spats twirled a cane and informed the crowds, in too-cultured and simpering British accents, that "Those sweet Swiss singahs are now at the Vienna Café." The bewildering international effort and the affected tones infuriated country boys who remembered Seattle as a man's town.

At the Hawaiian Building youths and maidens in native costume and *lei* wreaths strummed their ukuleles and steel guitars and sang beautiful island songs. But Hawaiian music and moonlight had not yet been publicized; the music and song fell on deaf ears or were judged barbaric. The Hawaiians had not yet come into their own. Shortly before the exposition a Southern-bred officer of Seattle's Chamber of Commerce was given the honor of welcoming a visiting Hawaiian princess and her retinue of island beauties. The southerner did not know anything about the islands, but he knew that princesses are always blondes. He waited proudly until the steamer docked and the bronze island beauties were pointed out to him. Then he yelled, *"Niggers!"* and ducked away through the crowd. He did not return to the Chamber of Commerce until the exotic visitors had left the city.

The Alaska-Yukon-Pacific Exposition was held on the new grounds of the University of Washington. The university had moved from its old site on Denny Hill to its present location between Lake Union and Lake Washington, and it was part of the plan that the exposition should do something for that institution. The university was short of buildings and its campus was mostly forest. It was expected that the exposition would leave a cleared campus and buildings suitable for a university. The result was only half satisfactory. The timberland was cleared and turned into a beautiful park, but the exposition buildings were not suited for university purposes. The only building of importance was the rustic forestry building, with a mezzanine floor and columns of gigantic fir logs, and the students were none too happy with that legacy. In spite of the Paul Bunyan dimensions of the building the students recognized it as an outmoded log cabin, and presently it was full of termites.

The students' complaints were bitter, but growth and change were already at work. Before another generation had passed, the student body of twelve thousand was provided with the stone and brick city of Tudor Gothic buildings that mark the spot where Seattle paid tribute to Alaska and the Yukon and the islands of the Pacific.

CHAPTER XVII

Present and Future

AT THE BEGINNING of settlement the Pacific coast was a long and narrow island frontier cut off from the rest of America by a sea of wilderness. That wilderness sea was slowly filled in by an Eastern frontier pushing west, and a Western frontier pushing east; it became dotted with islands of settlement and bridged with railroads. Seattle started in isolation as complete as that of Plymouth, Massachusetts; and in the process of surviving and growing its citizens developed hardihood and enterprise, a remarkable capacity for community action, and a spirit of undefeated youth.

Somewhere along the line, isolation vanished and Seattle merged with the rest of America. There is no exact date for the event, because it was a gradual process, but it occurred in the years between the gold rush and the World War. Northern gold diminished and became of less importance; but its value was more than made up for by the exploitation of other minerals, fish, and timber, which were a part of Alaska's wealth. Seattle was the established gateway to Alaska, and her northern trade was permanently established.

With the vanishing of isolation the pioneering period was over. Seattle was securely established and tested, and it was safe for the investment of capital. The Morgan and Guggenheim interests took over Alaska shipping; the Chicago, Milwaukee and St Paul came through Snoqualmie Pass to give Seattle its third transcontinental railroad; the L. C. Smith Company built its forty-two story building on Yesler Way, the tallest building west of Chicago at the time. It marks the spot where young Cornelius Hanford saw attacking Indians rise from behind a fir log when he went back, dutifully, to close the cabin door. Cornelius Hanford saw the skyscraper rise twice as high as the forest that he remembered, and he knew that Seattle had grown up.

Today a new stream of gold flows north through Seattle as Alaska is fortified and a beginning made at colonization and development. Until now Alaska has had a history of exploitation that has only marred the surface of tremendous resources. With the application of more intelligence and less greed, still greater wealth will flow out of Alaska; it will be more constant and there will be less blood in the stream. But whichever way the tide flows, whether Alaska is being developed or exploited, the current helps turn Seattle's mill wheel.

Seattle shared in the World War with much the same experiences and emotions as the rest of America. She also built ships. Twenty shipyards, employing forty thousand workers, thundered with the sound of rivet guns and drills and the volleying of hammers. Skinner and Eddy, the largest yard, turned out seventy-five steel vessels of up to ten thousand tons capacity, and the yard's master builder worked himself to death in the process. In a little over three weeks after the laying of their keels, eight-thousand-ton vessels were on the ways, ready for launching. Some days half a dozen ships were launched in quick succession, with an almost continuous plunging sound like boys diving into a swimming hole.

A steady stream of new vessels went out of Puget Sound; and when the war ended suddenly there was an embarrassing number of ships building and on hand. Thirty of the overstock remained in Seattle. They were moored in a silent tier in Lake Union, in the heart of the city, along with Sound steamers that were falling into disuse with the coming of more and more motorcars and ferries. There were also tiers of schooners and barkentines, and a British slave clipper, built of wrought iron in the year that Seattle was founded. Most of the windjammers had been pressed into use during the war. With its insatiable demand for bottoms the war had given them one final fling before they were brought to moorings beside the leftover freighters that had never lived.

The ships came into the heart of the city through the ship canal which the Government had opened from the Sound in 1916 and completed to Lake Washington the following year. It was the ship canal that Mercer had prophesied at the Fourth of July picnic in 1854, when

Present and Future

Seattle was a village of twenty cabins. That day Mercer had named *tenas chuck* "Lake Union," because it would unite Lake Washington and Puget Sound. Soon after that Harvey Pike had taken a wheelbarrow and shovel out to Union Bay on Lake Washington and started digging a ditch to connect the two lakes. In the sixty-odd years between the conception of the canal and its completion, the weaver's dream of a ship canal had never died in Seattle. Citizens had dug at ditches with their own shovels, and they had formed canal-digging companies on shoestring capital; they had tried to interest outside capital, and they had fought in the state legislature and in Congress for appropriations.

The ship canal had been the battle and the dream of two Seattle generations; then the Government dug the canal, handsomely, and built the locks at Ballard that are replicas of locks in the Panama Canal. Now Seattle lies between a great salt-water harbor and a still greater harbor of fresh water. Some of the city also floats on Lake Union in floathouses, which are sometimes close-packed, dingy tenements and sometimes comfortable homes with lawns and gardens at the shore end of the gangplank. Plump black coots and mallard ducks and tame ducks of exotic breeds swim in front water-yards or paddle round to back doors to be fed. Seaplanes take off from the lake, and seaplanes land on it and taxi home. Amateurs build boats on the shore; Government and commercial vessels come in to drydock; and big freighters and small yachts pass through on their way to Lake Washington or Puget Sound. With the passing of vessels through the locks to the sea the water of the lake has gradually grown salt, like the blood of the fresh-water people who founded the seaport.

The harbor of Seattle has had its hours of color: its sea-land battle in 1856 and its rush of sailing ships. In the late 'seventies and 'eighties it saw yearly invasions of Indians on their way to the hop fields of the Puyallup and White River valleys. They came in fleets of canoes, sometimes a hundred canoes towing behind one steamer, and before going on they paused like birds of passage on Ballast Island in the harbor. The island was jettisoned gravel from San Francisco's Telegraph Hill—San Francisco earth exchanged for Puget Sound lumber that became a part of San Francisco. In the gold rush years there was the great parade of new ships and ships from around the Horn and the ghosts of old ships risen from their graves to take part in the mad rush to the north. In 1904 Seattle launched the battleship *Nebraska* from the Moran yard. That same year there loomed up in the harbor the tremendous bulk of Jim Hill's *Minnesota*, the largest freighter in the world, built to extend the caravan roads of Asia to Seattle's door. In 1906 the city welcomed a very small craft which had just realized an older dream. She was Roald Amundsen's auxiliary cutter, *Goja*, and in her three-year drift in the ice from Greenland to Alaska she had negotiated the fabled Northwest Passage sought by Juan de Fuca, Heceta and Quadra and Captain Cook. In 1909 the last of McKay's clipper ships bowed to progress as the *Glory of the Seas* was cut down to a floating cannery for Alaska. In 1920 the hulk was brought back for the salvage of her copper fastenings. On the beach at Duwamish Head she blazed up at the end of her days: oak impregnated with copper and brine; a beacon of colored fire burning in the night; a farewell to the *Glory of the Seas* and the great days of sail.

The hills of Seattle surround Elliott Bay and the avenues of the city rise, tier on tier, like rows of seats in an amphitheater. Seattle is served by a hundred steamship lines, but some vessels go to the lakes, obscured by the headland of West Point as they enter or leave the ship canal; others come no farther than Smith's Cove Terminal at the far northern end of the bay; the rest are minimized by the great bay and piers scattered along six miles of water front. And the mosquito fleet is a memory.

From earliest times Seattle has been a shopping center for the surrounding country, and until the 'twenties most of the shoppers came to the big city by water. Behind closed eyelids any but the very young can see the view from the waiting room of the old Colman Dock: large steamers and small from every port on the sound, like a flock of white birds flying in every direction; coal smoke and wood smoke and snapping flags and gilded eagles on pilot houses and the solemn waterfalls of stern-wheelers going away with their convoys of gulls. Today those steamers are a memory: *Flyer, Greyhound, H. B. Kennedy, Tacoma, Sioux, Verona, Bainbridge, Tolo*, and a hundred others. The people who traveled in them, and their children, enter and leave the city on highways clogged with traffic, and finding a parking place in town takes more time than docking a steamship. For those who have water to cross, there are efficient Diesel and Diesel-electric ferries—craft without color or personality or even the proper seagoing smell. Actually, Seattle has gone a step further and achieved a ferry with individuality: the sheet-metal, aluminum-painted, Diesel-powered *Kalakala*, streamlined for a speed of sixty miles an hour which she does not make. The motor car has killed the steamboat and created the ferry in its own image, with something of its own smell.

As Seattle quickened with progress, she became a part of America. A Ford assembly plant was built near Lake Union; Sears, Roebuck and Company put up their gigantic branch building on Utah Avenue; Woolworth's and the J. C. Penny stores came to town; and the *Post-Intelligencer* was added to Hearst's chain of dailies. And Seattle became less the earlier Seattle. But what had moved in was America, and if Seattle was less Seattle she was more America. The docile mare, Tib, is suited to industry and efficiency, and her black coat is a foil for chromium trimmings.

But Tib's teammate is also deathless. Seattle is a strong union town; the Teamsters' Union is the ruling group; and Seattle's first teamster drove the legendary span. The stallion has been known to wander back to the gasoline-smelling stables of the Teamsters' Union and whinny provocatively. In 1919 he thundered through the streets when the harbor and mills were silent and no streetcars or jitney busses ran and restaurants were closed; and the only official traffic in the streets consisted of motor trucks mounting machine guns. The trouble was a product of after-war disillusionment and world unrest, but the immediate excuse was a dispute over shipyard wages. A general strike was called for February sixth, and the committee in charge announced that it was the beginning of a movement leading to "no one knew where." But the strike did not lead anywhere, and after tying up the city for three days it was called off. With Seattle's tradition for being able to have a great deal of excitement at a minimum of personal damage, no one was hurt.

In the summer of 1923, the Pacific battle fleet lay in the harbor in full dress, waiting to be reviewed; and the crowded city waited with flags and flowers and bands and Boy Scout and military uniforms. But the guest of honor did not arrive. After hours of waiting the crowd heard news vendors shouting hoarsely on the street corners and extra newsboys scurried about with black-headed extras. The President's ship had been in a collision on the way down from Alaska; he was delayed.

The ship docked in the afternoon, and there was a grand parade. Sidewalks were packed, buildings were dressed in bunting and flags, and the Liberty Theater was featuring "The Spoilers." President Harding rode in a white automobile that was blanketed with flowers and draped with bunting. Seattle cheered and cheered, and the President waved his straw hat and smiled, but all was not well. President Harding smiled and waved, but he looked terribly pale; and the white automobile, with its drapery and blanket of flowers, rolled by like a hearse. Later in the afternoon, at the Stadium, the President made his last address; then he went on to San Francisco to die.

On August thirteenth, 1936, trouble broke out at William Randolph Hearst's *Post-Intelligencer* plant. The management discharged a dramatic critic and a photographer. According to the management it was because of insubordination and incompetence. According to the discharged men it was because of their activities in the interest of the American Newspaper Guild. The critic and the photographer were discharged, and the twenty-seven members of the new Guild declared a strike.

A strike of twenty-seven employees out of a total of six hundred and fifty sounds like a tempest in an ink pot; but it held something inflammable that boiled over onto the stove like the glue in the paint shop. The Seattle Labor Council supported the strike; and in what happened afterward the fine points of dramatic criticism were obscured, but the drama was immense. Longshoremen and seamen swarmed up from the docks; loggers with needle-calked boots streamed out of the woods; and teamsters left their trucks to make a picket line three deep around the *Post-Intelligencer* plant. Members of the mechanical unions declined to pass through the sharp-shod, two-fisted picket lines. The presses stopped; bricks flew; and loyal employees were marooned in upstairs floors or manhandled in alleys while trying to slip out for something to eat; and some of them went to the hospital. Dave Beck of the Teamsters' Union was accused by the *Times* of instituting gang rule in the city, and Beck replied with a libel suit for a quarter of a million dollars.

The National Labor Relations Board held hearings while the newspaper plant remained marooned in a sea of hard-boiled pickets. The board decided that the dramatic critic and the photographer had been discharged for Guild activities and it ordered their reinstatement. Hearst appealed the decision and tested the Wagner Labor Relations Act. Seattle's Mayor Dore declared that Mr Hearst was "Public Enemy Number One," and he expressed the hope of getting Hearst and his paper out of town.

The Supreme Court found the Wagner Act constitutional, and a strike settlement was arranged with the Guild. John Boettiger, the President's son-in-law, was appointed publisher of what had been a bitterly anti-New Deal paper, and after fifteen weeks of suspension the *Post-Intelligencer* resumed publication. The picket line of long-shoremen and seamen and loggers and teamsters raised its siege. Mr Boettiger invited the discharged photographer to rejoin the staff; he presumably would have done the same for the dramatic critic, but the critic had died six weeks before.

Seattle makes its folklore as it goes along, and it would be misunderstanding the city completely to identify the pale stallion with any single faction. Once he whinnied encouragement to the insubordinate volunteers who were ambitious to be Seattle's capitalists; he pulled one of the wagons at Steele's Landing when the whole town of Seattle went out to build its own railroad over the mountains; and he galloped beside Judge Burke and the locomotive that he borrowed from the outraged passenger train at the Lake Shore and Eastern station.

Within the lifetime of one man Seattle went through the whole process of American history. Roland Denny, son of Arthur Denny, was present at the landing of the pilgrims, and he lived to see the America of today. He was the youngest of the band from the schooner *Exact,* and he was crying in company with his mother when the women and children were rowed ashore in the longboat to the city of one roofless log cabin in the rain, with naked and half-naked Indians swarming along the beach to the landing place. At Alki he was fed on clam juice because there was not a cow within a day's journey of Elliott Bay. His memory went back to the siege of Seattle. He had been taken on board the sloop-of-war *Decatur,* whose batteries bombarded the dark, smoke-jetting forest with cannon balls and grapeshot and shells that *mox poohed.*

Roland Denny watched the village of Seattle emerge from the wilderness and expand into a great city. On the bright day of October fourth, 1924, he rounded out his observations by flying over the city in a Navy plane. As a distinguished citizen he had been granted special permission, and he made the flight in company with instructor Major Muhlenberg of the Sand Point field on Lake Washington.

The seaplane lifted off the lake and roared up into the sky. Roland Denny had seen plenty of planes in his later years, but he had never imagined himself up in one, and it was like a journey in a dream. Beyond the flattened foothills of the Cascades he saw the snows of Mount Rainier come out clear, and the tremendous, pyramidal base of the mountain. . . . Then the plane swung and flew high over a park, over the university campus, its shadow skimming the sunlit grass with infinite speed. Down there was a ribbon of water: the ship canal, with a freight steamer on it, like a well-made toy, trundling through the city to the

sea. On the flattened hills around the lakes and on the shore
of the bay was the village of twenty families that he remembered—grown out of all recognition and beyond all
keeping track: a city of three hundred thousand people;
height-flattened skyscrapers and streets dark with toy
motor traffic. Even one who had watched it from the beginning could not explain how it had all got there, and
when it had happened. . . . Toy boats packed together
like sardines near one end of a lake: Shipping Board
steamers, too late for the World War, rusting in Lake
Union. Uncle Tommy Mercer's farm used to be over
there, and Uncle David Denny's next to it, and the rest was
forest.

Roaring through the sky over the city was like looking
at the map of a city to be—a map that came to life in a
dream of flying. The shadow of the plane dipping down
into streets and flickering over housetops with infinite
speed, skimming over the rippled water of Elliott Bay.
Over there, Bainbridge Island, with the foothills beyond,
and the snow of the Olympics; ahead, dividing the mouth
of the Duwamish, Harbor Island, with its wharves and
warehouses. Fort Lander blockhouse was on that island,
and the river, flowing by on each side, came out of the
dark forest and the valley of terror. Johnny King, the
delicate-faced boy on the *Decatur*, had come down that
river at night with his sister and little brother and a
friendly Indian. In the valley behind them houses were
burning and dead settlers were lying in their clearings or
cremated in the ruins. Now the valley is in golden sun-

light, with towns and market gardens and some of the richest farm land on earth. . . .

The plane tilted and swung as it roared west, high above a rounded point of land with city streets: Duwamish Head and West Seattle, with the city spreading wherever there was land. Ahead, another point of land with a lighthouse at its tip, reaching out into the Sound, and a deserted bathing beach. The shadow of the plane flashed across the sands of Alki like the shadow of a flying bird, touching for one instant on the years of life. Then the plane tilted and swung into the sky again, roaring back over the bay and over the city in the high sunshine, its shadow racing over streets and buildings like an idle finger zipped along a picket fence in passing, touching for one instant on the years of life. . . .

When Roland Denny died on June thirteenth, 1939, war was making up in Europe; the King and Queen of England had just said good-by to President Roosevelt at Hyde Park; the Japanese Army in China was becoming unruly and threatening foreign concessions; and American college boys were swallowing live goldfish. . . .

The story of Seattle is a story of courage and enterprise rewarded by success that has its taste of dust. The city fought its way out of the wilderness to share in the blessings of civilization—and civilization has become the sharing in larger wars and larger depressions—and larger anxieties. The pioneers did not push back the forest as far as they supposed, and the woods of the world are full of fighting savages. Seattle had courage when she stood alone, and she has plenty of courage as a part of America; but the world has grown incredibly complex, whereas thinking has remained relatively simple.

The city offers great opportunity for the enjoyment of life, with its lovely summers and mild winters, its surrounding mountains and forests, and its infinite variety of salt water and fresh, and water and land interpenetrating. Seattle people enjoy life as much as they can, and more than most people; but some ingredient is missing, or there is too much of too many things, and life falls short of its possibilities. There is so much loveliness, and so little peace and security for its enjoyment.

When your children's children think themselves alone in the field, in the store, the shop, upon the highway, or in the silence of the pathless woods, they will not be alone. . . . At night, when the streets of your cities and villages shall be silent, and you think them deserted, they will throng with the returning hosts that once filled and still love this beautiful land. The white man will never be alone.

The white man is never alone, and he is therefore always more or less thwarted in his enjoyment of this life. It is not because of any curse wished on the race by the old Duwamish chief, Seattle. The white man is not haunted by the Indian dead but by the living of his own race. With the rest of America, Seattle asks, "When shall we have a secure world to go on with our unfinished destiny? When shall we have security of mind to enjoy this beautiful land?"

On her seven hills Seattle waits for the answer; a city of

nearly half a million, only seven miles and ninety years from the landing of the pilgrims. On the other side of the Sound, Chief Seattle is dust under his white marble cross with its obscure legend; and under one of the hills of the city Madame Damnable sleeps in the unavailing earth, a ponderous effigy of stone with a Mona Lisa smile of satisfaction on her face.

Over the mighty hills of the city gallop Seattle's guardian spirits. They pause on Queen Anne Hill, which was their old pasture, and look toward the sea from which they came at the beginning of time. Or was it yesterday? The forest has been cut down and there are strange ships in the harbor, and bombers roar through the sky on trial flights from Boeing Field. They stand and snuff the changing breeze: the docile black mare, uneasy in an age of growing violence, and the pale stallion with the ready heels and a spirit that has never been broken. They stand there, questioning; riderless horses, ready for what Apocalypse may come.

INDEX

Index

Index

Index

Index

Index

Index

Index

Index